"If you want to understand how the science of spirituality can help you transform and heal, this is an important book to read."

—Deepak Chopra, author of *You Are the Universe*

"Dr. Yusim has given therapists and clients wonderful spiritual tools to bring head and heart together as we journey within psychotherapy and outside the consulting room. She shows how intuition, intellect, and innocence can take us to higher goals. Therapists can work on themselves. Clients can share what they discover in this book with their therapists. In these times of stress and disconnection, we need the spiritual dimension to go reunite with our authentic selves."

—Richard P. Brown, MD, associate clinical professor in psychiatry, Columbia University College of Physicians and Surgeons

"Dr. Yusim's book is refreshing. She is a psychiatrist who goes far beyond drugs to help us feel healthier, happier, and more empowered in whatever we do. Incorporating universal spiritual wisdom and the new worldview of quantum physics, she takes people out of the illusion of separateness and powerlessness into recognizing who and what they truly are and have the power to accomplish."

—Henry Grayson, PhD, founder, the National Institute for the Psychotherapies, founder, Synergetic Therapy Institute, author of *Mindful Loving*, *The New Physics of Love* audio series, and *Your Power to Heal*

"Rich with timeless wisdom, *Fulfilled* is a thoughtful and engaging manifesto on living an authentic, meaningful, and love-filled life. Dr. Anna Yusim writes with such depth of heart that you will feel as though you've made a new friend; one you can trust fully to guide you toward deeper dimensions of your own brilliance, calling, and…of course, fulfillment."

—Katherine Woodward Thomas, *New York Times* bestselling author of *Calling in "The One"* and *Conscious Uncoupling*

Fulfilled

Fulfilled

How the Science of Spirituality
Can Help You Live a Happier,
More Meaningful Life

ANNA YUSIM, MD

Foreword by
EBEN ALEXANDER, MD,
Neurosurgeon and #1 *New York Times* Bestselling
Author of *Proof of Heaven* and *Map of Heaven*

GRAND CENTRAL
Life & Style

NEW YORK · BOSTON

Grand Central Life & Style
Hachette Book Group
1290 Avenue of the Americas, New York, NY 10104
grandcentrallifeandstyle.com
twitter.com/grandcentralpub

First Edition: June 2017

Grand Central Life & Style is an imprint of Grand Central Publishing. The Grand Central Life & Style name and logo are trademarks of Hachette Book Group, Inc.

The publisher is not responsible for websites (or their content) that are not owned by the publisher.

Library of Congress Cataloging-in-Publication Data

Names: Yusim, Anna, author.
Title: Fulfilled : how the science of spirituality can help you live a happier, more
    meaningful life / Anna Yusim, MD ; foreword by Eben Alexander, MD.
Description: First [edition]. | New York : Grand Central Life & Style, 2017.
Identifiers: LCCN 2017003007| ISBN 9781455596799 (hardcover) | ISBN
    9781478915850 (audio download) | ISBN 9781455596782 (ebook)
Subjects: LCSH: Spirituality. | Mental health. | Happiness.
Classification: LCC BL624 .Y86 2017 | DDC 204/.4—dc23
LC record available at https://lccn.loc.gov/2017003007

ISBNs: 978-1-4555-9679-9 (hardcover), 978-1-4555-9678-2 (ebook)

Printed in the United States of America

LSC-C

10 9 8 7 6 5 4 3 2 1

A Note on Confidentiality

I owe a great debt to the patients, friends, and colleagues whose stories grace these pages. Although these stories are based in fact, I have heavily disguised each person's identity, life circumstances, and histories in order to protect their privacy. In most cases, I have created patient "composites," or a combination of multiple different patients' stories, histories, life circumstances, inner struggles and, occasionally, fictional elements to maintain the disguise. For those stories based on a specific patient, each patient has read his or her story, offered his or her thoughts and editorial feedback, approved the disguise when relevant, and provided oral and written consent for publication.

This book is dedicated to the three people
who taught me the meaning of love:

My mother, Alice

My father, Leonid

My husband, Jesse

Contents

Foreword by Eben Alexander, MD   xiii

Introduction: How It All Began   xv

PART I AUTHENTICITY

Chapter 1: Reclaiming Your Life   3

Chapter 2: Owning Your Truth   20

Chapter 3: Embracing Your Shadow   37

Chapter 4: Living Your Purpose   47

PART II SOUL CORRECTION

Chapter 5: Improving Relationships   71

Chapter 6: Releasing Addictions   91

Chapter 7: Transforming Fear   112

Chapter 8: Harnessing Personal Power   130

PART III PART OF SOMETHING GREATER

Chapter 9: Synchronicity   157

Chapter 10: Consciousness   175

Chapter 11: Interconnectedness   202

Chapter 12: Immortality   224

Conclusion: Where to from Here?   251

Acknowledgments   255

Notes   259

Foreword by Eben Alexander, MD

Advances in medical science in the last half century have engendered profound enhancements in our abilities to diagnose and treat a wide variety of human ailments. Paradoxically, such "advances" have also been, on occasion, more of a giant step backward—they have *impeded* actual progress. A prime example from my point of view is the tendency in the field of psychiatry to be seduced down the black hole of "promissory biochemical materialism;" that is, to see all of the vast spectrum of human mental expression as a field in which prescribing the right medication for anxiety, depression, or psychosis is all one needs to do in providing "mental health." I do not question that some of the advances in psychopharmacology have provided a true blessing to many patients in very dire straits. However, I think that the simplistic approach of just prescribing the right medication, especially over the long term, has often been more of a profound disservice to patients. In contrast, a broader psychospiritual approach that actually addresses underlying causes of mental illness, not so simplistically viewed as just "biochemical imbalances," might offer greater success and overall wellness than the more limited biochemical-only approach.

Thus I find Dr. Anna Yusim's book *Fulfilled* to provide a most welcome breath of fresh air, injecting vibrant life into the modern management of mental wellness. As a brilliant and very insightful psychiatrist in New York City, she has the experience and intelligence to assemble a remarkable series of cases from her busy practice, offering a treasure trove of insight and guidance to all humans, no matter where they exist along the spectrum of mental health.

Going beyond the limited purview of the conventional biochemical approach, Dr. Yusim's psychospiritual perspective incorporates the role of our relationships with others and lifetime patterns of behavior as indicative of a much grander overall structure and purpose. Through a valuable array of experience and analysis, she reveals the fundamental spiritual nature of who we are. Her richly psychospiritual approach allows a much deeper sense of connecting with one's higher soul to manifest its free will, bringing one much more in alignment with his or her true purpose through addressing the lessons he or she came to this world to learn.

Although this book would be of great value to many practicing psychiatrists, it is written in a beautifully personal and engaging style that is most inviting and accommodating for the everyday reader. Dr. Yusim's no-nonsense discussion of numerous instructive cases from her practice, especially in the setting of her compassion, intelligence, and spirituality, allows one to come away with a much richer understanding of the value of a spiritually based psychiatric practice, not to mention a wealth of insights about the deeply spiritual nature of our mental worlds. Everyone should take her lessons to heart in improving his or her own overall well-being.

So, without further ado, I wish you a fascinating journey of discovery and fulfillment through the rich substance and engaging exercises in Dr. Yusim's profound tour revealing the deeply spiritual nature of our psyches.

Bon voyage!

Introduction

HOW IT ALL BEGAN

The privilege of a lifetime is to become who you truly are.

—CARL JUNG

My life as a psychiatrist gives me a privileged glimpse into people's inner worlds. I become the bearer of secrets revealed to no one else, of the unspoken that remains when the ticking clock of daily life pauses for breath between seconds. With this work comes huge responsibility. At times I am witness to some of the most heartbreaking revelations or exhilarating triumphs of my patients' lives. More than once I've been forced to stand at the precipice between life and death with a fragile human being as they make the ultimate choice.

Knowledge and training can give you some preparation, but I believe the true work of healing comes not from the mind, but from the heart and soul. While I learned a great deal about the healing process through my training at Stanford University, Yale Medical School, and the NYU Psychiatry Training Program, the most important lesson was never taught in school.

Compared to many of my colleagues in psychiatry, I work with my patients in a unique way. I want much more for my patients than to bring their symptoms into remission or to alleviate their pain and suffering. What I seek in our work together is complete healing and fulfillment for each and every one of my patients. My own personal life and my work with more than one thousand patients in my private practice in New York City has taught me something very important about the healing process: *True healing and lasting fulfillment require a spiritual transformation as well as a clinical outcome.*

Together in a room with my patient, we are two souls connected in a mission of growth, healing, and transformation. This is not purely cerebral work, but deeply intuitive work of the soul. For me, this is much more than a profession; it is a calling.

Often patients come to me in times of great pain in their lives. Sometimes they find my door after being startled to realize they have been living their life all wrong and want help to make a change. At other times they invite me to join them on their journey after silently suffering from insomnia, fatigue, anxiety, deep sadness, or some other torment that at last has become too much to bear.

As I sit quietly with my patients, wondering what makes them tick, what brings them joy, what causes them pain, I feel more connected to my soul's purpose than I do at any other time in my life. It is deeply fulfilling for me to watch my patients gather the courage to make real and lasting changes in their lives, release their self-destructive tendencies, choose to live more fully and align themselves with the deepest part of who they are.[1]

PHYSICIAN, HEAL THYSELF

Through my life and work, I have come to realize that we are all on healing journeys at all times. The healers and individuals I have come to trust most in this world are those on a lifelong healing path, as opposed to those who claim they have "arrived."

Over the years, I came to see that every patient who comes into my life is a reflection of me in some way. As the Apostle Luke wrote, *"Medice, cura te ipsum."* ("Physician, heal thyself.")[2] Every patient is also a teacher. Everything I have ever helped my patients to transform is a reflection of something I have also needed to transform in myself. I call this the mirror principle. Sometimes it is astonishing to see one patient after another presenting with the same complaint, only to realize that this is the crux of the problem I've been grappling with in my own life at the time. This is an essential and humbling part of the therapy process.

As a therapist and healer, I believe that I can take my patients only as far as I have gone myself. For this reason, I believe it is particularly important to continually work on myself, grow as a person, and strive to move beyond my own personal limitations. The more I can help myself, the more I am able to help my patients.

Like many of my patients, I spent years living the life I was *supposed* to live. Not my real life—not the life I *wanted* to live. Truth be told, I didn't even know what life I wanted to live; I never bothered to check in with myself because I was too busy living the life that I thought was expected of me.

My real life would've been in sync with who I really am and compatible with happiness and fulfillment. Rather than feeling like an imposter waiting for my real life to begin, I would have felt a satisfying sense of authenticity. Instead, I was navigating from one false moment to the next by constantly trying to say and do all the things I was supposed to. But despite all the right words and the people-pleasing smiles, my heart cried out that something was missing. I could only hope that my real life was out there somewhere. But I hadn't found it yet.

In a few short years after becoming a psychiatrist, I had accumulated all the elements that, by societal standards, were supposed to make for a good life in New York City: work I really enjoyed, lots of friends, healthy and loving parents, and a loving relationship with a very good man. I was doing it right.

Then why was I so unhappy?

Rather than questioning the ideas I had about what I was *supposed* to be doing with my life, I blamed myself. How ungrateful and entitled was I if this kind of life didn't make me happy?

Over the years, many patients from all walks of life have come to me with the same complaints: "I'm unhappy and I don't know why!" or "I'm unhappy and have an inkling as to why but am not sure I can or want to change it!" It was not for lack of trying or lack of intellect that many of my patients and I could not figure out why we felt unhappy. As a physician and psychiatrist, I had all of these healing tools under my belt. So why couldn't I heal myself?

OF SCIENCE AND SPIRIT

Had anybody told me ten years ago that I would become a "spiritual" person, I would have laughed. My mother has always been a spiritual seeker, while my father, by contrast, has always had a much more rational bent. When I was younger, my mom would always tell me about her spiritual pursuits but I, at that time, related more to my father, espousing a belief that anything that could not be seen and measured could not possibly be real.

At a time when yoga was largely unknown to most people in Russia, my mother sought out and studied yoga. When it was difficult to procure books on esoteric subjects in the bookstores of USSR-era Russia, my mom scoured the black market for books on Judaism, Hinduism, Buddhism, and other spiritual and religious pursuits. Incredibly ambitious from an early age, she became the swimming champion of Moscow at the age of fifteen, after which she went on to be on Russia's national swim team while studying mathematics at Russia's top college, Moscow University. Her drive to succeed was paralleled only by her thirst for spiritual knowledge and wisdom, which has continued to this day.

It's not that my father isn't spiritual or does not believe in God. He just does not have the natural faith and certainty that my mother does. As a biomedical engineer and physics professor with a scientific approach toward life, his views on religion and spirituality are equally rational and scientific.

My father's sense of spirituality comes from our religion, Judaism. Anti-

Semitism was rampant in Russia, where I lived until we emigrated to Chicago when I was five years old. From the time of my father's boyhood, being Jewish in Russia gave him an identity and connection to strength, struggle, and survival. My father's father was sent to jail during Stalin's regime for being Jewish. An uncle on my mother's side was sent away to Siberia for the same reason and never heard from again. As a young schoolboy, my father got into frequent fistfights with other boys making anti-Semitic remarks. My father's Jewish identity was strengthened, in part, by constantly having to defend it. In this way, my father's connection to Judaism is about family, history, and culture, rather than about God and transcendence.

Both rational and spiritual in their own ways, my parents' conceptions of spirituality were, ultimately, irreconcilable. I think this is one of the reasons they got divorced when I was fourteen.

As I was growing up, I identified more with my father. Outgoing, talkative, and friendly, he always had many friends and loved to tell stories and make jokes. My mother, in contrast, was quieter, more reserved, and more introspective. As I grew older, these qualities would become a greater part of my identity.

Coming from a long lineage of mathematicians on both sides of my family, I fell in love with math at an early age. While I played volleyball, basketball, and soccer in high school, I was also an avid member of the math team (i.e., I was a nerd) and was preparing for a career in mathematics.

But in college I became fascinated by the neuroscience research of Dr. Robert Sapolsky, who studied the effects of stress on the brain (a topic relevant to any college student!). My passion turned from the innate beauty and symmetry of numbers to the inherent complexity of the most mysterious organ in our body—the human brain. In my junior and senior years at Stanford, I labored tirelessly and with great fascination in Dr. Sapolsky's laboratory. At the same time, I began studying philosophy. The beauty, symmetry, and logic of philosophy enraptured me in much the same way as mathematics. To combine my fascination with the brain with my passion for philosophy, I ultimately chose to pursue a career in psychiatry. But first I took a few years off to live a little, see the world, backpack through Europe, and work in the so-called real world as a management consultant.

In this way, my life progressed to Yale Medical School, where I sought out every opportunity possible to continue seeing the world through international research and clinical work abroad. I did a pediatrics rotation in South Africa, a primary care rotation in rural Ecuador, a dermatology rotation in Austria, an obstetrics rotation in India, and a three-month research rotation in Thailand, studying the connection between heart disease and depression in the Thai population. While research and clinical fellowships paid for some of these trips, the rest was paid for by hard-earned cash I got from being a guinea pig in numerous psychological and medical studies at Yale, where they hooked me up to IVs and took MRIs of my brain, among many other things. (That was an adventure in and of itself.)

Through these experiences, I discovered that traveling the world and learning about different cultures, particularly underserved communities, gave me a sense of fulfillment unlike anything I had experienced before. I chose to do my psychiatry residency at NYU, where I continued to pursue international research, this time in Rwanda, studying post-traumatic stress in genocide survivors. All this time, the idea of devoting my life to spiritual pursuits, or even finding fulfillment in spirituality, could not have been further from my mind.

MY DARK NIGHT OF THE SOUL

Everything was progressing according to plan until my life hit a bump. My psychiatry residency was proving to be a struggle. For the first time in my life, I was in trouble academically. As a conscientious, hard-working perfectionist, it shook me to the core, and I felt like a total failure.

Introduction: How It All Began

As the earth was shaking beneath my feet, I realized that the man I was crazy about was emotionally unavailable and would likely never make himself emotionally available to me. This experience was a reflection of what I call the "mirror principle": We don't draw into our life who and what we want; we draw into our life who and what we are. I was attracting emotionally unavailable men because a part of me was emotionally unavailable. This, I would later learn, was one of my *soul corrections*. Before I could attract the kind of man I wanted, I had to open my own heart to love and become emotionally available myself.

The painful convergence of these events brought on what I call my "dark night of the soul."

Feeling confused and lost, I did the one thing I knew would reconnect me to myself: I went backpacking in South America. Traveling alone in a foreign place has always allowed me to step outside the many roles I play in my daily life and see myself and the world anew. This time was no exception.

Alone in Iguazu Falls in Argentina, my everyday defenses finally slipped away. When I felt the pain that had built up behind them, it took my breath away. Deep in the mist of the Argentinean waterfall, I realized that the perfect life I'd so carefully and deliberately constructed held little meaning for me amidst my shame, anger, pain and, at the core of it all, my lack of authenticity. Admitting my inner pain, even to myself, shook my sense of who I was.

In retrospect, I had been feeling this way for a long time. Years earlier, I had been in a five-year relationship with a wonderful man, yet I couldn't figure out why I did not feel happy. Unable to figure it out and feeling pressure from him to get engaged, I ended the relationship, concluding that perhaps I would be happier with somebody else. For many years before, during, and after that relationship, I looked for the source of happiness outside of myself—in the men I dated, the work I did, and the accomplishments I achieved. I did not want to admit to myself how sad and alone I truly felt inside. The emptier I felt, the more I relied on these external markers of success. On the surface, it looked like I had everything going for me. Admitting my inner pain, even to myself, would shake up the public perception of perfection I had worked so hard to cultivate and desperately craved to believe.

WHEN THE STUDENT IS READY, THE TEACHER WILL APPEAR

Upon my return from South America, I started searching; I did not know for what. Whatever I was searching for, it was something my soul deeply needed and wanted for a long time. Thus began my journey inside myself. This journey proceeded down a long and winding road: soul searching at ashrams in India, learning Buddhist meditation in Thailand, spiritual pilgrimages to Israel, working with shamans and healers in South America, and ultimately, finding my way back to New York to start therapy with a new psychiatrist who would become an important mentor in my life and remains so to the present day.

In the midst of my search, I had a vivid dream one night of a sign that said "Kabbalah Revealed." My mom studied Kabbalah and had once sent me some books, so I checked my bookshelf for a book called "Kabbalah Revealed." There was no such book on my shelf. "Oh well, just another dream," I thought.

Some people believe dreams are created by the brain randomly throwing together memories and recently experienced material. But as a psychiatrist, I share Sigmund Freud's view that dreams are "the royal road to the unconscious." Moreover, I believe dreams are created by the soul as a way of helping the dreamer tap into their own inner wisdom. Our dreams mirror where we're at in our lives and what conflicts we are grappling with at the time. So what exactly was my soul trying to communicate to me through my Kabbalah dream?

I pondered this dream for a while thereafter without any resolution. Imagine my surprise when three weeks later, en route to meet a friend for dinner, I saw that exact sign from my dream. It was the New York City Kabbalah Centre. Skeptical yet curious, in the last year of my psychiatry residency, I signed up for the introductory class to study Kabbalah. I was still searching, for what I did not know.

They say that when the student is ready, the teacher will appear. Apparently, I was finally ready. Looking back at this now, I am struck by the perfection of the timing, or synchronicity, in the form of my Kabbalah dream. I had just about completed the formal part of my medical education. Fully equipped with my armamentarium of Western medical knowledge from top schools, I was ready for my spiritual education to begin.

The Kabbalistic principles I began to learn were in sharp contrast to much of what I had learned in medical school. Kabbalah teaches that what we see in this world is less than 1 percent of the true reality. Traditional Western medicine holds that what we see with our eyes and perceive with our senses is 100 percent of reality and that ultimately everything can be observed, measured, and known. If there is something that we cannot see or meausre, it's simply because we still lack sophisticated enough tools to accomplish this.

Gradually, I allowed myself to consider the possibility that the world we live in may be far more vast and complex than I had ever imagined or understood; that what I studied in medical school only scratches the surface about the nature of life, the world, and human consciousness.

Fascinated by this new insight and feeling it resonate with me on a very deep level, I subsequently devoted myself to the study of Kabbalah, which can also be thought of as the science of miracles and the principles of energy. Never letting go of my own natural skepticism and the finely honed analytic reasoning of a medical doctor, I began to make inquiries into the way in which the world of spirit interacts with the world of science. My attempt to reconcile these two very different perspectives has been a central part of my life purpose for the past ten years, and it is precisely what motivated me to write this book.

As a trained physician, I've always been in awe of the power of science to help us understand the most complex of processes, to the finest grains of detail, more of which is discovered and understood every day. But in spite of its far reach, I still find something lacking in its explanatory power. While my scientific training gave me frameworks through which to view the world, it didn't give me a sense of purpose or peace. Over the past ten years, my embracing of spirituality has helped me see larger patterns of meaning and to bring purpose and peace to my daily life and my practice of psychiatry. Just like encountering more cases of patients in medicine has allowed me to better diagnose medical and psychiatric disorders, encountering more instances of spiritual guidance has helped me to better diagnose existential and spiritual crises, often defined by lack of authenticity, connection, and purpose.

IN SEARCH OF FULFILLMENT

This is not a book about Kabbalah, or any specific form of spirituality for that matter. It is a book about connecting to the deepest part of yourself. It is a book about thinking outside the box (whatever metaphorical "box" you inhabit or perspective you espouse) and expanding your consciousness to look beyond the self-imposed limitations you have created for your life. It is a book about finding fulfillment, whatever your definition of fulfillment may entail.

Each person's definition of fulfillment is unique. For some, this involves vibrant health, a loving intimate relationship, meaningful work, financial security, children and/or a home of one's own. For others, this includes a connection to a Higher Power, being part of a supportive community, and the presence of creative outlets for self-expression. Just as an individual's definition of fulfillment is unique, so is the journey of growth, healing, and transformation. I cannot prescribe what you need to be fulfilled, but through this book I can help you identify what is most important and provide you with a bunch of tools and guideposts, spiritual and otherwise, to get there. I will share with you what has been integral to my own journey in the hope that it will help you on your own journey to fulfillment.

Part of my definition of fulfillment involved finding my life partner. One of my biggest fears was that my quest for fulfillment was, in essence, a fool's errand; that I would never be truly fulfilled in this way. I was too complex, demanding, difficult, or unlovable. But, thankfully, life has proved me wrong. The journey to getting here involved learning to balance self-acceptance with a disciplined optimism, which was another part of my *soul correction*. At times my journey was arduous and doubt-filled. At others it was fun, exciting, and reward-ing. An unanticipated part of my journey involved becoming a spiritual person along the way. Through my inquiry, I've been introduced to my soul, the part of me underneath the masks of perfection I had been wearing for so long. In wearing masks of perfection, we put on a good face when interacting with oth-ers and pretend we have everything under control—our careers, our love lives, our parenting, our perfectly decorated homes, and everything in between. For me, removing this mask was not an easy process, as so much of the world I had created for myself was predicated upon this mask.

Removing my own mask has led to an unexpected discovery: I really liked the person underneath. Imperfect and often scared, that part of me was wait-ing for many years to be acknowledged and heard. This isn't to say that I don't appreciate external affirmation or accolades or that I'm no longer tempted to wear the old masks of perfection. As an imperfect human being like the rest of us, I can certainly slip back into my old patterns. But now I have a spiritual compass of which I was previously unaware that serves as welcome friend and helpful guide when I need it.

When I finally did acknowledge and remove my mask, an amazing thing happened. I felt happy with my life for the first time. Truly happy. The kind of happiness that does not go away even when life is hard. It was only by standing in alignment with the deepest, most authentic part of myself that I was finally able to be me and, subsequently, feel complete and fulfilled.

MASK REMOVAL 101

So how does one remove a mask they may not have even realized they were wearing? This process is different for everybody, and this book will take you through several approaches. For myself, the process involved daily check-ins with myself, along with prayer and personal conversations with a Higher Power. I also began surrounding myself with like-minded individuals, exploring spiritual communities, voraciously reading books about this new world I was just discovering, and seeking out role models I admired. Through this process, I began asking for and receiving guidance from the spiritual world. Up until this point, I had primarily sought guidance and affirmation from the material world in the form of praise from others and professional accolades and accomplishments.

Now, in my daily check-ins, I start my day with some moments of quiet reflection, asking myself, "How am I feeling right now?" "What do I want?" and "What do I need?" In asking these questions, I look for spiritual guidance through not only my mind but also my heart and my body. In fact, my mind asks the questions and often my heart and body respond. For example, is my heart feeling heavy or light? Is there a tightness in my neck and shoulders, or is energy flowing freely through my body? I go through a similar process when I encounter a new situation or when I'm faced with a decision to make.

As I got better at listening to this spiritual guidance, which some may call intuition, I began to use it in my work with patients. Prior to going to my office, I ask for spiritual guidance on how I can best help each patient I will see that day. As my day progresses, I also ask for spiritual guidance in moments when I am unsure of how to proceed. So ultimately, I draw upon both what I am hearing and sensing from a patient while in therapy sessions with him or her *and* spiri-

tual guidance I receive during and in between our sessions. This book will eluci-
date how I integrate these two complementary ways of knowing. While medical
training taught me the former, my spiritual practice has led me to the latter.

AN UNEXPECTED OUTCOME

As I began to regularly seek out spiritual guidance in my work with patients,
I became more attuned to their inner worlds and my intuition expanded in
ways I could never have anticipated. I started having thoughts flash through my
mind about a particular patient minutes before he or she called, even if it was
someone I had not heard from in years. My patients started showing up in my
dreams, often providing insights into how best to help them in therapy. Sometimes during sessions, I felt certain words or phrases enter my mind that didn't
seem logical in light of what we were discussing. When I cautiously brought
these up, however, it usually led to a breakthrough in our treatment. I describe
some of these experiences in the chapters to come.

The most surprising of all of these experiences occurred in 2012 while I was
traveling through the Ukraine. It was there that I learned a difficult, profound,
and inspiring lesson about authenticity and being part of something greater.
After a long day of touring and sightseeing, I went to bed happily exhausted.
That night, with no apparent trigger or warning, I woke up suddenly at 2:00
a.m. drenched in sweat, my heart beating a million miles a minute. Patients had
described having such experiences to me in the past, but up until that night, I
had never personally experienced a so-called midnight panic attack.

Something felt terribly wrong, but I had no idea what it was. Had I had a
nightmare? I tried to dig back into my unconscious, but whatever had woken
me up was inaccessible. My heart kept beating as the beads of sweat poured
down my face. What was going on?

Now fully awake, I turned on the lights and felt compelled to check my e-mail. I was shocked to discover that two minutes prior, at the exact moment I had awoken, one of my patients, Hans, a brilliant young violinist with whom I had been working for the past two years, had sent me an e-mail contemplating suicide! I called him immediately.

Hans was furious at me! A few weeks prior, a senior colleague gave me some advice about my treatment with Hans. His advice went against my intuition, but I made the mistake of following it anyway because I deemed him "older and wiser." Big mistake. That decision had set off a series of events that spiraled into places I could never have imagined. Hans held me partially responsible for the depths of his despair. He felt the one person he could rely on for emotional stability had betrayed his trust.

I felt riddled with guilt, took responsibility for my mistake, and wholeheartedly apologized to Hans for my role in what had transpired. Being able to talk through his feelings with me lessened his despair, smoothed Hans's emotional pain, and gave him hope that we would work this out. We spoke daily during my trip and, upon my return, began to work through the rift this experience had created in our treatment.

Because Hans and I had a very strong connection, we were able to overcome this challenge together, confirming my belief that a strong therapeutic alliance could surmount even the greatest challenges in treatment. Undeniably, we both learned a great deal from the experience. One of the lessons for me was to give more credence to my intuition and be wary of ceding my power to others, such as "older and wiser" authority figures.

My unexpected awakening at 2:00 a.m. in the Ukraine ultimately led to an even greater awakening: that the Universe was supporting my patients and me in strange and unexpected ways, even if and when I made mistakes. The synchronicity of this event was confirmation to me of how we are connected to something greater than ourselves that protects us in often incomprehensible ways.

Despite this powerful realization, I was still dumbfounded by what had just transpired. Was it purely coincidence that I woke up in a panic at the exact moment my patient had e-mailed me? Or were Hans and I somehow inexplicably interconnected even while five thousand miles apart? Was this what people described as telepathy? I had no idea how to make sense of what had just occurred.

I could not help but wonder, did other psychiatrist have "telepathic" experiences like this? I began speaking with colleagues and combing the medical literature. Yes, a few brave souls had dared to publish on this subject, which meant that probably many more had similar experiences but chose to keep quiet for fear of being judged or discredited by the medical profession.

This book is one of the products of my quest to better understand what happened that fateful night and how "telepathic" and intuitive experiences of this nature can be cultivated and enhanced in the service of healing.

THE SCIENCE OF SPIRITUALITY

In much of medicine, there is a long-standing, unfortunate split between science and spirituality. Sigmund Freud, the eminent Austrian scientist, neurologist, and founder of psychoanalysis, described belief in God as delusional and religion as a "universal obsessional neurosis."[3] Although Freud wrote about "the oceanic feeling," the unspeakable wholeness, limitlessness, and awe when one becomes aware of a connection to something greater than oneself,[4] he admitted to having never experienced this feeling personally.

In contrast, Swiss psychiatrist Carl Jung acknowledged the spiritual connection as the central core of the human experience. He believed that life has a spiritual purpose beyond material goals, which entails discovering and fulfilling our deep innate potential.[5] Jung believed that we are born whole and lose this sense of wholeness as we go through life. Connecting to this unity and our own transcendent nature was, for Jung, the way of restoring our inherent wholeness.

Albert Einstein may have best reconciled Freud and Jung's opposing viewpoints when he wrote, "Science without religion is lame; religion without science is blind."[6] Science is always searching for that which is objectively measurable, quantifiable, testable, and repeatable. In contrast, spirituality, by definition, is transcendent, subjective, and therefore difficult to measure and reproduce. It is not surprising, therefore, that spirituality means different things to different people. British professor of religion and theology Christopher Cook offers a nice comprehensive definition:

> *Spirituality is a distinctive, potentially creative and universal dimension of human experience arising both within the inner subjective awareness of individuals and within communities, social groups and traditions. It may be experienced as a relationship which is intimately "inner," immanent and personal, within the self and others, and/or as relationship with that which is wholly "other," transcendent and beyond the self. It is experienced as being of fundamental or ultimate importance and is thus concerned with matters of meaning and purpose in life, truth and values.*[7]

Generally, but not always, spirituality entails an individual's internal sense of connection to something "more," something beyond oneself, which could be perceived as a Higher Power, God, or the Universe, but could also be a more general sense of the sacred, a universal consciousness, a shared global purpose, or the interconnectedness of all life. For some, spirituality entails a belief in positive human values like hope, trust, love, persistence, and faith.[8] Some people's spirituality is deeply informed by participation in organized religions, while others describe themselves as "spiritual but not religious."

I specifically use the term "spirituality" rather than "religion," even though for some people the two are equivalent. Religion generally refers to participation in or endorsement of practices, beliefs, attitudes, and sentiments that are associated with an organized community of faith. In contrast, spirituality is something people can connect with in a number of different ways, including prayer, meditation, yoga, church services, spending time in nature, religious rituals, personal conversations with God, or other forms of acknowledging and/or embracing something greater than themselves that holds deep personal meaning. Belief in God is not a prerequisite for spirituality; many atheists and agnostics consider themselves to be very spiritual people.

Exactly how spirituality reduces the incidence of mental health problems and disease is not completely understood. But then again, neither is the mechanism of some of the most powerful psychiatric medications. We know from observing cause and effect simply that they work.

More than 90 percent of adults express a belief in God, and slightly more than 70 percent of them identify religion or spirituality as one of the most important influences in their lives.[9] Many studies have shown that spirituality improves physical health, mental health, and subjective well-being, while reducing addictions, psychological distress, and suicidal behaviors.[10]

A study of ninety-five cancer patients found that spirituality was associated with less distress and better quality of life regardless of how threatening the cancer was to their life.[11] People who attended church weekly were less likely to be hospitalized for any reason, and when they were, spent less time as inpatients than those who went to church less frequently.[12] Religious and spiritual commitment has been associated with reduced incidences of depression in the elderly,[13] quicker, more thorough recovery from depressive illness,[14] and less alcohol dependence.[15] In a study of 659 adults with alcoholism, undergoing a spiritual awakening was a strong predictor of sustained remission.[16]

These studies suggest that physicians can enhance their effectiveness as medical healers by considering, inquiring about, and attending to the spiritual needs of their patients. One research study found that while only 10 percent of psychiatrists believe spirituality is important in their practices, 65 percent of patients with depression, anxiety, and other psychiatric conditions indicate that they want spirituality to play a part in their treatment.[17] A survey of patients hospitalized for medical reasons found that 77 percent of patients reported that physicians should take patients' spiritual needs into consideration, and 37 percent wanted physicians to address religious beliefs more frequently.[18] A large survey of cancer outpatients in New York City found that a slight majority felt it was appropriate for a physician to inquire about their religious beliefs and spiritual needs, although only 1 percent reported that this had occurred. Those who reported that spiritual needs were not being met gave lower ratings to quality of care and reported lower satisfaction with care.[19]

But what is it exactly about religious and spiritual commitment that helps people? Many things. Being a member of a supportive religious or spiritual community provides consistent and positive human connection. Religion and spirituality often connect people to something greater than themselves, including a higher purpose. And spiritual practices frequently include messages about healthy living, life-affirming beliefs, and encouragement during difficult times.[20] When it comes to addictions, qualities that protected against alcoholism included an attitude of thankfulness or gratitude, social involvement in a community of like-minded individuals, a belief in the involvement of God or a Higher Power in the person's life, and a belief in God as judge.[21]

Belief in God or a Higher Power can serve as a positive and secure relationship in one's life[22] or compensate for a lack of other positive social supports.[23] The way you view your relationship with God can also affect your mental health and recovery. For instance, people who took a collaborative rather than dependent religious coping style (working with God rather than waiting for God to fix things) showed greater improvement in their mental health and recovery.[24]

In many different ways, spirituality has been shown to support and enhance mental and physical health and healing.

THE QUANTUM PHYSICS OF HEALING

Quantum physics has begun to offer fascinating new insights suggesting that the world is more complex than we had previously imagined. Some say that it offers the beginnings of a scientific mechanism, still largely unproven, through which the world of science converges with the world of spirit. According to quantum physics, at a level of reality that is invisible to the human eye, everything and everybody is interconnected with one another and to all living organisms. This interconnectedness may be at the core of why I sensed my patient was in trouble five thousand miles away.

Through his famous equation, $E=mc^2$, Einstein scientifically proved that energy and matter are two expressions of the same universal substance. The universal substance is the primal energy of which we are all composed. This means that in addition to being cellular and physical beings, we are also beings of energy, existing in a field of subtle electromagnetic energies that communicate with one another at all times. This energy field is the cornerstone of our being and our consciousness.

The implications are profound: our perception that we are separate from each other may be no more than a delusion. It was Albert Einstein who made the salient point:

> *A human being is a part of the whole, called by us "Universe," a part limited in time and space. He experiences himself, his thoughts and feelings as something separate from the rest—a kind of optical delusion of his consciousness. The striving to free oneself from this delusion is the one issue of true religion. Not to nourish it but to try to overcome it is the way to reach the attainable measure of peace of mind.*[25]

In keeping with Einstein, the term "Universe" will be used throughout this book to reference the connectedness of all living organisms.

A PLACE FOR MEDICATION?

A disconnection from one's soul may present in many ways: anxiety, depression, obsessions, excessive worrying, suicidal thoughts, self-destructive behaviors, psychosis, mania, addictions, and phobias, among many other presentations I may see in my medical office. Traditional medical and psychiatric practice may attribute the above symptoms or illness to chemical imbalances in the brain that need to be fixed with medications. A deficit in serotonin leads to depression. Prozac increases serotonin and so cures depression. It's as easy as that. Or is it? In many cases, although medications can treat the symptoms resulting from a disconnection from one soul, they rarely treat the underlying cause, which is the disconnection itself. Only by looking inside oneself and aligning with the deepest part of yourself can you address the root cause of the problem instead of the symptoms that result from it. Complete healing and fulfillment entails unearthing the root cause of the pain.

In my medical practice, only about half of the patients I treat are on medication, which is a relatively low percentage for a psychiatrist. For certain patients, however, medications are a lifeline without which they feel they could not survive. Work of the soul is hard to do, even impossible, if you are so depressed that you cannot get out of bed, or so sleep-deprived from insomnia that you can barely function, or so anxious that you cannot leave the house, or in an opiate withdrawal so painful that you don't know if you will even survive the day. Engaging in soul work is necessary for complete healing, but it is predicated on first being able to function in this world. When clinically indicated, psychiatric medications can sometimes be the very tools that allow one to emerge from the darkness.[26]

In the chapters that follow, I do not focus on the use of medication, which is beyond this book's scope. Instead, I delve deeply into the psychological and spiritual tools I have used with my patients and in my own life, to help them and myself connect to our souls, transform the core beliefs that are no longer serving us, and find greater fulfillment.

EXPLORING CORE BELIEFS

When I meet a patient for the first time, I spend a great deal of time exploring their core beliefs: how connected, if at all, do they feel to something greater than themselves? How aligned do they feel with their life choices? How authentic do they feel in their day-to-day interactions with the people in their lives? How honest and in touch are they with themselves? I often ask them if spirituality is a part of their lives. The answers I receive are quite varied, ranging from multiple patients who outright disavow any interest or belief in spirituality or any greater being or purpose, to another patient who may tell me that she was raised Catholic, hated the repression she felt in Catholic school, converted to Judaism when she married her husband, and then became a devout yoga and meditation practitioner.

In my work with patients, I have found three core misperceptions responsible for much of their pain and suffering. First, they are unaware of or disconnected from their own souls. Second, they give away their personal power. Third, they feel alone and disconnected from everything and everybody. These misperceptions keep them from being fulfilled. As patients move from these misperceptions to connecting to their souls, taking their power back, and embracing their interconnectedness with everybody and everything, they move closer to experiencing a fulfilling life.

1. Authenticity

Aligning with your authentic self is the first key to living a fulfilling, joyful life. To do so, you will need to shift:

FROM: I am unaware of my soul

TO: I am deeply connected to my soul

2. Soul Correction

Understanding and taking personal power back is the second key to creating a fulfilling life. To do so, you will need to shift:

FROM: I give away my power

TO: I take my power back and create the life I want to live

3. Part of Something Greater

Feeling connected is the third key to creating a fulfilling life. To do so, you will need to shift:

FROM: I am disconnected and alone

TO: I am interconnected with everybody and everything

As you move through each chapter of the book, you will learn more about each of these implicit core beliefs. Within each chapter, I include exercises to help you apply these principles to your life. Part 1 focuses on cultivating authenticity. Before we can begin to align with our authentic self, we have to first access our intuition. This still, quiet voice can only be heard when you can silence or tune out your thoughts and emotions. It can sometimes be difficult to distinguish the voice of intuition from two other inner voices we all possess: the voice of instinct and the voice of reason. While each of these voices serve a different function in our lives, they all must be heard and acknowledged to live a balanced and fulfilled life.

Another part of cultivating authenticity is filling your life with purpose and meaning. Meaning comes from multiple sources, two of which are your soul corrections and your soul contributions. Soul corrections are the specific challenges your soul needs to work through or correct in this lifetime in order for you to become the best version of yourself. This version of yourself is calmer, connected to your values, and resilient when faced with challenges. Soul contributions are the unique ways you choose to use your talents, skills, abilities, passions, desires, and experiences in the service of others. For example, one of my soul contributions is being an empathetic listener, and I use this ability in my work with patients every day. All of us have come into this world with multiple soul corrections and contributions to make. Part II focuses on four of the most common soul corrections I encounter in my psychiatry practice: improving relationships, releasing addictions, transforming fears, and harnessing personal power.

Albert Einstein said, "The most important decision we make is whether we believe we live in a friendly or hostile universe." Opening yourself to spiritual guidance in a friendly universe is a powerful catalyst for growth, healing, and transformation. Part III, Part of Something Greater, discusses ways to accomplish this, including becoming open to synchronicity (i.e., meaningful coincidences), elevating your consciousness, embracing your interconnectedness, and exploring the soul's potential for immortality.

FROM ONE TO MANY

I know that I am not alone in having lived much of my life out of alignment with who I really am. If these words speak to you on any level, this book is for you. I am writing this book for introspective seekers who are just beginning a journey of introspection and those who have done a lot of work on themselves over the years, perhaps with therapy, yoga, meditation, acupuncture, various forms of medication, or other modes of self-help. Despite being better off than where you started, you may still find yourself falling short of true healing and fulfillment. If you are reading these words, maybe you feel an emptiness in your life that you do not know how to satiate. You may look like you "have it all," yet deep down—in those rare moments when your defenses fall away and you stand naked, honest, and alone before yourself—you return to a sad and lonely place, aware of a deep inner void and with no idea how to fill it. This book will give you a road map to healing the old obstacles that have plagued you and cultivating new ways of living in the world that will change your point of view. It will help you tune in and listen to the voice of your soul, your best friend and greatest guide.

As you begin your journey, I encourage you to set one intention of how you would like your life to change over the next year. Your intention may be to release something from your life that blocks your fulfillment. It may be to date only emotionally available men or women or meet your life partner by the end of the year. It may be to find a new job that is more in keeping with your authentic self and aligned with your soul. It may be to find a community of like-minded people and friends with whom to share your life, to see an improvement in your health, or achieve greater financial abundance. Your intention may be anything that will bring you greater fulfillment. Your intention does not have to make sense to anybody else—only to you and your soul.

Our souls are the blueprint we bring into this world of how we are meant to grow, change, evolve, transform, and meaningfully contribute to humankind over the course of our lives. Once we learn to hear our soul's whispers and uncover its deepest longings, it will guide us to a life of meaning and fulfillment.

I share the story of my process with you in hopes that some of what you read here will resonate in your own life. Perhaps my story is not just "my" story, but is a part of "our" story—the human journey toward finding our true selves and our unique places in this world. By cultivating authenticity, aligning with your soul, and embracing our interconnectedness, I invite you to join me in taking your very first step toward greater fulfillment.

PART I

Authenticity

FROM: I am unaware of my soul

TO: I am deeply connected to my soul

It takes courage to grow up and become who you really are.

—E. E. CUMMINGS

1

Reclaiming Your Life

Who looks outside, dreams.
Who looks inside, awakes.

—CARL JUNG

The last thing my patient Beatrice expected at a business convention in Venezu-
ela was a tarot card reading. But when a woman named Maria approached her
on the street and offered her a reading ("I'll tell you anything you want to know
about your love life," she promised), Beatrice could not resist.

Even after three years, Beatrice still had a burning question about Pavlos:
Was he "the One"?

Maria sat Beatrice down, spread the deck across the table in an arc, then
told her to ask a question she would like answered and draw one card from the
deck. Beatrice held her breath and asked the question that was still gnawing at
her soul: Was Pavlos "the One"?

On the card Beatrice chose, a couple was intertwined. A woman's head
was bent back in surrender; a man stood behind her with his arm around her

shoulders. His hand gently touched her cheek. Beneath their feet, the title read: *Los Enamorados.*

Brushing back her long dark hair, Maria looked down at the card, then back up at Beatrice. "This is the Lovers card," she said. "It represents the man with whom you could be happy on every level." Yes, Pavlos could have been, or perhaps still can be, "the One."

The love Beatrice was waiting for had arrived! Normally, that would have been more than she could've hoped for. But as far as Beatrice knew, Pavlos was gone.

Yet again Beatrice had betrayed her fondest dreams and sabotaged her love life. Instead of dancing for joy, she started to cry. It was an existential cry of brokenness, pain, and deep disconnection from her true essence. Once she started, she couldn't stop.

She cried all week, though not because she'd lost a man she barely knew. After all, this man was never hers. So why did he still hold such a place in her heart?

Eventually, Beatrice's skepticism about tarot readings rose to her defense. Why should she believe a single card could tell her anything important about her life? But even as she mounted her arguments, she could not shake the gnawing feeling that the tarot card was right; she had lost the love of her life.

Beatrice had met Pavlos at a business conference in Hawaii three years before. When their eyes met, she felt as if he were looking deep into her soul. It was only a few seconds, but it felt like an eternity. The handsome man standing before her was an entrepreneur from Greece with scruffy blond hair, a warm smile, and gentle blue eyes.

A surge of romance rose inside her. "He may be 'the One'! My soulmate!" It felt so real, except that Beatrice sang herself that same lyrical refrain about once a year—every time she felt a "soul connection" with a man.

Finding someone to love had been Beatrice's deepest longing for as long as she could remember. She had dated many men, but it never seemed to work out. Even so, she wanted it more than anything else in the world. If being a hopeless romantic were a science, she'd win the Nobel Prize.

Pavlos and Beatrice had made an instantaneous but deep connection with each other—the sort of connection Beatrice had never experienced with anyone else. They talked and laughed, then laughed and talked some more, oblivious to their inebriated colleagues dancing to a surreal mix of hot-blooded salsa music and old Frank Sinatra tunes like "My Way."

Pavlos had wanted to keep the magic going. As he walked Beatrice to her hotel room that night, he pulled her close for a kiss. Beatrice felt fireworks. He was not ready to say good-bye. Still gazing into her eyes, he murmured, "Would you like to spend more time together? Maybe come out and look at the stars with me? I am not ready for tonight to end." His words echoed perfectly everything that Beatrice thought but was afraid to admit.

Everything was going so beautifully. Then, for some inexplicable reason, Beatrice said no. That was their last goodbye. She chose to walk away and never contacted him again, though the memory of Pavlos still lingered wistfully in her heart and mind three years later.

Over the years, Beatrice didn't ask herself "Where is he now?" but "Why did I say no?" Her actions that night were one of many examples from her life of acting against her true self. The most authentic version of herself yearned for love and connection more than anything else. Yet when the possibility presented itself, something unexpected happened. Instead of embracing the opportunity, she pushed it away. She was stuck in a repeating pattern. In her heart, she said yes. In her life, she said no.

All of us face critical decision points where we can choose to be authentic or not, to act with courage or with fear, to align with our true selves or with who we think we have to be.

Have you faced moments like that? Are you living a life that is aligned with who you are? Or do you feel like you've somehow ended up in a life that isn't really your own?

Sometimes we've been faking it for so long, we can't even imagine what it would feel like to live life as our truest selves. One way to evaluate it is to ask yourself: What would you be doing with your life if nothing stood in your way?

We live in a world where our sense of who we are is often defined by how much money we make, whom we marry, where we live, and what we do. Instead of being seen for our true selves, we're known by our job titles—as doctors, lawyers, teachers, dental hygienists, grocers, construction workers, business owners, musicians, or athletes. These labels are reinforced a thousand ways by our culture, until, eventually, it's easier to think of ourselves as people who do certain kinds of jobs than to explain who we really are.

The great psychoanalyst Donald Winnicott warned of the dangers of letting other people's expectations take on too much importance, thereby "overlaying or contradicting the original sense of self, the one connected to the very roots of one's being."[1] Whether those expectations come from our culture, our society, or our loved ones, we can't afford to sacrifice our true nature to meet their standards. That is what it means to "live someone else's life."

Once we do that, we lose the ability to feel spontaneous or alive. Our lives feel fake, not real. Although we may look fine, even great, on the outside, we quietly suffer from the sense that we are dead or empty inside. According to Kierkegaard, the deepest form of despair is when we choose to be someone other than ourselves.[2]

FROM LABELS TO WHOLENESS

When I initially ask patients to tell me about themselves, they often give me their name, title, occupation, or marital status. Although this information is important, healing doesn't come from external labels. Many elements factor into who we are. These elements are beholden to the unseen rules of intellect, emotion, and spirituality much in the same way that our physical selves operate according to physical laws. Healing involves engaging every aspect of a person—both physical and nonphysical—in an integrated whole.

My own journey away from emotional and psychic pain has taught me that no matter what kind of pain brings people into therapy, we will have a better chance of alleviating that pain if we are aligned with our most authentic selves.

Strangely enough, to one degree or another, many of us wear a mask in early childhood to be accepted by and to please others such as our parents, siblings, friends, and teachers. In doing so, we hide our precious, but vulnerable, true selves. Gradually, we find ways to use this false mask to ward off anxiety, to help the family deny its problems, or even to keep ourselves safe from harm. As time goes on, the mask brings us so much acceptance and sense of belonging that we lose track of who we once were. We've hidden our true self so well that even we can't find it![3]

Beatrice didn't even know she was wearing a mask until one day she realized how unhappy she felt despite doing everything that *should* make her happy. A natural-born *empath*, or somebody particularly attuned to the feelings of others, Beatrice had lived her whole life pleasing others: first her parents, then her friends, then her teachers, then her boyfriends. Her parents had wanted her to follow in their footsteps and become a teacher, even though she wanted to go into business all along. But it was only after working as a teacher for five years and not feeling fulfilled that Beatrice finally went back to school for a business degree. Her parents wanted her to marry her high school boyfriend, Doug, so she did, even though she knew walking down the aisle that it was a mistake. Two years later, they got a divorce. At that time, Beatrice swore to do away with her people-pleasing ways. Now older and wiser, Beatrice had removed her masks and was working hard to be true to herself but, as in the example above, this still proved to be a challenge when it came to her love life.

Adopting a false self is a very human defense. Our survival depends on it, or so we are taught to believe. For centuries, this pattern has been commonplace, as penned by the nineteenth-century Austrian poet Rainer Maria Rilke: "No one lives his life. Disguised since childhood, haphazardly assembled from voices and fears and little pleasures, we come of age as masks."[4]

What Rilke didn't acknowledge was: we have a choice. Recognizing our tendency to conform to the expectations of our culture, our community, our parents, and even our own inner critics is a step toward reclaiming our true natures.[5]

In fact, living in an authentic way is a great relief. It frees us from the pressures of striving (and failing) to be someone else. Instead, it allows us to be transparent and to connect more deeply with other people. In *The Drama of the Gifted Child*, Alice Miller explains that, when the true self is set free, the sense of emptiness disappears and "an unexpected wealth of vitality is now discovered."[6]

In my own practice, I have had the privilege of helping numerous patients who feel they have been living someone else's life. Often they come to me at a time of great darkness. Something precious has been lost—a loved one, a cherished hope, an important job, or even their good health. Many have been silently enduring pain, anxiety, fatigue, or deep sadness for years. One day the suffering is too much to bear, and they ask for help.

LETTING GO OF SELF-DECEPTION

Blatant self-deception always comes at such a high cost that the obvious solution is to simply be honest with ourselves. But sometimes we just can't, or won't, or don't know how, or don't want to. In no situation is this more commonplace than when we fall in love, which always involves some form of conscious or unconscious self-deception. In his book *Love's Executioner*, existential psychiatrist Irvin Yalom writes, "Love and psychotherapy are fundamentally incompatible. The good therapist finds darkness and seeks illumination, while romantic love is sustained by mystery and crumbles upon inspection."[7]

When it comes to love, honesty is at a disadvantage. That's because the brain reserves its most delightful chemical concoction for the infatuation stage of a relationship. Falling in love produces a natural high. The euphoria is triggered by a number of brain chemicals called neurotransmitters, including dopamine, noradrenaline, and oxytocin.[8] Dopamine floods our system with pleasure. Norepinephrine enhances our experience of joy. Then, as if that wasn't enough, oxytocin, often called the love hormone or trust hormone, amplifies the effects.[9]

For most species in the animal kingdom, this giddy romantic feeling lasts only a few minutes or hours—days or weeks at the most. For humans, these chemicals stay active in the brain for twelve to eighteen months, stoking our intense feelings of love.[10]

In the throes of that glittering infatuation, it is nearly impossible for any of us to see clearly. Even if we did see warning signs in the other person, we would find it unusually hard to believe that they were reason enough to forfeit such a positive and reinforcing feeling. As a master in the art of infatuation, my patient Beatrice could certainly attest to this fact. It was only after enduring many rounds of these intoxicating yet self-defeating infatuations that Beatrice was finally able to extricate herself from this pattern. Soon after, she met the love of her life and they have been happily married for the last four years.

The trouble with infatuation is that it wears off. Unfortunately, before it does, many couples enter more committed unions (e.g., marriage and other unions), have children, and promise to live "happily ever after." By the time the mist of infatuation clears and any warning signs come into full view, their lives are intertwined in ways that have legal, social, financial, occupational, and emotional ramifications. The temptation to "paper over the cracks" is strong. Married friends will often encourage them to work things through and/or overlook their partner's faults to keep their marriage intact.

Two of my patients, Jessica and Elisa, had multiple things in common. Both were beautiful, stylish women. Both were married to ambitious, successful men who had endowed them with elegant lifestyles in Manhattan. And both husbands were cheating on them. The clues weren't subtle, yet neither Jessica nor Elisa wanted to admit what they knew. Accepting the truth meant facing their fears, risking an unpleasant confrontation, and perhaps even sacrificing other aspects of a life they enjoyed. Denying the truth allowed them to remain in a state of relative comfort and complacency.

Jessica initially maintained that she and her husband, Pascal, both loved each other too much to be unfaithful. The woman in question was another executive at his consulting firm. If she kept him late at the office, called him in the night, and stood too close for Jessica's comfort, it could still be explained as a working relationship. Yet as the evidence mounted and friends began to ask awkward questions, Jessica was forced to be honest with herself.

When she confronted Pascal, he denied the affair, but over the coming weeks, he came to realize that he was putting his marriage at risk. The hope of renewing the love they had felt in the past made him willing to end the affair and join Jessica in couple's therapy. Together they worked to rekindle the love and passion in their marriage.

For Elisa, marriage had increasingly felt like a trap. She had fallen in love with a prominent cardiologist during her freshman year in college and dropped out of school to start a life with him. She noticed the way the female doctors and nurses flirted with him at the hospital. She'd even heard the rumors about his revolving door of affairs. But she told herself that once they got married, Jeremy would give it all up for her.

That never happened. Even worse, she soon began to feel like an accessory to his busy life, with no life of her own. Since Elisa had been raised to believe that getting married was the only way to be normal and happy, she was slow to admit to herself that she wasn't happy at all. What did that say about her? Was she not normal? Was she a bad wife? Had she failed?

In therapy, we worked together to help Elisa admit the truth about her relationship without condemning herself. After several agonizing years, she filed for a divorce from Jeremy, although he never admitted the truth about his affairs. After discovering that the traditional wisdom about getting married didn't necessarily apply to her, Elisa broke the mold again by going back to finish her college degree at the age of thirty-five.

After finding the courage to be honest with themselves, Elisa and Jessica were able to get in touch with their authentic selves, confront the difficult feelings they had worked so hard to avoid, and ultimately, work to reclaim what made them feel happy and fulfilled.

THE LIMITS OF AUTHENTICITY

In some contexts, authenticity can be somewhat of a luxury. In the United States and abroad, many individuals live within cultures where maintaining the bonds of families and communities is considered far more crucial than pursuing individual dreams or authenticity.

Nancy Rosenberger's book *Japanese Sense of Self* explores the commonly held distinction between the Western sense of self being relatively individualistic, and the non-Western sense of self being grounded in a sense of collectivism and defined in relation to others: mother-daughter, brother-sister, father-son, and so on. This begs the question of whether there is a single underlying authentic self that is the essence of the person, or whether the self is instead a collection of "masks," each tied to a particular set of social circumstances.[11] If we consider possible "selves" as systematic components of the self-concept, we can conceive of an authentic self that is diverse and multifaceted without being fake, wishy-washy, or incoherent.[12]

When I first met Lee, she was a twenty-three-year-old student from Singapore. She asked me to help her resolve her struggle between what she wanted to do with her life and what her family wanted. Fascinated by artifacts, relics, and cultural landscapes from an early age, Lee always dreamed of becoming an archeologist. She had been accepted to several graduate programs in the United States, but her family couldn't understand why she refused to give up this "foolish" pursuit of a career and go back home to take care of her aging parents. Her father, Huang, took her plans very personally. Raising a daughter who defied the traditions respected by everyone he'd ever known made him feel like a failure as a father. Did she feel no love or loyalty to her family? How could she abandon her parents to pursue her own selfish desires?

In our work together, Lee and I spoke at length about what it means to live your life authentically. In time, Lee decided that continuing her education would open the door to the life that was right for her. As I had come to expect in this work, aligning with her authentic self generated a profound new sense of clarity for Lee. She felt empowered as never before and even gained the courage and strength to stand up to her father. However, her dream never came to fruition. When Lee returned home to Singapore to share her decision with her family, her father went into a rage and literally beat her into submission. Like a prisoner in her own family, Lee tragically had no choice but to comply with his rules. Lee's hope of being able to convince her father of the rightness of her path was dashed. Fortunately, though, I was able to continue to work with Lee to help her chart her own path forward, a path so courageous that she knew it would take all her strength and self-understanding to stick to her own authentic self.

While anyone in Lee's circumstances can certainly develop an intimate connection with the inner self and listen daily to its truths, there may be real constraints that prohibit them from stepping outside their cultural norms. An individual's role in shaping his or her destiny may be limited by other responsibilities: caring for loved ones who are aging or ill, struggling to bear financial burdens, or meeting other familial, cultural, or societal obligations. The challenge in these situations is to find ways to live the most authentic life possible within those constraints, which can be incredibly difficult at times.

Mahatma Gandhi taught that, "Happiness is when what you think, what you say, and what you do are in harmony." But the sad reality is that the integrity and authenticity described by Gandhi are not always possible, as illustrated in Lee's case. As Lee and I continued to work together, I helped Lee come to terms with her situation, accept her father's limitations in supporting her, and figure out how to live the most meaningful life she could within the cultural norms of her society.

Lee ultimately became a science teacher in Singapore and married a very good man. Two years later she and her husband moved to the United States. A year after that, Lee went back to school to finally begin actualizing her dream of becoming an archaeologist. Although Lee's life did not unfold entirely as she had once hoped, she has ultimately been able to live a fulfilled and authentic life nevertheless.

Below is the first of a series of exercises included in this book to help you not only understand but experience some of the concepts in the book.

Exercise: What Do You Most Deeply Want?

In order to remove self-deception and align with the deepest part of yourself, you must know who you are and what you most deeply want. This exercise will help you to identify and access this crucial piece of information through the act of meditation.

Meditation is a state of contemplation, focused attention, and awareness that originated thousands of years ago as a practice that improves spiritual and emotional well-being. This discipline teaches the practitioner to examine thoughts, feelings, and sensations in a nonjudgmental fashion with the goal of achieving a state of inner peace, physical relaxation, and psychological balance.

Literally thousands of scientific papers have elucidated the benefits of meditation for both psychological and physical health. The practice of meditation has been shown to reduce general stress, anxiety, and depression,[13] substance abuse,[14] and pain[15] while improving medical conditions like diabetes, heart disease, high blood pressure, and high cholesterol,[16] multiple sclerosis,[17] Alzheimer's disease,[18] to name a few.

Throughout this book, meditation will be one of the many tools we use to help put the ideas of this book into practice. Cultivating a meditation practice takes time and discipline, and you should be patient, especially when just starting out. Because many of you may be doing this exercise for the first time, it may be challenging at first, but I encourage you to stick with it because the rewards will be well worth the effort you put in.

To begin this exercise, remove any distractions from your environment so you can surrender fully to the process. Put on comfortable clothing in your favorite part of your home or a beautiful place in nature. You may want to light some candles and incense, or put on some relaxing music to help create a peaceful atmosphere.

Keep a journal nearby so you can write about your experiences in a stream-of-consciousness format, which I will guide you through in the following exercise.

Read these directions all the way through before starting this meditation.

The meditation begins with a breathing technique to calm your mind and body. This system of breathing floods your brain with oxygen, which gives your body the signal to relax. Once you begin, you may yawn or feel tired. This is normal. Just focus on your breathing and envision your whole body relaxing. When you are ready, sit in a comfortable position, then begin.

1. Close your eyes and take several slow deep breaths:
   - Inhale through your nose for the count of two.
   - Hold your breath for the count of four.
   - Exhale through your nose for the count of eight.
   - Repeat the above for ten breaths.

2. Once you feel yourself relaxing, ask yourself the question: *What do I most deeply want?*

3. Then let the answers come to you. They may come instantly or slowly, as you continue to focus on your breathing. If the answer does not come immediately, gently ask yourself the same question again. The answer may present itself to you in words, images, a visceral sensation, a gut feeling, or another way entirely. Be open to the ways your answer may show up. If the answer does not come to you in this meditation, you may want to repeat the meditation again tomorrow, as today you have planted a seed into your subconscious mind that will slowly grow and evolve into an answer over time.

4. Once you have your answer, imagine that you are able to actualize it. In your mind's eye, imagine getting exactly what you most deeply desire.

5. Now invoke all of your senses: How does this feel? What does it look like? Sound like? Smell like? Taste like? Experience all the feelings and sensations of having your greatest desire fulfilled.

6. Now return your awareness to your breathing. See if you can go even deeper. Is there an even deeper sense of longing? Allow the feelings, smells, and sensations from your first wish to inform you and drive you even deeper as you begin the breathing technique again. Take five slow deep breaths:

   - Inhale through your nose for the count of two.
   - Hold your breath for the count of four.
   - Exhale through your nose for the count of eight.

7. Now ask yourself: *Now what do I most deeply want?*

8. As before, let the answer come to you. Once it does, invoke all five senses and feelings, imagining what it would be like to actualize this even deeper desire. How does it feel? Look? Smell? Sound? Taste?

9. Repeat this exercise as often as needed to access your deepest core desires.

10. Begin to do this meditation exercise once per week and see how your answers evolve over time. As you grow and change, so may your deepest desires.

The initial answers you obtain to this question may not be your core desires. For instance, the first answer you obtain may be "a burrito!" You have acknowledged to yourself that right now you most deeply want a burrito! This is important information. Take note of it. As you go further, you may discover that underneath your desire for a burrito is a much deeper desire for nurturance, sustenance, and care that many of us associate with food. What comes up as an initial desire may actually be a metaphor for something deeper.

Exercise: Stream-of-Consciousness Writing

Another way of accessing your inner truth is through the act of writing. For this purpose, I invite you to set aside a journal or notebook to chronicle your thoughts, insights, and inspirations as you go through this book. If you prefer to type, that's great too. The method we will use for much of our writing is the five-minute stream-of-consciousness writing method.

Stream-of-consciousness writing means that for five minutes straight, you will write from your heart and soul without lifting your pen from your journal or your fingers from your keyboard. Any and every thought that enters your mind will go down on the page. You will write for five full minutes without stopping, going back, editing, criticizing, judging, or becoming stuck on any one topic. You just let the thoughts, feelings, sensations, and images come to you and then put them into words. There is no right or wrong. There is no good or bad. You just do your best to put your truth—what you feel in the depths of your heart and soul at the present moment—into words.

If you feel stuck, take a deep breath and just keep writing. If you can, set a stopwatch for yourself so that you can invest fully in your writing without having to monitor the clock. There are no mistakes here. Perfection is the enemy of truth and authenticity, so please do this exercise as imperfectly as possible!

For the first topic, set your stopwatch to five minutes and write without stopping on the topic What Do I Most Deeply Desire? The Questions for Reflection are included as mere guideposts. As with life, let your writing take you where it may. You may end up somewhere much better than you could have imagined or planned.

Questions for Reflection

1. What did I learn about myself in the above exercise?

2. What do I most deeply desire?

3. Do I desire something even more deeply than that?

4. What surprised me in this exercise?

5. What is holding me back from actualizing what I desire most deeply?

6. If I wanted to actualize my deepest desire, what would my first step be?

LEAVING THE CAGE OF SMOKE AND MIRRORS

While some of us have stumbled through the trials and tribulations of inauthenticity en route to discovering who we really are, others discovered their authentic selves in more mysterious and unexpected ways. For some, a meta-phorical door opens suddenly one day and they have the choice of whether or not to walk through it.

Fernando Broca was raised in a devout and traditional Catholic family in Mexico City. He could never have imagined a wise old grandfather he had never met traveling a thousand miles to find him at the age of eighteen and tell him what he was meant to do with his life: become a shaman!

Fernando had had premonitions throughout his life: "Before this happened I had already had dreams about this man I did not know. I knew I had a call-ing but did not understand what that calling was. When I was younger, indig-enous healers would come up to my family and tell them I was one of them. This scared my family because we were devout Catholics and did not know this other world. But when I spoke to this grandfather, I understood that his heart was good and he had a good intention for me." At the age of eighteen, Fernando made the choice to leave behind the world he knew and began training as a sha-man, which he has been doing ever since.

When asked how exactly he was "discovered," Fernando explained that "when my teacher [the wise grandfather] prayed, he sensed that far, far away was the spirit of a young person that had a vocation for speaking to God. And he began looking for this spirit and finding the heart which possessed this intention. This is how he found me."

Although Fernando never felt particularly inauthentic prior to his shamanic initiation ("I never thought about this then…"), when this unexpected door opened for him, he knew in the depths of his soul that this was the path he was meant to take in life. Since the age of eighteen, he has been living a life of authen-ticity, healing, and connection to something greater than himself as a shaman.

While there are many different types of shamans in the world, a shaman is generally defined as an individual who lives at the interface of the physical world we live in and the spiritual world above. By having an influence in the spiritual world through prayers, rituals, and sometimes the use of natural herbs, shamans create change in the physical world. An age-old spiritual principle first noted by pagan prophet Hermes Trismegistus on the Emerald Tablet describes this phenomenon: "As above, so below."

Having had a traditional high school education in Mexico, with only limited access to the spiritual world, Fernando was understandably quite skeptical when he first began studying the tools and techniques of shamanism. Shamans treat ailments and illness by healing people at the soul level. By mending the soul, the shaman restores the physical body of the individual to balance and wholeness. The restoration of balance results in the elimination of the ailment.[19]

When asked why human souls are "broken" and need mending in the first place, Fernando elucidated the shamanic explanation:

According to shamanism, human beings fell asleep and an energy came and created a cage of smoke and mirrors. When we open our eyes while we are asleep, we believe that this cage was reality. We forget that outside of this cage exists a living and breathing natural world of the spirit.

Human beings, while they are half awake, prefer to stay inside the cage because it is secure. The cage gives us control. The cage gives us power. People think that if they have a lot of money and a strong cage, they are superior.

But life shows us that this is not so. We all die. We all get sick. We all have people that we love that pass away. The security of the cage is an illusion. But people prefer to stay asleep usually because the cage becomes familiar and comfortable. The idea of leaving the cage becomes frightening.

The courageous individuals decide to free themselves from the cage... They venture into the world of spirit and soul to discover who they truly are.[20]

2

Owning Your Truth

The greatest discovery of my generation is that human beings can alter their lives by altering their attitudes.

—WILLIAM JAMES

Aligning with your true self will bring a new level of authenticity to your life. But this is easier said than done. The reality is that every one of us must work to balance competing elements inside us.

We are complex creatures with many faculties: logic, instinct, emotion, and intuition, to name just a few. Where these different faculties reside in the brain and body has been a topic of great research and debate for centuries. In the fourth century BC, Aristotle considered the brain to be a secondary organ that served as a cooling agent for the heart and a place in which spirit circulated freely.[1] Toward the end of the sixteenth century, philosopher René Descartes believed the pineal gland, a small gland in the center of the brain, was the seat of the soul.[2]

In the 1960s, physician and neuroscientist Paul MacLean proposed a three-part model of the brain that emerged in the course of evolution to house many of our faculties: a *reptilian brain* in charge of survival functions, a *limbic brain* in charge of emotions, and *a neocortex* in charge of abstract, rational thinking. Although oversimplified, this model has nevertheless proved interesting and useful.[3] But one of the things this model does not address is something deeper that supersedes our logic, emotion, and instinct and connects us to our true self: our intuition. With advances in science and technology, our theories of where certain human faculties are housed in the brain are constantly evolving.

More than a century ago, William James, one of the founding fathers of modern psychology, identified two primary modes of thinking: associations and true reasoning. We can think of them as instincts versus logic, or as snap judgments versus analyses. Instincts or snap judgments are lightning fast, effortless, and mostly unconscious. This mode of thinking operates when you know something without really knowing why. Logic or analytical thinking is more of a process we use to reason things out, like solving a math problem or writing an essay. These processes are slower, more deliberate, and very conscious.

In *Thinking, Fast and Slow*, Daniel Kahneman, an experimental psychologist who was awarded the Nobel Prize in economics in 2002, describes the cognitive errors we often make, believing we are using logic (the deliberate, slow-thinking, analystical system) whereas in fact we are using instinct (the fast, emotionally laden, ingrained system). In other words, we often act on instinct, then come up with ways to justify it to our logical, rational minds.[4]

At its best, this gives us a built-in system of checks and balances. But it doesn't solve the deeper problem of when to trust instinct and when to go with what seems more rational. There is pressure in both directions. "My gut's telling me to go for it!" we say to ourselves. "Does that make any sense?" and then we think it through. If both our instinct and our logic agree, we're free to act. At its worst, this system gives us heightened powers of self-deception. When people say, "You're just rationalizing!" it may mean that we're trying to pretend we acted logically, when in fact we acted on impulse.

Remember how my patient Beatrice said no to Pavlos, the handsome Greek entrepreneur in chapter 1, even when she desperately wanted to say yes? It can be argued that she was using logic to rationalize her instincts. When I asked her why she said no, she gave me three very sensible-sounding rationalizations:

Rationalization #1:

She really liked this guy and wanted to take it slow.

(That makes perfect sense, right? Who could fault her for that?)

Rationalization #2:

She had a presentation the next day and needed to rest.

(Even more sensible! Not to mention, responsible. How could that be wrong?)

Rationalization #3:

She was being swept away by a passionate delusion of connection with a man who didn't even really know her.

(What good could possibly come of that? Logically speaking, this is not how healthy relationships begin.)

These rationalizations sound sensible, logical, responsible, and certainly reasonable. Moreover, if Beatrice were your daughter, your friend, or your patient, you probably would have told her that she did the right thing. Why then was Beatrice regretting her decision *years* later?

Despite it being perfectly rational and reasonable to turn down Pavlos, Beatrice knew in her gut that to say yes was not merely impulsive, and the rationalizations she gave herself for saying no made no sense at all. She hadn't known Pavlos long, but her instincts and her deepest feelings were both telling her that she really liked this man. She was divorced, alone at a business convention for three days, looking for the right partner at this particular point in her life, when Pavlos came along. In the short time they spent together (several hours of talking that evening), she learned that Pavlos was divorced as well and looking to find the right partner. In essence, the above three rationalizations were just stories Beatrice constructed afterward in an effort to relieve her regret and explain to herself why she said no to this man she really liked. So why did Beatrice *really* say no?

THE CULPRIT OF SELF-SABOTAGE

If anything feels inauthentic in retrospect and fills you with regret, there is one primary culprit: fear. It is an emotional response that has evolved to ensure our safety. In the modern world, we no longer need to escape from saber-toothed tigers, but we face other dangers. If we stand too near the edge of a precipice or find ourselves in a dangerous part of town, we rightly feel afraid. Anytime we venture into the unknown, we feel fear, whether it is because a loved one has been diagnosed with a disease or because we have voluntarily agreed to go base jumping and have lost our nerve.

More often the stakes are emotional, but the consequences can have far-reaching effects. When a man takes the risk of confessing his romantic feelings to a close friend, it can cost him an important friendship. If an employee reports the unscrupulous actions of her manager, she may end up getting fired herself. Concerned parents, despite their best intentions, may lose contact with their adult child if they confront him about his drinking problem.

In all these cases, the danger is real. As if that weren't enough, we can also be plagued by *perceived* dangers. When our fear is based only on perception, it is known as "stress" or "anxiety."

As confident as Beatrice appeared on the outside when she spoke to Pavlos, she was filled with anxiety on the inside. She was afraid of how deeply she resonated with this man who appeared to have many of the qualities she was looking for in a partner. Rather than enjoying the prospect of being with a man who was offering her everything she dreamed of, obsessive thoughts filled her worried mind, taking her out of the present moment with Pavlos and into her own inner world of fear, anxiety, and neurosis. Unfortunately, this was a pattern Beatrice knew well. Pavlos was not the first "no" she had regretted long after the fact. For all the years Beatrice had been searching for love, she was also unconsciously pushing it away.

Sometimes what we most want can be the very thing that we fear most. For Beatrice, nothing created more fear and anxiety than the possibility of having her greatest desire fulfilled. Her instincts must have sensed this and immediately geared up for self-sabotage.

Even as she was gazing into Pavlos's eyes, that familiar voice inside her head was worrying. *What if he's 'the One'? But what if things don't work out? Worse yet, what if things* do *work out?*

Beatrice was afraid of having her heart broken if Pavlos didn't feel the same way. Having been through one divorce already, she was also afraid of a repeat scenario: another painful breakup. Beatrice had only recently given up her people-pleasing ways in the service of living an authentic life. Another fear of hers was that falling in love would cause her to lose sight of her true self once again. In all these scenarios, Beatrice was being driven, first and foremost, by fear. But fear, by its very nature, is often an illusion. I like the mnemonic FEAR: False Evidence Appearing Real. The majority of what we most fear never comes to fruition.

What is even more painful than failure, abandonment, uncertainty, loss, and rejection is the fear of regret that comes with not having truly lived. This is precisely the role fear plays in our lives. It stops us in our tracks, makes us succumb to our internal demons, and keeps us from taking the risks necessary for living a full, authentic, courageous life.

As Dr. Lissa Rankin writes in her book *The Fear Cure*: "Courage is not about being fearless; it's about letting fear transform you so you come into the right relationship with uncertainty, make peace with impermanence, and wake up to who you really are…[C]ourage stems from inner peace and it empowers you to live in alignment with your soul's values."[5]

But Beatrice didn't know any of this at the time. She unwittingly let fear make her decision for her, then tried to rationalize it.

When we unwittingly act out of fear, it creates flawed thinking that leads to flawed actions. We see only what we want and expect to see, leading us to make snap judgments based on familiar patterns of the past and deliberately ignore evidence to the contrary. The result is what Kahneman kindly calls "cognitive illusions."

These same instincts evolved to save us by making quick decisions. Too much uncertainty or doubt would stop us in our tracks when we needed to be picking up speed to escape those saber-toothed tigers!

With Pavlos, Beatrice's fear-based instincts were right on track. They quickly and efficiently summed up the danger of the situation at hand. Here was a very handsome, intelligent, charismatic man. She felt a soul connection. He appeared to like her. He said he wanted to spend more time with her. One whiff of that and her instincts shouted: *Run! Before it's too late! Warning!!! Men like this have broken your heart in the past! Danger!!!* Her heart raced. Her pupils dilated. Her breath quickened. She acted on instinct, succumbed to her fears and immediately said: "NO!" A deeper, reflective, slow-moving logic never had a chance to intervene until it was too late.

By letting fear-based instincts steal the show, Beatrice trapped herself in her own history, completely discounting the possibility that Pavlos could be different from all the other handsome, charismatic men she had previously met. What if, this time, they mutually liked each other and it actually worked out? As Dr. Kahneman says, our instincts, in their continual search for patterns, can make the same "pattern recognition" error and engage in the same repetition. Again and again and again.

DANGEROUS PATTERNS

My patient Slava, an attractive Russian electrician in his forties, had his own pattern in relationships. No matter how much he tried to do things differently with women, the same thing happened every time: he felt rejected.

Slava's seductive charms were considerable. After a period of avid flirtation and romance, women would invariably fall for him. It was not until they started dating that things went wrong. Something would happen that upset Slava: one woman did not call him back quickly enough, another canceled plans at the last minute, and a third smiled too warmly at a passing stranger. The offenses were often innocent, but each one set off alarm bells in Slava.

When Slava was just five years old, his father abandoned him and his mother. It left a deep wound that never fully healed. Whenever he invested his hopes in someone he loved, he lived in fear that they would inevitably abandon and reject him as he felt his own father had.

Had he allowed himself to be vulnerable and confessed his sense of pain, fear, and rejection, or asked the women to explain their behavior, he might have made an authentic connection with them. But that early loss of his father had had such an impact that he saw the same experience everywhere, as if it were a truth about life. His deepest desire was for these women to prove him wrong. And when they failed, it was yet another devastating blow.

The cycle was so painful that Slava became hypersensitive. At the slightest sign of abandonment, Slava fell headlong into his accustomed rage—not over what they'd done, but over what he assumed it meant. It was nearly impossible for him to think that their actions were innocent; he was consumed by the righteous pain of a five-year-old boy abandoned forever by the father he loved.

No matter how true that abandonment had been in the past, it was not a truth about life. These women wanted to love him, but as long as Slava gave in to his unconscious, instinctual reaction, they couldn't get near him. The way to break this habitual pattern was for Slava to consciously challenge the cognitive illusion. That meant *not* acting instinctively, but taking a deep breath to give the wisdom of his own logic time to kick in.

Thoughts are not facts. We can't believe everything we think. When our logic is overwhelmed by the fear, pain, anxiety and anger churned up by our instincts, Tibetan Buddhist master Tsoknyi Rinpoche says we should acknowledge the feelings, then say to ourselves: "Real, but not true."[6]

Acting on that realization, Slava might allow himself to consider other options: "Maybe this woman's smile is an innocent sign of the very warmth I love in her—not a sign that she wishes she were with someone else" or "Is it possible that something really did come up that prevented her from calling sooner or made her cancel our plans?" In my patient Beatrice's case with Pavlos, had she given herself time to think it through, she might've asked herself: "Do I really want to reject this man, or am I just repeating an old pattern that is no longer serving me?" Every time Slava found a new way to reenact his most painful childhood trauma or Beatrice met another handsome (potential) heartbreaker, their brains went on high alert.

The good news is, when we interrupt our habitual reactions and allow ourselves to see other options, we literally create new patterns in our brains to support us. Engaging in *any* intense activity over time changes the neural pathways in our brains. Learning any new habit or way of being affects the connections between the neurons. Research has shown that the growth of new neurons continues throughout our lifetimes in a process called *neurogenesis*, or the rebirth of the brain.[7]

Exercise: What Stops Me from Living My Truth

As in the prior chapter, I invite you to do another stream-of-consciousness writing exercise. Set your stopwatch to five minutes and write without stopping on the topic What Stops Me from Living My Truth? The Questions for Reflection are included as mere guideposts. As with life, let your writing take you where it may.

Questions for Reflection

1. If I allowed myself to fully live my truth, how would my life be different than it is now?

2. What are my most common rationalizations? What purpose do they serve in my life? How do these rationalizations keep me from living my life fully?

3. What am I really afraid of? When does my logic most often disagree with my instinctive reaction?

HEALING OUR BRAINS

Now we know that continual exposure to positive thoughts and rewarding environments measurably enhances our ability to change and grow.[8] Numerous studies have shown, for instance, that positive experiences in therapy alter the brain in constructive ways that can help people change their lives as well.[9] By challenging our old ways of thinking, we can directly counteract the negative patterns we've built in the past.

Strange as it seems, it's often easier for us to live in the familiar world of our fears than to leave ourselves open to the unknown of each moment as it occurs. The fear of the unknown is deeply buried in our reptilian brains. If we had not instinctively been afraid of wandering into deep, dark caves or slowing down with caution around blind corners, our species might well have been extinct long ago. But in our time, most of us have the luxury of overriding these old fears in comparative safety and freeing ourselves of their constraints. We no longer need to huddle in the sanctuary of our comfort zone.

As Susan Campbell, PhD, says in her book *Getting Real*, experiencing *what is* demands that we set aside our fears. This is the only way we can have a true, authentic connection with another human being. By releasing our fears, expectations, and wishes, we can truly embrace the here and now. This means relinquishing our beliefs about what should or should not be going on, what we expect, what we are prepared for, what we interpret, and what we judge as acceptable.

If we are reluctant to do this, then the connection we make is not with the person in front of us but with our own past: our fears, expectations, wishes, and projections. Staying in the world we know—no matter how painful and dangerous it is—gives us an illusion of control. Paradoxically, this illusion of control keeps us stuck in the same self-sabotaging patterns until we recognize what's going on and are able to finally release our fears and make different choices.

Thanks to new technology, like the functional MRI, which shows activity of the brain in real time, we now have our first clue as to which efforts are the most effective in breaking off old reactions and restoring our brains to vibrant health. These studies prove that love, journaling, and meditation all enhance the health of our brains and help release us from the destructive patterns of the past.

- **Love may stimulate brain health.** The release of oxytocin, or "the love hormone," stimulates the growth of neurons in the brain and may offset the effects of stress.[10]
- **Journaling about trauma has physical benefits.** After writing about traumatic experiences four days in a row, people showed fewer illnesses, better immune function at the cellular level, and a more positive mood.[11]
- **Meditation improves regulation of pain.** Using detached observation in meditation allowed patients to "uncouple" pain from an emotional reaction of alarm over ten weeks of regular practice.[12]

A loving, supportive environment combined with meditation and a means of self-expression (like journaling) can be ideal for healing the traumas of the past and finding a balance between logic and instinct. To get in touch with our most authentic selves, we can go even deeper and connect with our souls.

HEALING OUR SOULS

Many people are surprised to learn that Freud considered psychoanalysis to be "the science of the soul." Unfortunately, his English translator minimized the spiritual implications when he translated the German word for "soul" (*seele*) as "mind" and the German word "spiritual" (*seelische*) as "mental." So instead of reading about "the science of spirituality," English-speaking people read Freud's work on "the mental science."[13] It is time that we bring back the science of spirituality that Freud originally intended.

As my own personal journey has proven to me time and again, fulfillment entails connecting to your soul. One way to do this is by accessing your intuition. The word "intuition" comes from the Latin *intuir*, which means "knowledge from within." It is a subjective mental experience that gives us information about the present moment by enabling us to tap into our true self. Intuition can provide us with the answers to the most important questions in our life. It is that inner voice that breaks through to show us the right way when we are about to make wrong decisions. Using our intuition allows us to access wisdom about our life that we may have been completely unaware we possessed. This knowledge can only be revealed by looking within.

It can sometimes be difficult to distinguish the inner voice of intuition from the inner voice of logic. The voice of the intuitive mind is calm, quiet, and peaceful. Its guidance is steady and unwavering. It operates in the service of our inner wisdom, rather than being dependent on moods, thoughts, or emotions. This inner voice is courageous, willing to do what is needed in a given situation, despite fear.

The voice of the logical mind is what we often refer to as "clear headed." It evaluates situations and strives to resolve problems in the most effective ways possible. When emotions are swirling and the outside noise of other people's opinions threatens our well-being, the logical mind carefully takes one step after another to get you safely to your destination.

It is nearly impossible to hear the voice of intuition in the everyday tumult of life's demands. But a daily contemplative practice such as journaling and/or meditation, as through the exercises in this book, will allow you to hear this voice. Once you become aware of this voice, begin to pay attention to all aspects of it. Is it a loving voice or a harsh voice? Is it a caring voice or a controlling voice? Is it a compassionate and gentle voice or a harsh and punitive voice? Is the voice high or low in pitch? Soft or loud in volume? Masculine or feminine in tone?

This inner voice exists within each of us; it has always been there and is actually communicating with us all the time. Sometimes we hear it and sometimes we don't, but it is never silent. Building a rapport with your inner voice can become an invaluable resource in your life. If you've ever had moments of doubt, or made decisions out of sync with your own best interests, you will find you inner voice especially helpful. Checking in with what you really think and feel about any situation can enable you to avoid mistakes and ensure that you're living a more authentic life every day.

The first time I became aware of my inner voice, I realized that it was the voice of an angry male drill sergeant! This was the voice of my logical mind. It spoke to me in clear, concise language and directives. Perhaps I feared that if I were not so demanding of myself, I would shirk my responsibilities and not live up to my expectations of myself. So I unconsciously created a demanding, powerful, masculine inner voice to help me accomplish my goals and ambitions. My friends suggested that perhaps this masculine inner voice was the voice of my father. But my father is kind and gentle—anything but a drill sergeant.

Only later, by regularly checking in with myself and quieting my thoughts, did I discover the inner voice of my intuitive mind, which spoke much more softly—in images, hunches, gut feelings, intuitive flashes, or bodily sensations. It often emerged as I wrote in my journal, flowing as a stream of ideas emerging from a deeper awareness than my conscious mind. Whenever I began to feel this inner voice emerge, I would relax, listen, and receive its guidance.

Later I came to realize that my drill sergeant self was my own personal illusion of control. Although this aspect of myself may indeed have helped me to achieve some of my goals, it did so at the cost of alienating me from love and compassion for myself. Over time, I learned to soften the cadence of my inner voice and to address myself more softly and lovingly. I was able to do this only after I had made the conscious decision that I no longer needed my drill sergeant self in every aspect of my life.

Even today I have not let it go completely. Sometimes it still helps me get things done quickly and efficiently. But over time I have begun to soften my inner voice, realizing that a more intuitive, feminine approach does not compromise my ability to accomplish my goals and actualize my potential.

Fulfillment entails being able to balance our logic *and* intuition. Over time we can develop the ability to tell which one is appropriate in a given situation. Releasing the instinctual, fear-based patterns that no longer serve us enhances our tolerance for ambiguity and makes us more aware of the present. A tolerance for the uncertainties of life is critical for creativity, richness of experience, and freedom from fear-driven repetitive patterns.[14]

As you begin to build a connection with your inner voice, you will find that it enhances your life with love and compassion. By learning to let go of the illusion of control, we gain *real control* over the choices we make. Instead of allowing old, outdated assumptions to rule our lives, we can experience the freshness and vitality of every moment.

Exercise: Daily Check-Ins

Start by putting aside as much time as you are able, perhaps ten minutes daily, then eventually build up to twenty minutes. One of the best opportunities to enter your inner sanctuary is in the early mornings, so you can check in with yourself before you begin the day. If the morning hours do not work for you, choose a time that is more appropriate for you.

The secret to finding the time for a daily check-in is to make it a priority. You will always find a time if it is your priority. In the words of novelist Anne Lamott, "Almost everything will work again if you unplug it for a few minutes, including you."[15]

Be warned: With any exercise that allows your intuitive mind to surface, your logical mind will make its presence known. It will remind you that you have no time for this. You have too much work to do. There is a to-do list waiting for you. Reassure your logical mind that you have set aside time for this and it will significantly improve the quality of your life. When you are ready, you can begin the exercise by following these steps:

1. Wash your hands and face (a metaphorical "cleansing" from your daily routine).

2. Sit in a comfortable position with your eyes closed.

3. Take a deep breath. Notice your even breathing rhythm, in and out.

4. Connect to your body, becoming aware of what sensations you currently feel.

5. Ask yourself, gently and lovingly, "How am I feeling right now?" Then let the answer come to you, slowly or quickly, as you continue to breathe and feel your body. Do one or more of these possibilities reflect

how you feel? Happy, sad, bored, warm, fearful, uncomfortable, anxious, dubious, worried, pained, restless, confused, in love? If the answer does not come, take a few more deep breaths and ask yourself again, always gently and lovingly.

As you engage in this exercise, the answer may not come for the first few days, perhaps even weeks. As you slowly cultivate this daily practice, your inner voice will begin to break through and finally become heard.

INTUITION AND THE SOUL

Many believe that learning to hear one's inner voice and cultivating one's intuition is synonymous with connecting to one's soul. But what exactly is this mysterious entity we call *soul*?

Since the beginning of time, human beings have been on a quest to understand this arcane and esoteric concept. In many cultures, religions, and philosophies, the soul is believed to be the transcendent or spiritual part of a human being. In Hinduism, the Sanskrit word most closely corresponding to soul is *Atma*, which can mean God, the higher self or universal consciousness. The Bahá'í Faith believes that "the soul is a sign of God, a heavenly gem whose reality the most learned of men hath failed to grasp, and whose mystery no mind, however acute, can ever hope to unravel".[16] Because there is no commonly agreed-upon definition of *soul* from a scientific standpoint, seeking to define and understand it is a challenge for us mentally driven humans.

According to shaman Fernando Broca, the soul is composed of two parts. The first part of the soul, known as the spirit, unites all of humanity together with the divine. The world *spirit* comes from the Latin word *spiritus*, which means "breath." Our spirit, like our breath, unifies us with all of humanity. This is what people are speaking about when they say that we are all interconnected, or "one unified soul."

The spirit is the essence, energy, and divine spark that corresponds to the highest form of what we are. It is the part of us that is pure, perfect, and divine. About the first part of the soul, Fernando says,

When I think of the soul, I think of something pure; completely luminescent and perfect. It cannot learn anything because it already knows everything. It cannot grow because it is already in its most evolved form. So the process of making your ego, your mind and your conscience recognize the soul is a process which in spirituality is called "the process of waking or enlightenment." It is the recognition of the divine light within us.

Certain cultural traditions, including shamanism, believe that this part of our soul is the repository of wisdom, love, and experiences gleaned across many incarnations. Growth and transformation of our soul occurs over many lifetimes through the lessons we learn and choices we make.

In contrast, the second part of the soul is what defines our unique essence, otherwise known as the "self." It is what differentiates us from every other human being on this planet and is the basis of our unique soul corrections (the main lessons we have come into this world to learn) and soul contribution potentials (what we will contribute to humanity over the course of our lifetime). In this way, the first part of our soul unites us with all of humanity and connects us to the divine, while the second part encapsulates our uniqueness.

According to Indian yogi and guru Paramahansa Yogananda, soul wisdom is revealed to human beings through the agency of intuition. Intuitive wisdom can be thought of as the direct perception of truth and appears naturally at those times when our mind is calm. Intuition is not developed by amassing knowledge through the intellect. All power of knowing borrows its ability from intuition. One goal of yoga and meditation is to calm the mind in order to allow yourself to sense the infallible counsel of the inner voice, and thereby connect to your soul. The highest expression of intuition is that by which the soul recognizes itself as a part of something greater: the knower, knowing, and known exist as one.[17]

3

Embracing Your Shadow

We find that—by opening the door to the
shadow realm a little and letting out various
elements a few at a time, relating to them,
finding uses for them, negotiating—we can
reduce being surprised by shadow sneak attacks
and unexpected explosions.

—CLARISSA PINKOLA ESTÉS

As human beings, we are all prone to self-deception. One of the most common ways we deceive ourselves is by blaming others for our own feelings. When Sigmund Freud noticed this tendency for emotional displacement, he called it *projection*. Acknowledging and accepting certain feelings within ourselves creates too much anxiety, so we deny what we feel and instead project these feelings onto others. This is all done outside of our conscious awareness.

Envy is a common projection. If someone is uncomfortable with feeling envious, they may mask the feelings even from themselves and assume instead that they're uncomfortable because *other people are envious of them.* Rather than identifying the envy within themselves, they only see the envy in others. Sometimes people with low self-esteem choose to believe that others are insecure, rather than becoming aware of their own insecurity. Bullying is a prime example. The bully projects his own feelings of vulnerability onto his target, while failing to recognize his own personal sense of inadequacy. A woman who is habitually rude or selfish may constantly accuse other people of being rude or selfish, while not seeing anything wrong with her own behavior. In this way, a projection often reverses the truth.

When we engage in projection, none of us does it deliberately. Unconscious defense mechanisms like this serve an important psychological function. We only project the feelings we find unacceptable—too shameful, too obscene, too dangerous.[1] By deceiving ourselves into thinking that someone else feels those things, not us, we protect ourselves from anxiety and dismay. It is a very human attempt to preserve our self-esteem.

Carl Jung preferred to see these projections as embodiments of ourselves, which he referred to as our shadow side. Since we all have shadows, Jung liked to use the term to refer to any part of our personalities that we have unconsciously rejected or disavowed out of fear, ignorance, shame, or lack of love. He wrote, "If you imagine someone who is brave enough to withdraw all his projections, then you get an individual conscious of a pretty thick shadow…Such a man knows that whatever is wrong in the world is in himself, and if he only learns to deal with his own shadow he has done something real for the world."[2] To this end, many spiritual teachings emphasize that one of primary ways we can change the world is by changing ourselves.

Because the shadow represents the part of us that we feel is "unlovable," it may be tempting to ignore this part of ourselves once we become conscious of it. However, what we resist persists. The harder we try to ignore it and push it away, the more powerful it becomes in our lives. Reclaiming our shadow sides requires us to follow our soul's call and inward response.

By learning to embrace our shadow sides, we become more fully ourselves. It is easily illustrated by the difference in a drawing of a flat cartoon figure or a fully realized portrait with shadows and all. It is impossible to live a fulfilled life as a virtual cartoon figure without every dimension of you. Two particularly common shadows that many of us, including myself, contend with are anger/aggression and dependency, as illustrated in the cases that follow.

THE SHADOW OF AGGRESSION

"My problem is *Jenson!*" Leo exclaimed as we started our session. "I'm sorry, I don't mean to shout, but I've had about enough of him!"

Jenson was the new guy, a computer programmer who had just joined the team at the company where Leo worked. It was hard for him to say exactly what it was that bothered him so much about Jenson that he tried to avoid him whenever possible. Leo could only describe him as "aggressive."

While it's not uncommon to dislike a colleague, it doesn't usually bring people to therapy. There was clearly something else going on. Leo had started to have panic attacks not long after he started working with Jenson. Our conversations soon revealed that Leo's father had been an exceptionally aggressive man. When he was angry, his father would explode in emotional tirades and start throwing things. Both Leo and his mother would cower and try to soothe him, suppressing their own emotions.

"No wonder he makes me feel this way!" Leo said. "He reminds me of my father." It was a significant realization, but it did not reduce his sense of panic. Only when Leo began to express his own feelings of anger and aggression, first in our sessions together and then through journaling at home, was he able to reclaim his shadow. Then his panic attacks began to abate.

Exercise: Identifying Your Projections

For this stream-of-consciousness writing exercise, set your stopwatch to five minutes and write without stopping on the topic Identifying Your Projections. The Questions for Reflection are included as guideposts.

Questions for Reflection

1. What bothers me most about other people?

2. How is this quality a reflection of something I do not like about myself?

THE SHADOW OF REBELLION

Casting yourself as a victim, as in the case of Leo, is one of the more popular uses of projection. Blaming others is always far more comfortable than noticing the ways that we ourselves are responsible for our lives. Another common projection is when people are drawn to your prototypical "bad girls" or "bad boys" as romantic partners. If their own identity does not leave room for spontaneous wildness or bad behavior of any kind, the attraction may be almost compulsive. They are drawn not so much to the other person as to the missing part of themselves!

My patient Valerie is a good example of this. As valedictorian of her class in high school, Valerie had also been class president, prom queen, and head cheerleader. It was not a surprise that the skills she used to win hearts were the same ones she'd learned as "daddy's little girl." Always smiling sweetly and saying just the right thing, Valerie completely identified with being the "good girl."

At the age of seventeen, Valerie met Frank. He was her first love. Frank was ten years older than Valerie, rode a motorcycle, frequently used drugs, and had

had a few run-ins with the law, including some jail time. But none of this seemed to bother Valerie, who had been elated to find that they'd connected on every level. She'd never felt anything like it before. No one understood her like Frank. Something in Frank's cool, aloof, and often rebellious manner made Valerie feel excited, present, and complete all at the same time.

Unfortunately, six months into their relationship, Valerie discovered to her horror that Frank was seeing at least five other women. In retrospect, there had been many red flags that Valerie had chosen to overlook. Feeling trapped by her love for Frank and unable to leave him despite what she knew, Valerie stayed in the relationship for another year until Frank broke it off. She came to see me months later because she could not get Frank out of her mind. Whenever she saw a picture of him with other women on Facebook, she would go into tailspins and cry inconsolably.

In Valerie's eyes, she was the victim of Frank's heartless, unscrupulous ways. Frank uncaringly caused her great pain and she allowed herself to be hurt by him again and again. But this was only half the picture. Psychoanalysis tells us that people who can readily adopt the roles of "good girl" and "victim" like Valerie often have a hard time speaking their minds and owning their aggression.

Valerie disavowed her rebel side, the part of her that was tired of always having to be perfect, sweet, and nice. This was her shadow, the part of her that wanted to do whatever she damn well pleased. This part was angry, resentful, rebellious, and fighting to be free. But this part of Valerie's personality did not fit the "good girl" persona so she avoided experiencing the feelings it produced. Instead, she reclaimed that part of herself in her love for Frank, who fully and readily embraced his rebel "bad boy" side.

As long as a part of Valerie was cut off from herself, she could not heal. To get in touch with her inner voice, Valerie did daily check-ins and writing exercises to express her feelings. While Valerie could readily identify with her sadness, it was far more difficult for her to get in touch with her feelings of anger toward Frank. Because, in her mind, she was still the "good girl" and "good girls" don't get angry. She was afraid that not saying the sweetest thing she could think of at all times would mean turning into a rude, mean-spirited person.

Through her journaling, she identified the parts of her "good girl" behavior that were out of keeping with her true feelings. All those years of keeping a lid on her true feelings had caused a lot of negative energy to build up. Over time she started to disentangle herself from the role of victim she had previously played and express her feelings of anger toward Frank. Slowly but surely thoughts of Frank began to take up less space in Valerie's mind and she was able to move on with her life and, eventually, to a much healthier relationship with a new man. Jung wrote, "One does not become enlightened by imagining figures of light, but by making the darkness conscious."[3] In Valerie's case, accepting heartache, anger, and aggression was uncomfortable at first but liberating in the end. When it comes to the shadow, this spiritual principle is never more true: "What you don't own, owns you."

Exercise: Discovering Your Shadow Side

For the next two days, observe your judgments about other people. Whenever you find yourself feeling upset or annoyed by someone else's words or actions, write down the quality in that person that you find most bothersome. At the end of the two days, review your list. How are these qualities a reflection of your own shadow side?

THE SHADOW OF DEPENDENCY

For his part, all Jack wanted was love. Jack was a forty-nine-year-old gay male film producer in New York City with a gregarious, confident manner and a winning smile. In the film world, everything he touched turned to gold, resulting in multiple blockbusters. Despite his career success, however, his relationships never worked out.

A common pattern emerged when Jack started dating a new man. In the beginning, everything would go well. Soon Jack would think he had finally found his life partner. As he expressed those sentiments, things would take a turn for the worse. With a new level of intimacy and commitment, things would become more serious emotionally. Then, like clockwork, Jack's partner would become "too needy" in Jack's eyes, and Jack would end the relationship.

The strange thing was, these "needy" men were all successful, highly independent professionals. Something in his story didn't fit.

As a boy, Jack had grown up as the eldest son everyone depended on in a big Irish Catholic family. On the one hand, Jack thrived on being like a second father to everybody, because he loved taking care of people. Yet another part of him resented their dependency and demanded to know: "Why can't I find anyone I can depend on?"

When I asked Jack if any part of him identified with the neediness he perceived in the men he dated, his eyes teared up for the first time in therapy.

As a little boy, Jack desperately craved contact with his father, who was home for only a few days a month between international business trips. He always cried when his father left and waited for him to call, but his father rarely called while he was away and never said when he'd be coming home.

Throughout his childhood, Jack spent days, weeks, and months longing to see his father to no avail. He had to find a way to defend himself against the futility and pain of those emotions. Unconsciously, he chose to tell himself, "I don't need my father. I don't need anyone."

As a survival mechanism to protect himself from all the pain, Jack slowly learned to tuck away his needs, portraying to the outside world a perfectly constructed winning smile and air of confidence, success, self-sufficiency, and independence. For many years, this "false self" got him plenty of popularity, fame, and recognition. But deep inside, in those rare moments when he was finally honest with himself, Jack felt unhappy and alone.

When he started a new relationship, this unmet need was like a time bomb waiting to go off. There is a big difference between being "needy" and having needs, but Jack didn't think about that. His own childhood need for his father's love and affection had caused him too much pain.

Any time a man Jack was involved with expressed his own needs, Jack winced from the memory of his own pain. Rather than bring back the whole saga, he defended himself by pushing it away—inadvertently pushing the men he loved away at the same time.

By beginning to identify and listen to his inner voice, Jack was able to feel what was actually happening in his relationships and his life. That awareness shifted things in the context of the relationship he and I had established. As if a fog had cleared, Jack realized that the men who loved and needed him did not need to re-create the pain he'd felt about his unmet needs as a boy. His own unconscious associations were creating that. Once he stopped projecting that old story onto his boyfriends, his fear of their dependency evaporated. The next time he found a viable life partner, he was finally able to embrace a fulfilling, long-term relationship with him.

In suppressing our darkness, we are also suppressing our greatest light. By denying our ugliness, we lessen our beauty. By denying our fear, we minimize our courage. By denying our greed, we reduce our generosity. When a projection is reclaimed, it is like a revelation of the self. As Jung said, "To confront a person with his shadow is to show him his own light."[4] Only by integrating the shadow and making peace with our unlovable parts can we learn to fully love ourselves.

Exercise: Guided Meditation for Relaxation

As you did in the exercise in chapter 1, remove any distractions from your environment so you can fully surrender to this process. Put on comfortable clothing and go to your favorite place in your home or a beautiful place in nature.

You may want to light some candles and incense, or put on some relaxing music to help create a peaceful atmosphere for yourself. Keep a journal nearby so you can write about your experiences.

Read these directions all the way through before starting this meditation.

This system of breathing floods your brain with oxygen, which gives your body the signal to relax. Once you begin, you may yawn or feel tired. This is normal. Just focus on your breathing and envision your whole body relaxing.

When you are ready, sit in a comfortable position, then begin. Close your eyes and take several slow deep breaths:

- Inhale through your nose for the count of two.
- Hold your breath for the count of four.
- Exhale through your nose for the count of eight.
- Repeat for ten breaths.

Now, with your eyes closed, imagine yourself walking inside the basket of a hot air balloon. As you step inside the basket, the hot air balloon slowly begins to rise and take you to a new world far above the clouds that you never knew existed. As you visualize your hot air balloon rising beyond the horizon, imagine your body getting progressively lighter and lighter. Eventually, the hot air balloon stops and you step out into a beautiful new land you have never seen before.

Lush green plants and a brilliant blue sky beckon you forward as you begin to walk and explore this beautiful new landscape. Notice the trees, flowers, animals, sky, clouds, garden, forest, and anything else that your secret new space has within it. This is the land of your unconscious. You can create in your mind whatever would feel most peaceful, beautiful, serene, and relaxing to you. You can also re-create in this space a place from your past that you associate with freedom, serenity, and peace.

How do you feel to be in this new space? What colors do you see? How does it feel beneath your feet? How does it smell? What are you wearing? Is the sun shining? Take a minute to look in all directions and notice what else this special space holds in store for you.

As you walk around, create a sacred meditation space in your new landscape where you can come to find all the answers you've ever desired. Now take five slow deep breaths:

- Inhale through your nose for the count of two.
- Hold your breath for the count of four.
- Exhale through your nose for the count of eight.

This will bring you into an even deeper state of relaxed awareness. While in a state of meditation, reflect on one or two of the following questions:

1. What am I most afraid somebody will find out about me?

2. What's the biggest lie I ever told myself?

3. What's the biggest lie I ever told someone else?

4. What parts of myself do I own and express fully?

5. What parts of myself do I hide and why?

After you've taken the time to reflect on these questions, write down your reflections in your journal.

4

Living Your Purpose

If you don't know what you're living for, you haven't yet lived.

—Rabbi Noah Weinberg

"What is the meaning of life?" It is one of the central questions posed by philosophers, theologians, scientists and writers since ancient times. Many of us wonder about it in high school or college but soon get caught up in what we're doing and forget to ask why we're doing it. As life goes by, the question returns again and again. Caught up in the obligations of our lives, it is easy to lose track of what matters most to us. As we go through the motions of meeting our responsibilities, our lives can become so stagnant that the question comes back to us in various forms: Why am I doing this? Why does it matter? What do I really want? What is my purpose?

YOUR SOUL CORRECTION

It is possible to choose a life with greater purpose by aligning with your authentic self. Every person comes into the world with a specific purpose that is unique to that individual, as well as a general purpose that we all share. These are our

47

soul corrections, or what our soul has come into this world to correct. Often these corrections will lead to some of the most important lessons we learn in life. In fact, kabbalists believe that the "correction of the soul," or *Tikkun HaNefesh* is our primary purpose on earth.[1]

I often tell my patients they can identify the area that is most in need of a soul correction by asking, "What is the source of greatest pain in my life?" Ordinarily, we all do everything we can to avoid pain. But when it comes to growth and healing, pain can be our best friend and greatest guide. As Joseph Campbell said, "Where you stumble, there your treasure is."[2]

When recurring struggles and pain emerge that interfere with our lives, they draw attention to the types of soul correction we need. The area most in need of soul correction is the thing that keeps coming up again and again, much to our dismay. Often these patterns are what Freud called repetition compulsions— unconscious and self-sabotaging behaviors that we may feel at a loss to change. Transforming and clearing this "baggage" is precisely how we achieve our *soul correction*. In Part Two of this book, you'll learn more about four of the most common soul corrections I encounter in my private practice: improving relationships, releasing addictions, transforming fears, and harnessing personal power.

There are also several soul corrections we all share. One of these is to align with our soul rather than our ego. We always have a choice to align with light, goodness, optimism, hope, love, kindness, and generosity—the qualities of the soul. We can also just as easily focus on darkness, fear, pessimism, anger, hatred, jealousy, pride—the qualities of the ego. The founder of the Kabbalah Center, Rav Yehuda Ashlag, teaches that the Universe will support the choices we make. Follow the light, and we will be pushed toward more light. Follow the darkness, and we will be pushed toward more darkness.[3] One of our soul corrections is to become better able to align with light, love, and expansion rather than darkness, fear, and stagnation.

So how do we do this? We have two choices. We can either achieve this proactively or reactively. Changing ourselves proactively means identifying those aspects of our lives where we are aligned with our ego, that part of us that keeps us small and constricted. Proactive change entails first identifying the ways in which we are falling short of being the best version of ourselves. This recognition is an accomplishment in itself. Just to see ourselves clearly and make the decision to change is a huge step forward. It is our nature as human beings to be dominated by our egos at times. To depart from this mindset and commit to growth and transformation is actually quite amazing—it does not happen to everybody.

Many people never develop the inner clarity that allows them to differentiate between who they are, as compared to the person they want to be. These people too will undergo their soul corrections, yet rather than doing so proactively, they will often do so reactively. Reactive transformation occurs through pain and suffering as we react to the external circumstances of our lives. Pain and suffering are inevitable parts of life. We will all feel pain. We will all suffer. Yet the more proactive growth we are able to achieve by overcoming the limitations of our egos and expanding our consciousness, the less pain and suffering we will have to endure. A large part of pain and suffering is not about the obstacles we encounter, but our reactions to those obstacles.

So how do you enable proactive growth to occur? By identifying exactly that which is *most difficult, fearful, and uncomfortable* for you to do in a given situation, and doing precisely that. Comfort and complacency are the enemies of growth and transformation. Growth entails choosing the path of *most* rather than *least* resistance exactly because it enables you to expand. In this way, you grow as a person by holding back your reactive, ego-based responses and allowing your proactive, soul-based responses to emerge.

I am not implying here that you must repress or deny your difficult feelings. If somebody truly upsets you or pushes your buttons, you are denying your true feelings if you say, "I'm not upset" or "What they said wasn't that hurtful." Being proactive does not mean being in denial. Like we discussed in the previous chapter, welcoming in your difficult feelings is an important part of befriending your shadow side, the part of yourself that you may view as unlovable and therefore be tempted to deny or disavow. By learning to recognize and observe difficult feelings without reacting to them, you slowly train yourself to align with your soul instead of your ego.

If somebody does truly upset you, the proactive response would be to honestly acknowledge how you feel—"I am upset" or "What they said was hurtful"—and then *not* revert to your usual response. Proactive growth means going against your nature. If your typical response would be to lash out in anger, the proactive response may be to restrict your reaction, pause, take a deep breath and, once you're feeling calmer, discuss how you're feeling with the person involved, if that is appropriate. If your typical response would be to shut down when things get heated, the proactive response may be to restrict that reaction, pause, take a deep breath, and be open and honest with the other person about how you're feeling. In contrast, if your typical response would be to ignore the whole thing and sweep it under the rug, the proactive response may be to restrict that reaction, pause, take a deep breath, and honestly ask yourself, "How does this really make me feel? Am I running away from my emotions? What feelings am I trying to avoid by sweeping this under the rug?" Going against your nature is not easy. It is a disciplined and concerted lifelong practice, the mastery of which requires time, patience, and maturity. While going against your nature may feel uncomfortable, it is the most effective way to transform your reactive, ego-based responses to proactive, soul-based responses.

To help you practice responding to life's challenges in a proactive way, I've included an adaptation of the Kabbalistic Proactive Formula in our next exercise.[4]

Exercise: Using the Proactive Formula

The Proactive Formula is a powerful way to transform your response in a given situation from a reactive, ego-based response to a proactive, soul-based response. The following four steps will help you to put the Proactive Formula into practice:

1. An obstacle occurs. This could be absolutely anything that upsets you or stresses you out. Observe your reaction to the situation. How does it make you feel? Where do you feel the pain, sadness, anger, tension or stress in your body? Focus on the feeling as you breathe in and out for a count of five. Sometimes just the act of neutral observation, taking a step back from an emotional situation, is enough to release the pain, sadness, anger, tension or stress you're feeling.

2. Recognize this obstacle as an opportunity for growth. Realize that your reaction—not the obstacle—is the real enemy. Although we cannot always change the obstacles that come into our lives, we have the free will to respond from a place of soul instead of ego. Ask yourself, "How would I typically respond in a situation like this?" "What would be the reactive, ego-based response in this situation?" "What would be the proactive, soul-based response?"

3. Shut down your reactive response and connect to your soul-based response. You could do this in a number of different ways:
   a. Imagine what somebody you respect and admire might do in this situation. Usually one's hero or role model would take the high road and express a more elevated point of view and understanding of the situation.
   b. Focus on somebody or something you love and why. Hold a picture of the beloved person or object in your heart as you breathe in and

out for a count of five. As you bring love into your heart, it often becomes easier to respond from a place of soul rather than from a place of ego.

    c. Take responsibility for the obstacle. What role might you have had in bringing this obstacle into your life? By taking responsibility for our obstacles, we can often conquer the difficult feelings they bring up.

    d. Ask for help from above—from God, a Higher Power, the Light, or the Universe—in silently saying the following prayer or request to yourself, "Please help me connect to my soul."

4. Now with knowledge, responsibility and a higher consciousness, you're ready to respond in a proactive way. How do you feel after having responded proactively in this situation?

Being proactive requires taking a pause, observing your feelings, taking responsibility for your response, and choosing to go against your nature. In contrast, being reactive allows you to put our head in the sand, to remain stuck, feel like victims of circumstances, and be powerless in the face of adversity. When my patients are faced with a choice, I often ask, "Which one requires the greater stretch from you?" The greater the stretch is, the greater the growth and transformation you will experience.

YOUR SOUL CONTRIBUTION

How often are we afraid to say what we truly believe because it is all too important how the world perceives us? Sometimes we're so busy trying to look good that we forget who we really are. As William Shakespeare said, "This, above all, to thine own self be true."[5]

In this vein, another soul correction we all share, if we choose to accept it, is to live authentically and find a way to reveal our unique *soul contribution* to the world. Your soul contribution, sometimes referred to as your *calling*, is the unique way you choose to use your talents, skills, abilities, passions, desires, and experiences in the service of others. This may include choosing a profession or career which centers on helping others, fighting for a social cause, giving to a charity you believe in, improving the world, or nurturing and raising children. The possibilities are endless.

Inherent in the concept of soul contribution is the idea of giving and sharing. The more we give of ourselves, our talents, skills, and abilities, the more we are able to actualize our full potential. Because no one can be like you, it is important to develop the courage to live authentically and purposefully and, at the same time, allow others to do likewise. Identifying your soul contribution, which educator and author Katherine Woodward Thomas calls your soul's purpose, is a vital stepping-stone to fulfillment. She writes,

Discovering our soul's purpose is rarely an event, although epiphanies do happen. More often than not, it's a process that requires patience and perseverance. In order to discover it, you must pay attention to what stirs your passions, lights you up, and just comes naturally. When you are living inside your soul's purpose, you are often in flow. You lose track of time. You feel alive, useful, of service, and a part of all that is.[6]

Though we may not always be aware of it, I believe that the deepest craving in all our hearts is to live for something greater than ourselves. We are instinctively searching for a purpose that transcends the boundaries of our own personal lives. It is a deep, very human hunger that we can only satisfy by believing we are living in such a way that, by the end, we will have made the contribution we have come into this world to make.

Exercise: Identifying Your Soul Contribution

I now invite you to do a stream-of-consciousness writing exercise on the topic Your Soul Contribution. Set your stopwatch to five minutes and write without stopping, beginning with the first thought, impression or vision that comes into your mind and working through as many as time allows. Do not censor any thoughts, writing down even unconnected single words that come to mind. Just keep writing! If you find yourself wanting to write for more than five minutes, continue to do so until you feel like you have written all that you wanted to say. If you get stuck on a prompt or thought, don't worry! Move to the next one and see what emerges. Alternately, if you'd like to focus on just one thought or subject during the five minutes, that's fine, too. You can revisit this exercise as often as you'd like and look across your writing from various sittings to see if repetitions, patterns, or contrasts emerge.

Questions for Reflection

1. When do you feel most alive? What do you love to do? What are you passionate about?

2. When you were a child, what did you want to do when you grew up?

3. What comes most naturally to you? What have people always told you that you're good at?

4. What unique talent, skill, ability, or interest can you share with others?

5. What is your soul contribution?

The above exercise can be done together with the exercise in chapter 1 titled "What do you most deeply want?" These two exercises will help you identify your soul's deepest longings, which are key to understanding how you can best be of service to others and the world.

Patients frequently come to me trying to understand what they are supposed to be doing with their lives. They may be at the beginning of their lives, having just completed high school or college, trying to figure out their life's next chapter. Some feel extreme pressure to move forward yet simply cannot take the next step, feeling held back in their lives by an intangible yet palpable sense of fear, confusion and inner conflict.

Other patients come to me mid-life or mid-career, realizing that they are not as fulfilled in their work as they had hoped, and contemplating an important life change. Or they may feel like they've accomplished what they've wanted in a particular profession or industry and are ready for their next challenge. Making dramatic transitions mid-life almost always involves soul-searching, sacrifice, and inner conflict. But sometimes the pain of staying where you are exceeds the potential pain of uncertainty and change. Dramatic transitions do not always come into our lives by choice, either. Sometimes life hands us challenges—our company folds, we get fired, we're forced to move—and we're left with the question of how to make do.

In my work with patients at this stage in life, I have seen senior executives become college professors and stay-at-home moms, investment bankers become actors and writers, teachers and consultants go back to school to become healers, to name a few. I've seen patients take big risks and reap even bigger rewards. But I've also seen failure, loss, and people recognizing that things weren't really so bad after all, but only after they had made their transitions.

The potential for failure is the undeniable price of risk. But choices of this nature are never truly failures or mistakes if you learn from them and gain a sense of clarity about your soul contribution in the process. Sometimes you can only know what you're supposed to do or where you're supposed to be by going in the "wrong" direction. We learn about what we want by experiencing the opposite. These are our blessings in disguise.

Even if we find a purpose that feels meaningful or is what we'd love to do, we can easily talk ourselves out of it, or get distracted and move on to something else. As Henry David Thoreau famously wrote in *Walden*, "The mass of men lead lives of quiet desperation."[7] It's true of most people, even today, but if that kind of life was enough for you, you wouldn't be reading this book. You sense, as I do, that there has to be so much more to life than that.

Pausing to question the path you're on is a vital part of living a fulfilled life. The key is to let the process of questioning, and the subsequent answers, matter and to take the answers to heart. Your mind may argue against it, but our minds do not always know what's best. It's better to open your heart and listen for that still voice that answers from your soul. Poet and novelist Hermann Hesse said it best:

> *Everyone had only one true vocation: to find himself...to discover his own destiny, not just any destiny, and to live it totally and undividedly. Anything else was just a half-measure, an attempt to run away, an escape back to the ideal of the masses, an adaptation, fear of one's own nature.*[8]

Until Joseph Jaworski found his genuine vocation, he lived life in the fast lane as a top international corporate lawyer. Living in a huge house, making loads of money, earning a great reputation, having girlfriends in every city, and gambling, he blindly believed that he was making his contribution. The day his wife asked him for a divorce was the beginning of his "dark night of the soul."

Darkness ultimately led to his renewal as he began to see the world anew and open himself up to a form of universal guidance of which he was previously unaware. The moment this universal guidance entered Jaworksi's life was the day he quit his law firm to follow his heart and actualize a dream to start the

American Leadership Forum (ALF), a nonprofit organization whose mission is to join and strengthen diverse leaders to better serve the public good. The interesting part of Jaworski's journey is that when he finally decided to start the ALF, he knew nothing about leadership curriculum and development. He had much fear and uncertainty. Yet he forged onward and succeeded, with a little help from above. In his book *Synchronicity* he writes,

> *If we are truly committed to follow our dream, there exists beyond ourselves and our conscious will, a powerful force that helps us along the way and nurtures our growth and transformation. Our journey is guided by invisible hands with infinitely greater accuracy than is possible through our unaided conscious will. [Joseph] Campbell says it is the "supernatural assisting force..."*[9]

GUIDANCE FROM THE UNIVERSE

What is this "supernatural assisting force" about which Joseph Campbell speaks? Is there really such a thing as guidance from the Universe? Or is our wish for guidance merely an embodiment of our desire to forsake our free will once and for all and be rescued by a supreme being? Can we ever know for certain? If so, how? If not, then what are we to believe?

An interesting answer to this oft-pondered question comes from seventeenth-century French philosopher, mathematician, and physicist Blaise Pascal. Pascal's Wager posits that we as human beings base our lives, to some degree, on whether or not God exists. For our purposes here, God may be interchangeable with any Higher Power. Based on the assumption that the stakes are infinite if God does in fact exist (for instance, the promise of eternity in heaven and the possibility of infinite guidance from a Higher Power) and that there is even a small probability of this, Pascal argues that the rational decision is to live as though God exists and seek to believe in God. If God does not actually exist, the losses are finite. Whereas if God does exist, the gains are infinite. Rationally speaking, it pays to be a believer.

Many physicians have sided with Pascal. In her book *The Fear Cure*, Dr. Lissa Rankin writes: "The universe may be orderly and meaningful even if we don't understand how it operates, and we may be protected by a loving Universal Intelligence that guides us through outer signs and inner knowing." My life and the lives of my family, friends, and patients have been filled with guidance in the form of outer signs and inner knowing.

A therapist friend of mine had a patient, William, who discovered her practice through a "sign" of this nature. While William was looking for a therapist, he brought home a book from the local library and found the therapist's card between the pages. Interpreting this as a sign, he called her to book an appointment the next day. He's now been working with her for two years. How her card got inside that library book, the therapist has no idea. I was so taken with this story that I considered a new marketing strategy for my own practice: leaving business cards in random library books!

I received a "sign" of guidance after a particularly grueling overnight shift during my psychiatry residency. As I left the hospital beyond exhausted, I wondered yet again if I had made the right decision to be a doctor. I loved the study of medicine and I loved working with patients. But whenever I was squeezed between the chaos on the ward and utter sleep deprivation, I had my doubts.

A few months earlier, I had my first encounter with Kabbalah. The pursuit of spirituality was still new to me, but walking home that day as the sun was just beginning to rise, I decided to embrace my spiritual self and ask the Universe for a sign. Under my breath, I silently asked, *Universe, please give me a sign that I am on the right path in life… that this is really what I'm supposed to be doing with my life.*

Just as I turned the corner at the next block I saw a small crowd of neighbors huddled over a crumpled body on the street. At this hour, the street was mostly empty except for the occasional taxi. I ran to the scene and saw an elderly woman who had fallen out of her wheelchair when it inadvertently crossed over the curb. The few people on the street had all rushed to help. As we straightened out her wheelchair, I started asking her a few questions to assess her state of mind: Was she okay? Was she in pain? Had she hit her head? She said she was fine but had hit her head slightly. We erred on the side of caution and she agreed to stop by the emergency room, conveniently located a block away, to make sure there was no damage.

"Thank you!" I said to the Universe, as I headed home. Although tentative, I was blown away at how quickly I had received what clearly qualified as a "sign." It was my first test of this new spirituality. Encountering and being able to help this woman was the confirmation I needed at that moment to quell my doubts. Despite the grueling nature of residency, this moment energized me and helped me keep going when future doubts arose.

Sometimes, guidance from the Universe may take an unexpected form: something that appears quite negative may turn out not to be so. Correctly interpreting this kind of pattern once saved my friend Patrick's life. In the summer before he started law school, Patrick got into two freak car accidents in close succession, which left him wondering why death seemed to be following him.

In the first accident, Patrick was driving at the speed limit on the highway in a small compact car, and out of nowhere, a driver lost control of his car and slammed into Patrick's car head-on! About six months later, Patrick was a passenger in a car, and as the car accelerated to merge onto a highway, the steering wheel mysteriously malfunctioned and the car swerved haphazardly across several lanes of high-speed traffic, ultimately falling into a ravine and flipping several times. It was a well-maintained car, and again, the accident seemed like a total fluke.

In the two incidents, Patrick suffered some minor injuries, but overall he felt very lucky the injuries weren't worse and he was grateful to be alive. Beyond the physical damage, he did feel quite shaken. These accidents left him fearful of driving, given that injury and the potential for death now seemed like unpredictable and real possibilities around every corner. It also left him asking, what is the Universe up to? Is it my time to go soon? What is going on?

One week after the second accident, Patrick had been planning to travel by plane with several others to a developing country to do volunteer work. Although he was physically intact after that second accident and really didn't like to disappoint others, he decided uncharacteristically to cancel the trip because he was still feeling a bit shaken up. Although he tried to find a replacement, no one was available to go in his place.

Then Patrick heard the most devastating news. The plane that he would have been on had crashed and everyone on board had died. He was shocked, saddened, and dealing with grief, yet also was in disbelief that the second freak car accident had, ironically, saved his life!

GUIDANCE THROUGH PAIN

Things are not always what they seem. As Patrick's story illustrates, what causes us pain can work to our advantage, even though we cannot always appreciate or understand it at the time. My patient Ilse's story illustrates this principle in a slightly different form.

One day a soft-spoken, no-nonsense Swedish woman who was the CEO of a nonprofit organization to help children with cancer came to see me for an evaluation. Ilse had been suffering from such terrible stomach pains that she had been forced to miss a week's work every few months for years. Despite an extensive medical evaluation, the cause of her symptoms couldn't be identified. After her fifth visit to the gastroenterologist all the lab results were still negative, so she was sent to me for a psychological evaluation.

Ilse was the very opposite of the people who feign an illness to take time away from work. She prided herself on having an iron will that allowed her to accomplish anything she set her mind to. Her superiors agreed. Her reputation at her nonprofit was stellar. She had raised more money and advanced the mission of her nonprofit more than any other CEO in the organization's thirty-year history. Ilse was always the first in the office and the last to leave. Having to take time off for a stomachache was almost as onerous to Ilse as the stomach pains themselves!

As you can imagine, for a woman who had managed to take complete control of her life in every other way, feeling powerless was completely unacceptable. She was determined to get to the root of the problem.

We first discussed the possibility that her stomach issues could have had their roots in her travels. The summer before her symptoms began, she contracted giardiasis, a parasitic infection, while establishing a cancer program for children in India. Even though Ilse had received the appropriate treatment, her stomach was never the same again. However, giardia alone could not explain why Ilse's symptoms were particularly bad in times of high stress, with months of symptom-free periods in between.

Ilse and I began to consider the possibility that perhaps her stomach issues had some sort of adaptive value. What if they were somehow providing her with relief from an emotional conflict?

In exploring this possibility, we talked about a concept that medicine calls primary and secondary gains. A primary gain gives us something we want. But as human beings, we are often conflicted about what we want. We may want one thing, but also want its opposite at the same time. As Freud observed, sometimes we can be completely unaware of many of our deepest desires.

It's not uncommon for a patient to initially deny that they are getting any benefit from an illness whatsoever. After all, who wants to be sick? The truth is, sometimes it's worth it, especially if it gets us something we want or need. This is often something we may initially believe is unacceptable to us or those around us. This could include permission to slow down, make lifestyle changes, reduce stressors, and remove ourselves from relationships and situations that are harmful to us and our well-being.

Secondary gains are the benefits we get by sidestepping challenges until we are ready to face them. If a first-time father who feels anxious about interacting with his children finds he doesn't have time anyway, because he has to work through the weekend, then working weekends is reinforced. He may genuinely want to spend time with his kids and genuinely have to work, but the situation helps him avoid his anxiety. Secondary gains are rarely conscious. It doesn't mean people are faking it or trying to manipulate the situation. It's simply the way our minds and bodies work together to get us what we need precisely because we may not be consciously aware of what we most deeply desire.

Ilse strongly identified with her self-image as an iron-willed, ambitious hard worker. What she needed was more time and space to care for herself. But that was not a part of her master plan. Needing care connoted weakness to Ilse. And she was not weak!

Only through debilitating stomach pains could Ilse justify the need to take care of herself. From her body's point of view, it was a brilliant solution. It allowed her to avoid guilt and offered the secondary gain of allowing her to give herself the rest and care she needed.

Growing up in Sweden, Ilse had lived in the shadow of an older brother who was the "golden child." In the parents' eyes, he could do no wrong. To make up for it, Ilse worked twice as hard and accomplished twice as much to get her parents' approval, but they never noticed. They had already decided how they viewed her and had no intention of changing their assessment. It was as if they were saying, "Don't confuse us with facts. Our minds are made up!" Finally realizing she was never going to get their approval, Ilse moved to the United States when she was thirty-two. She pushed herself to achieve great things, and kept her foot on the gas at all times. Except when she got sick.

"Is it possible that this stomach pain is the only excuse you'd accept for taking your foot off the gas?" I asked her.

"These pains aren't imaginary," Ilse insisted.

"I know that," I assured her. "I'm just wondering what other choices your body would have if it needed you to take a little time off? Would you do it for anything less than the most debilitating illness? What other choices did you leave yourself?"

Ilse shifted uncomfortably in her chair, realizing that the very pride she took in pushing ahead no matter what had cut off her options. There were few reasons she would accept for missing work. Her love of work and drive to excel had painted her into a corner where only abject sickness could get her to slow down. It was an important realization.

Over the coming months, Ilse and I worked to bring more balance into her life. It was perfectly all right to keep her foot on the gas most of the time, as long as she gave herself time to relax with a leisurely lunch in the sunshine or a stroll through Central Park once in a while. Otherwise, frankly, she'd face the consequences. Her unconscious mind was at least as strong and determined as she was. If it had to intervene to get her to slow down, she knew it would.

As Ilse's life became more balanced, her gastrointestinal symptoms slowly began to recede. In times of extended stress, she still has occasional symptoms, but their frequency and duration is much improved. And Ilse's degree of understanding of the nature of the problem is much greater.

This case is another example of where things are not always what they seem. Debilitating stomach pains were actually the cry for help from Ilse's body and unconscious mind that finally led Ilse to slow down and lead a more balanced and, ultimately, more fulfilling life. In this way, Ilse's pain was guiding her to accomplish one of her *soul corrections*—cultivating self-love and self-care.

RESISTING THE GUIDANCE

It helps to have faith in the friendly Universe described by Einstein, though faith is not something that always comes naturally, especially in the face of pain—our own or that of others. Yet even the pain we experience and witness around us can be seen as part of our healing and growth process. When it is hard for us to appreciate or understand the guidance we are receiving from the Universe, we may frequently misunderstand and/or resist this guidance.

I have certainly experienced this many times. After I ended a five-year relationship in my early thirties, I began to develop a pattern of drawing into my life single men who were interesting, intelligent, charismatic, successful and, like clockwork, emotionally unavailable. They all truly believed that they wanted to marry the right woman, but deep inside they all had a deep-rooted fear of commitment. As you may know, these kinds of men are excellent pursuers. As long as I was not fully available to them, they were eager to pursue me. But as soon as I raised the question of a relationship, they ran like the wind.

Had I been really listening to the guidance the Universe was giving me, I might've known that I was drawing in the wrong kind of men. But, like Ilse, when I became fixated on something, I wanted it with all my heart, mind, and will. While my heart was gently coaxing my mind to let go of my plans and surrender to what was naturally unfolding in the relationship, my mind fought to retain control of the situation. I can tell you, I wasted a lot of my extra energy on this inner conflict. Telling me to let go of this obviously self-sabotaging pattern was like telling an addict to stay away from a drug. I was addicted to the drama, the excitement, the anticipation, and the pain that these men created in my life. And it seemed like there was nothing I could do, despite my best efforts, to kick the habit.

In time I realized that I needed to carefully reconsider my soulmate selection criteria. In certain areas, I needed to make it more stringent—no more ignoring red flags that signaled emotional unavailability! In other areas, like the long checklist of qualities I expected every man I dated to possess, I needed to loosen my grip.

After having my heart broken time and again, a deeply spiritual man with a beautiful soul and open heart walked into my life and swept me off my feet. At first I was confused by the experience. It felt very different from my prior dating history. Jesse was kind, generous, straightforward, and comfortable with his emotions. He did not play games. He was honest with me about how he felt and what he was looking for in his life.

At first it was a little overwhelming. Then I realized that was actually a good sign. It meant I was outside my comfort zone. Something had shifted. I had finally drawn in a different kind of man!

When we started dating, I was thirty-seven and Jesse was fifty-four, which is older than the men I had typically dated. He led a fascinating life as a model, photographer, and filmmaker that enabled him to live, work, and travel all over the world. I loved how his mind worked. He was a brilliant man and an original thinker. Having been on a spiritual path for his whole life, he was dedicated to growing as a person as opposed to being satisfied with a life of creature comforts and complacency. Most importantly, he had a deep capacity for love, which, truth be told, was quite frightening to me for some time.

I had been gathering around me all those emotionally unavailable men because a part of me felt safer avoiding emotional intimacy. If I was going to be available for all the love that Jesse was able to give me—and to reciprocate in turn—I was going to need to step outside my comfort zone and slowly open my heart.

Thomas Moore, author of *Soul Mates*, defines a soul mate as "…somebody to whom we feel profoundly connected, as though the communication and communing that takes place between us were not the product of intentional efforts, but rather a divine grace."[10]

From day one, this relationship was full of divine grace in the form of little unexpected coincidences or synchronicities. One of the most poignant signs was that, from our second date onward, an inner channel of communication opened between us. We finished each other's sentences and literally read each other's minds. Moreover, whenever I asked him a question, he would answer me honestly, no matter what. I loved how honest, real, and authentic he was.

As I slowly and cautiously eased into this relationship, I began to experience a level of comfort and familiarity I had never experienced before. The more I got to know Jesse, the more similar I realized we were on the soul level. We had similar values. We were both mission-driven and needed to make a difference in this world by helping humanity. We loved to work hard and valued originality and creativity. Quite often, the status quo felt stuffy and constraining to both of us.

Although the Universe's guidance in my love life had been a source of great pain to me, it ultimately led me to find my soulmate. We were married on July 10, 2016. Becoming open to spiritual guidance in a friendly Universe was, in this situation, a powerful catalyst for growth, healing, and transformation—even with the many painful lessons along the way.

Exercise: Exploring Pain

For this stream-of-consciousness writing exercise, bring to mind an area in your life in which you experience pain—this could be physical, psychological, or emotional pain. Begin by writing about this pain—when, where, and why does it occur? Describe it in as much detail as you'd like, using metaphors if helpful. Now, focus on the following questions:

1. What have I learned from this pain?

2. What, if anything, do I think this pain still has to teach me?

3. Am I resisting being guided by this pain? If so, how and why?

GUIDANCE AND PURPOSE

Many of my psychiatry colleagues, however, may view the stories in this chapter quite differently. From their perspective, hindsight is twenty-twenty. To them, perceiving "guidance" from the Universe is an attempt to construct a magical, sentimental meaning from a series of random, unconnected events. My skeptical colleagues would say that my desire to believe that the Universe is guiding me comes from a yearning to find order in what may otherwise be chaotic, random happenstance. My magical stories of divine guidance may actually be an unconscious defense against uncertainty and the unknown aspects of life. If the Universe is looking after me, like a loving father in the sky, I feel special and cared for. This argument speaks to the psychological benefits I receive from feeling guided.

As a psychiatrist myself, I certainly cannot discount this possibility. The two points of view are not mutually exclusive, however. In my extensive search for meaning and purpose in my own life and those of my patients, I have carefully considered Pascal's Wager and ultimately chosen to believe in a Higher Power. The psychological benefits for me, if indeed my belief is right, include a life of magic, wonder, and guidance. If I am right and there is something greater out there, the gains are tremendous. If I'm wrong, however, I'm no worse off than where I started. As per Pascal's Wager, the benefits of belief outweigh the costs of nonbelief.

I do not believe, however, that psychological benefits alone could account for the deep sense of fulfillment to be found in aligning with something greater than ourselves, be it God, a Higher Power, or the vast, majestic patterns that lie in the Universe. The more we are able to align with universal guidance, the more we can live from our authentic self and be guided to discover our soul corrections and soul contributions. In this way, we can move into the beautiful flow of life where random events may take on new meaning and seemingly inconsequential meetings may reveal themselves to be major turning points in our lives. As Harvard-trained author and mind-body medicine expert Joan Borysenko, PhD, wrote,

If you take a single step toward positive change, that divine energy will take a hundred steps toward you. New worlds and unbelievable possibilities will open up for you. The synchronicities that will begin appearing in your life will become a source of delight and amazement.[11]

PART II
Soul Correction

FROM: I give away my power

TO: I take my power back and create the life I want to live

I am not what happened to me. I am what I choose to become.

—CARL JUNG

5

Improving Relationships

What sages and mystics have purported for centuries is now being studied by neuroscientists and psychologists. Our own personal worlds are a reflection of who we are and what we think, feel, and dream. Our thoughts and emotions also have a profound impact on the people we draw into our lives. It is not surprising that in changing our inner worlds, we also profoundly change the people we attract into our lives. By changing ourselves, we essentially transform our relationships.

Everybody's soul correction includes improving their relationships in one way or another. In this chapter, we will focus on four of the most common relationship soul corrections: mirror images, repetition compulsions, poor boundaries, and lack of self-love and/or self-care.

MIRROR IMAGES

"I love beautiful women!" Sebastian told me as he leaned back in the leather chair in my office and began to catalog his conquests. He loved his wife (though hers was not the first name that came up), his adorable one-year-old twin daughters, his revolving door of mistresses, and his countless one-night stands. Since college he had made a habit of sleeping with at least one woman a night when he went out of town. He never remembered their names or kept their numbers. Although he "loved" them, they meant nothing to him.

A business colleague had recommended that Sebastian come to therapy to find out why he kept attracting women who only cared about his money. Since Sebastian enjoyed complaining about how all the women he loved tried to manipulate him, he was glad to give therapy a try.

As attracted to his exceptional wealth as he was to their exceptional beauty, Sebastian's gorgeous mistresses inevitably asked for favors: a car, an apartment, jewelry, and spending money. It was truly amazing to hear how many women wanted nothing from Sebastian but his money. Yet he had been using them as well. Sebastian was exploiting women who exploited men. Sebastian and the women he attracted were perfectly matched. It was my suspicion that, whatever wounds he hid beneath the highly polished facade he presented to the world, these women shared the same wounds. But introspection on that level was of no interest to Sebastian, who preferred to play the victim. "It's the women," he would say. "All of them are out to take advantage of me!"

As Sebastian's case illustrates, the world is our mirror. Everybody we attract into our lives is a reflection of us in some way. Rabbi Yisroel ben Eliezer, also known as the Baal Shem Tov, elaborated on this point in saying, "Should you look upon your fellow man and see a blemish, it is your own imperfection that you are encountering—you are being shown what it is that you must correct within yourself." If a certain person has come into our life, they have something important to teach us about ourselves. Recognizing the mirror-image nature of relationships is the first step in improving our relationships.

When the image we secretly hold of ourselves does not match the people we attract, it surprises us. But it shouldn't. In the 1960s, Dr. Maxwell Maltz, a renowned plastic surgeon, discovered even when his patients were visually transformed with a whole new face, the old doubts and insecurities that they hoped to escape still haunted them. It was only through soul corrections—or what Maltz thought of as an "emotional face-lift"—that their psychological scars and negative beliefs about themselves could be transformed.

Dr. Maltz wrote that who we think we are "has been built up from our own beliefs about ourselves. But most of these beliefs have unconsciously been formed from our past experiences, our successes and failures, our humiliations, our triumphs, and the way other people have reacted to us…"[1] From these we shape a sense of ourselves, but this may not be the most authentic version of who we are. By transcending past patterns that may have once been adaptive but no longer serve us today, we engage in the second relationship soul correction: resolving *repetition compulsions*.

REPETITION COMPULSIONS

Marina and Jacqueline both tended to compulsively draw partners into their lives who repeated old patterns from their childhoods. No one consciously sets out to find a romantic mate with the same qualities as an unreliable or abusive parent. Yet it happens again and again, in repetition compulsions, unless we can become conscious of the pattern and break it.

When Marina turned forty, she fell in love with a woman for the first time. Although she had never particularly thought of herself as gay or bisexual, there was just something about Andi that captured her heart.

Unlike the healthy, stable men Marina had dated throughout her life, Andi was elusive and unpredictable. She seemed to take life by storm, savoring every moment to the fullest. Instead of going out to dinner and a movie with a quiet stroll home, Andi took Marina to pop-up jazz clubs on the far side of town, where she danced and flirted shamelessly into the night. Marina saw that Andi was selfish, capricious, and unreliable, but she still couldn't get her out of her head.

What she didn't realize was that Andi had been dishonest from the start. She said she'd broken up with her girlfriend, Gabrielle, and wanted an exclusive relationship with Marina. It turned out that she was still living with Gabrielle, who knew nothing about their alleged breakup. To make matters worse, Marina discovered that when Andi canceled their dates at the last minute, she was going out with other women.

After Marina told her it was over, Andi kept calling and texting, trying to persuade her to come back. Although very clear that there was nothing to come back to, Marina herself couldn't understand why she still wanted so badly to make it work.

As we explored this pattern, I remarked on the striking difference between Marina's relatively stable relationships with men and the highly unstable relationship with Andi. That's when Marina told me about her parents. Marina's father had always been a gentle, kind, honest man, whom Marina had always been able to rely on. By contrast, her mother was capricious, explosive, dishonest, and completely unreliable. Since childhood, she had flitted in and out of Marina's life at whim, very much like Andi.

Like all children, Marina naturally felt a yearning to be close to her mother and secure her love, regardless of her mother's bad behavior. Because she could not repair the relationship with her mother, a part of her had been eager to try again with a similar kind of person. But, as Freud observed one hundred years ago, a *repetition compulsion* is doomed to fail. The only solution is to accept the loss, which for Marina would mean grieving the loss of the relationship she had yearned for with Andi. As painful as it may be, it is ultimately less painful than living the same sad story over and over again.

Jacqueline too was repeating the wrong story. A twenty-seven-year-old veterinarian, she claimed she wanted a good relationship with a man, yet she kept drawing abusive men into her life. At the beginning, the man would always be charming, charismatic, and chivalrous. He would wine and dine Jacqueline at the finest restaurants and adorn her with expensive gifts from exclusive stores. But as she became more attached, a pattern consistently emerged: the men became controlling, then emotionally and sometimes physically abusive.

As we began to work together, I learned that Jacqueline's father had been an alcoholic. When he came home late at night, he often beat his wife and children. Every time Jacqueline got involved with a similar kind of man, her unconscious mind was seeking to repair that important relationship with her damaged, abusive father.

For Jacqueline, breaking this cycle of abuse was one of her soul corrections. Fortunately, she was honest enough with herself to admit that this pattern was putting her life in danger. If she did not succeed in completing this soul correction, her next relationship could kill her.

By allowing herself to explore this pattern with me in therapy, Jacqueline began to see the pattern vividly. Since Jacqueline was a spiritual person, I encouraged her to pray for the help, guidance, strength, and courage to break this pattern in her life.

In her dreams, Jacqueline's late, beloved grandmother appeared, telling her it would all be okay. The following week Jacqueline dreamed that a peaceful, loving man she had never seen before took her hand. We both agreed it was a good sign.

Dreams may have many meanings. One possible meaning of our dreams is to represent our wishes for the future. The presence of these two dreams told me that Jacqueline's unconscious hopes, as represented by her dreams, were now in alignment with her conscious wishes. Prior to this, her unconscious hope was betraying her conscious wishes, which may be why she continually drew abusive men into her life. Jacqueline's dreams evidenced an important step toward resolving her repetition compulsion.

The next part of our work involved Jacqueline finding her voice and beginning to take responsibility for the men she was drawing into her life. Jacqueline began to see that she was not a helpless victim here; this was not "happening to her." She was creating it. That awareness allowed her to free herself from the victim mentality she had identified with for so long.

In the past, Jacqueline had unconsciously chosen men like her father because they felt familiar and exciting. She loved being wooed by them. The strength and charisma they appeared to possess was intoxicating. With every single one of them, there had been red flags warning her to turn back, but Jacqueline had closed her eyes.

Jacqueline and I talked about how her relationship with her abusive father had left her feeling unworthy of love. In order to take back the power she had given him to make her feel unworthy, she felt she needed to confront him.

Her father was now much older, weaker, and less volatile than he had been in her childhood. And now Jacqueline was an adult. But her father still seemed as scary and sinister as ever in her mind. So she needed courage to take this step.

The night before the confrontation, I had Jacqueline do an important soul visualization exercise. When she went to sleep, she would call on her father's soul to meet her own soul. All she had to do was put forth this intention before she went to sleep, as if in a prayer. I told her to ask for whatever soul reconciliation needed to happen between her and her father's souls to occur that evening, before they met the following day.

Anytime you ask for soul reconciliation, it is important to add "for the greatest good of all involved," as opposed to specifying a particular outcome you want. If you say something like, "I want Dad to realize just what a jerk he was all my life, feel horrible about it, and finally apologize to me!" the request will not be coming from a good place, but from a place of pride and ego. Instead, asking for a soul reconciliation would go something like this: "Please allow my father and me to heal our relationship for the greatest good of all involved."

By having her soul communicate with her father's soul prior to the meeting, I believed the most difficult work would already have been done in the "upper worlds" when she saw her father the following day. All she would have to do was follow suit in this world. As above, so below.

The exercise itself was profoundly cathartic for Jacqueline. This was the first time she had done soul work of this nature. She was shocked by how powerful it was.

When Jacqueline showed up at her father's home the following day, the very first thing he did was hug her! Jacqueline was shocked. Jacqueline's father had *never* hugged her or any of her siblings. Then both she and her father began to cry.

From seemingly out of nowhere, her father began to apologize to Jacqueline for all the ways in which he had failed her. She stood there listening and crying, absolutely dumbfounded. It was the first heart-to-heart conversation Jacqueline and her father had ever had.

Hours later, Jacqueline left for home and slept better that night than she had in years. Within a year Jacqueline drew into her life a very different type of man, one whose energy matched that kind, gentle energy of the man in her dream.

Exercise: Soul Visualization and Reconciliation

As you lay in bed before you go to sleep tonight, visualize your day tomorrow from start to finish. Do you have any challenging upcoming meetings, discussions, or confrontations that may benefit from a soul reconciliation exercise?

If so, invite the soul of the person or people with whom you will have the challenging meeting to join you tonight. Speak to the soul of this person from your own soul: honestly and authentically.

Ask for a soul reconciliation between your soul and theirs. Put forth this intention, as if in a prayer. Ask for whatever outcome you would like to come from the meeting, and make sure to add to the end of your request "I request this outcome or an even better outcome for the greatest good of all involved."

While it's important to put forth your ideal intention for the meeting, the outcome may be something even greater than you can imagine or visualize, as occurred in the case of Jacqueline, so adding this last clause opens the gateway for some divine intervention.

As with Jacqueline, our current relationship struggles are the product of childhood wounds that will echo throughout our lives. In the practice of Imago Therapy, co-developed by marriage therapists Dr. Harville Hendrix and Helen LaKelly Hunt, the Latin word "*imago*" refers to the unconscious image of familiar love.[2] That image can be a portal through which we can see both the wounds of childhood and our relationships as adults.

Our unconscious desire to repair the wounds of our childhood as a result of needs not met by our parents is to find a partner who can give us what our caretakers failed to provide. Whether our childhoods were happy or fraught with danger, our hearts dream of unconditional love. Each time we re-create an old wound, we hope for and expect a different outcome.

We seek to heal the wounds of our childhood by unconsciously re-creating the same wounds and triggering the same difficult emotions with our significant others in our adult lives. If our parents were overbearing, we may draw overbearing partners into our lives. Or else we may ourselves be overbearing to our partners. If our parents were neglectful or abusive, we may draw in abusive or neglectful partners, or ourselves be neglectful or abusive to our partners. If a parent abandoned us, we may repeat this pattern in our romantic relationships either by repeatedly abandoning our partners or living with a deep-rooted fear of abandonment.

In this way, how we are loved as children often impacts the way we are able to love ourselves and others as adults.

CULTIVATING SELF-LOVE

In our society, we often focus on beautifying ourselves on the outside by focusing on our bodies, hair, clothes, makeup, smiles, gestures, careers, achievements, partners, and homes. On the inside, we work to beautify ourselves through therapy, yoga, meditation, reading, poetry, art, and culture. So why does the self-hatred epidemic persist?

Part of the problem lies in our tendency to yearn for what we lack instead of being grateful for what is already in abundance. In reality, there is so much that is *right* in everybody's life. Most of us have eyes to see, ears to hear, food to eat, a bed to sleep in, legs to walk, clean air to breathe, clean water to drink, among many other things. These are simple things we take for granted. Yet we are consumed by obsessions about what we lack.

At the same time, we often focus on the qualities in ourselves that we lack too. Every time we do that, it makes it harder to love ourselves and find the fulfillment we so desperately crave. Sadly, self-hatred is one of the most common issues my patients contend with. It is more than just an epidemic in therapy practices. It is a societal ill that has taken over our culture.

When I first met Diana, she was a successful model whose face had appeared on national magazine covers for years. With her six-foot-two height, confident smile, and the grace of a ballerina, she was a sight to behold as she crossed her never-ending legs in my Eames chair.

She asked me for help with a problem I hear often from my patients: "I cannot stop comparing myself to others!"

As a child, Diana had been constantly bullied for her height. Since her father was a star basketball player in college, she was destined to be tall. But Diana always bemoaned the fact that she was taller than all the boys and winced when her classmates called her "giraffe." For years, she cried herself to sleep at night and dreaded going to school the next day.

Somewhere along the way she made the welcome transition from the ugly duckling to the beautiful swan that every sports team captain in high school wanted to date. By the time she graduated, she was voted "most likely to succeed."

Still, Diana was plagued by the feeling that she was not beautiful enough. An innocent stroll down a city street turned into a series of slights and insults in her own thoughts. This woman had more fashionable clothing; that woman had bigger breasts, a more shapely figure, whiter teeth, more confidence. It went on year after year until Diana finally sought my help. Change occurs when the pain of staying the same begins to exceed the pain of changing oneself.

In our work together, we focused on finding out where Diana's habit of constant self-comparison had originated. Diana's mom, Janice, had the same habit. Janice felt she had to always look absolutely perfect. Not a day went by when she was not preoccupied with manicures, pedicures, Botox, breast enhancements, liposuction, chin lifts—anything to keep up with the competition. Thanks to her frequent visits to the plastic surgeon, Janice looked thirty when she was fifty. No one ever believed she was Diana's mother.

Clearly Diana had adopted some of her mother's attitude. She never felt beautiful enough. She always sought to "improve" her looks, focusing on perceived flaws. Her friends obsessed over beauty in similar ways, reinforcing and even magnifying her own self-criticism. In our sessions, we began to challenge the narratives Diana had created for herself around beauty, femininity, and perfection.

Over time, Diana began to realize how maladaptive and downright painful some of her deeply held beliefs had been. She started slowly pulling away from the so-called mean girls who had been posing as her friends. Instead, she befriended people who she did not feel were always comparing themselves to her. It was difficult at first to not fall back into the habitual behaviors and thought patterns Diana had known all her life. Through vigilance, courage, and determination, she repeatedly picked herself up when she would slip back into her old ways.

As she changed, Diana began to attract very different friends into her life. These friends seemed to have no need to be perfect all the time, or gossip behind each other's backs. With a change of friends, she effectively found a support group for a change in her value system. Anytime she lapsed into self-criticism or perfectionism, her new friends laughed her out of it.

Although Diana can still fall into her old habits of self-comparison, it is no longer an obsession for her. Her new mantra is "I love and accept myself exactly as I am."

Exercise: Identifying Self-Criticism

Sometimes we deceive ourselves into thinking that our self-critical thoughts and behaviors are helping us implement positive changes in our lives. But the result is often the opposite. The more we criticize ourselves, the more we keep ourselves stuck in our old patterns. Change is difficult to implement in a climate of self-hatred. Moreover, loving and accepting oneself fully and completely does not imply complacency and stagnation, as some people may fear. It does not mean that we don't want to grow and change.

Quite the opposite is true. Usually, self-love and self-acceptance are necessary prerequisites for creating real and lasting changes in our lives. It is possible to love ourselves fully and completely exactly as we are, while at the same time work toward growing and evolving into the person we wish to become.

In this stream-of-consciousness writing exercise, we will begin to identify and release our self-criticism. In the exercises that follow, we will replace the self-criticism with self-love and self-compassion. Set your stopwatch and write for five minutes without stopping on the topic Identifying Self-Criticism. The questions below are included as guideposts.

Questions for Reflection

1. Identify three things about yourself of which you are critical.

2. When did you begin criticizing yourself for each of these three things?

3. Has this self-criticism produced any sustainable positive changes in your life?

4. How has this self-criticism affected your self-worth and ability to love and accept yourself?

5. How would your life be different if you replaced self-criticism with self-love?

PRACTICING SELF-CARE

For Diana, learning to stop comparing herself to others and surrounding herself with supportive (rather than competitive) friends was vital for cultivating self-love. For another patient, Bella, learning to love herself meant acknowledging that she was as important and worthy of care as all the other people in her life.

Everyone loved Bella. On top of being a devoted wife and mother of two boys, she also had a challenging career as a clinician and researcher in oncology at a prestigious medical center. Yet no matter how busy her life was, she unfailingly attended to the needs of others.

Bella was exceptionally good at taking care of all the people in her life, but not so good at taking care of herself. I have seen this pattern many times in my practice with physicians and other caregivers. For people in service professions, it is easy to forget that devoting your life to helping others should not mean sacrificing your own self-care.

After six months of feeling absolutely burned out and empty inside, Bella came to see me. "What would it mean to you to take radically good care of yourself?" I asked.

As soon as the words left my lips, Bella looked as startled as if I'd told her Martians had landed on Fifth Avenue. Amazingly enough, this woman who had devoted her life to finding myriad ways to take care of others had never thought about taking good care of herself.

In our subsequent sessions, we explored this question. Once she turned her attention to it, Bella had a host of ideas. After all, it was her specialty! Soon she was taking concrete steps to implement her answers: getting more rest every day, making time for herself, meditating, reducing her research responsibilities so she could focus on the clinical work she loved, and enjoying an occasional leisurely lunch with friends.

In the years since, Bella's energy has changed in remarkable ways. When she was out of sync with her own implicit core values, caring only for others but neglecting herself, she was constantly feeling drained. By caring for herself, too, she removed the obstacle that was obstructing the power of her authentic self.

Today it's possible to tell at a glance that Bella is no longer feeling tired and empty. Her life is every bit as busy as before, but now she is radiant.

Bella was always a kind, caring person. Yet it took concerted effort for her to truly care for herself the way she deserved. It is ironic that the most beautiful people among us often find it the most difficult to feel love and compassion for themselves.

For Bella, learning to love herself meant learning to care for herself as much as she cares for the others in her life. For Diana, it meant individuating from the beliefs, ideas, and self-perceptions held by her mother. We can only love others as much as we love ourselves. By cultivating our capacity for self-love, self-care, and self-compassion, we also enhance our ability to love others more fully and completely.

Exercise: Cultivating Self-Love through Mirror Work

For this exercise, you will need a mirror and a quiet place where you can feel safe and not be disturbed. This exercise, inspired by Louise Hay's *Mirror Work*, will take one minute of time.[3] I recommend that you do it at least three times per day for one week to achieve the full benefit.

Look into the mirror. Look straight into your eyes. Look straight into your soul. Now say the following affirmation:

> *I love you.*
> *I approve of you.*
> *I know you are doing the best you can.*
> *You are perfect just as you are.*
> *I love you.*

Regularly repeating affirmations like the one above is a powerful way to change our deeply held unconscious core beliefs. Doing this exercise may feel uncomfortable at first. Negative thoughts may surface. It may feel false or even cheesy. These are all good signs, because it means that you're going outside your comfort zone, and this is precisely where change begins. I recommend taking the time to journal and note whatever comes up for you in doing the mirror work and affirmations above.

ESTABLISHING HEALTHY BOUNDARIES

The final relationship soul correction we'll discuss in this chapter is individuation and boundary setting. For any healthy relationship, it is important to know who you are and what you believe, separate from what others expect from you and would like you to believe. In relationships with friends, lovers, husbands, wives, loved ones, and even ourselves, we all make constant adjustments, drawing and redrawing the lines between "us" and "them." This give and take in relationships is natural.

When Andrea came to see me, her soul correction was reflected in an unusual complaint: she felt *too close* to her daughter. All mothers and daughters have to learn to negotiate the delicate boundaries between them. On some level, they must ask themselves, "How close is too close? How far is too far?" Over the course of life, they delicately dance the dance to figure out the answers to these questions in hopes of finding a healthy balance that allows both of them to thrive and prosper.

When a mother and her daughter are each living authentic lives, it is much easier to know what appropriate boundaries feel like. In this case, Andrea had a very poor sense of who she was. Giving birth to Francine when she was only sixteen years old, Andrea didn't have a chance to grow up herself before becoming a mother. Now, fourteen years later, Francine was a boy-crazy teenager while Andrea, at thirty years old, was a completely devoted, loving, and caring mother. Andrea's own mother had been narcissistic and prone to alarming outbursts of emotion and blame. Andrea knew she wanted to rear Francine differently, but she didn't know what to do, except to love her with all her might.

In her eagerness to make up for her own childhood, Andrea completely lost herself in her role as a mother. It was not uncommon for her to tell her friends that Francine was "her life." If Francine stayed out late with friends, Andrea couldn't sleep. When Francine failed a test or had a fight with a boyfriend, Andrea suffered more than Francine did. When anything went wrong in Francine's life, Andrea would have a panic attack.

Andrea confessed that her attachment to her daughter had become so overwhelming that it plagued her day and night. The boundaries between them had merged until she could no longer tell where she left off and her daughter began. Both of them were caught in a pattern of overcare and codependency that was making them miserable. For Andrea, it had become truly incapacitating. Moreover, it became overwhelming for Francine to see how emotionally affected her mother was by her decisions. Francine would feel like she had to walk on eggshells around her mother and limit what she shared with her. Together Andrea and I began to work toward giving Andrea her life back.

Over time, Andrea began to gain insight into her codependent relationship with her daughter. But insight alone is not always curative. For some patients, insight into their self-sabotaging patterns is indeed the catalyst for making different choices and meaningfully changing their lives. For others, however, insight is just the first step to finally liberating themselves from the chains that bind them.

For Andrea, insight led to curiosity: if her way of doing things all these years wasn't working, what other choices did she have? This important question highlighted Andrea's recognition that she did indeed have a choice in how she behaved with her daughter. She was not destined to repeat the same self-sabotaging pattern the rest of her life.

Andrea and I identified female role models in her life who have healthy boundaries with their daughters. Andrea began to study their behavior like an anthropologist: What did they do differently? How did they respond when their child was upset? How did they set healthy and appropriate boundaries with their child in times of stress? After studying some of the behaviors of her role models, Andrea began to try some of their behaviors on for size. She started limiting her phone calls to Francine to once daily (whereas in the past they sometimes spoke four or five times a day). She also stopped asking Francine quite as many questions about her personal life. These behavioral changes were excruciatingly difficult for Andrea to make, and it took many iterations of trial and error for them to stick.

As I often tell patients, changing yourself is the most difficult thing you will ever do. But Andrea persevered and ultimately was successful. By giving Francine some more space, Andrea was able to create more space in her own life as well. The result of Andrea's boundary setting with her daughter was a healthier relationship that was still loving, supportive, and very close yet no longer codependent.

For Kimberly and her mother, Donna, the question was the same—how close is too close?—but the conflict manifested in a very different way. Kimberly was a seventeen-year-old high school student with a history of anorexia. Her father, Clarke, was a writer and stay-at-home dad, while her mother, Donna, was an investment banker and the family's primary breadwinner. Clarke was a kind and caring man, always engaged and attentive, while Donna was more emotionally aloof, always keeping her distance.

Donna, too, had a history of anorexia. Between them, Kimberly and Donna developed a very strange, destructive pattern, where only one of them would be anorexic at a time. Kimberly would starve herself for months, avoiding food altogether or forcing herself to throw up, until she was dangerously pale and sick. She would urgently seek out medical help, to her mother's relief. And then, just as Kimberly's anorexia started to improve, Donna's anorexia would worsen. And so it went, around and around. Neither one of them admitted to being aware of it, but the pattern was obvious from the medical records alone.

Since Donna's anorexia was more serious, she was often hospitalized and required the use of feeding tubes. She only began to recover as Kimberly started to show the signs of the disorder herself. Although they never spoke of it, Kimberly gradually learned that she needed to stay sick in order to keep her mother alive. If she ever got healthy enough to let go of her eating disorder, she unconsciously believed her mother might die!

In this case, as in many others, a repetition compulsion was passed on from one generation to the next. Anorexia and emergency trips to the hospital were only the external signs of the compulsion. Deeper still was a massive degree of self-loathing that was nearly impossible to shake as long as Kimberly believed her mother's life depended on Kimberly being sick.

Only by individuating from her mother was Kimberly able to extricate herself from the destructive codependency that she and her mother had unconsciously cocreated. Kimberly's anorexia began to improve only once she went away to college, several states away from her mother.

Without a solid, intact sense of self, it is difficult to know where your self ends and where another self begins. A clear sense of self enables you to set healthy boundaries in how you treat yourself. These often manifest as self-care activities surrounding sleep, food, exercise, hygiene, alone time, and other things that one needs to be healthy and feel good. When you set boundaries in how you take care of yourself, it becomes easier to set healthy external boundaries with the important people in your life. Without a clear sense of your authentic self or internal boundaries, it is difficult to set boundaries with the people with whom you are in a relationship.

Setting healthy boundaries with the people we love can bring us closer to who we really are by clearing away old beliefs and patterns that no longer serve us. Moreover, healthy boundaries enable us to get closer to others because, as the old adage says, "good fences make good neighbors."

Exercise: Self-Care and Healthy Boundaries

For this stream-of-consciousness writing exercise, set your stopwatch to five minutes and write without stopping, beginning with the first prompt and working through as many as the time allows. Do not censor any thoughts that come to mind—just keep writing! If you find yourself wanting to write for more than five minutes, continue to do so until you feel like you have written all that you want to say. Alternately, if you'd like to focus on just one prompt during the five minutes and do this exercise in multiple sittings, that's fine, too. You can revisit this whole exercise as often as you'd like and look across your writing from various sittings to see if repetitions, patterns, or contrasts emerge.

Questions for Reflection

1. In what situations do you find it difficult to say no? Why?

2. How do you feel when you say no to somebody who wants something from you?

3. In what ways do you take good care of yourself?

4. In what ways do you not take good care of yourself?

5. In what situations would saying no enable you to take better care of yourself?

YOU DESERVE LOVE

Countless soul corrections are possible in relationships with others. My patients often amaze me with their incredible resilience as they go through these soul corrections, trusting that their breakthroughs will improve their relationships on every level.

As you can see, the process of soul correction begins with building a loving, supportive relationship with yourself. Only then can you draw loving, supportive people into your life, whether they are friends, family, soulmates, partners, or colleagues. As the Buddha said:

> You can search throughout the entire universe for someone who is more deserving of your love and affection than you are yourself, and that person is not to be found anywhere. You yourself, as much as anybody in the entire universe, deserve your love and affection.[4]

Cultivating self-love involves identifying the ways in which you are lacking these qualities, offering yourself forgiveness, and learning new ways of living in alignment with self-compassion. This entails listening to yourself, getting in touch with your deepest desires, and setting good boundaries with the people in your life. And finally, it entails living your life from a space of love whenever possible. To echo the words of Mother Teresa, "It is not how much we do, but how much love we put into doing. It is not how much we give, but how much love we put into giving."

Living a fulfilled, authentic life from a place of love does not involve perfection. We will all fall short at times, especially when it comes to acting in the service of ourselves. For this reason, I end this chapter with an adaptation of a beautiful exercise in self-forgiveness from Jack Kornfield's *The Wise Heart*.[5]

Exercise: Offering Forgiveness to Yourself

To begin this exercise, find a comfortable place where you can sit quietly for the next five to ten minutes. Recite the following to yourself:

> *There are many ways that I have hurt myself and let myself down over the years. I have acted against myself, sabotaged myself, and withheld love from myself many times through thought, word, and deed, knowingly and unknowingly.*

As you do this, focus on your breath and feel your heart energy. One by one, picture the ways in which you have let yourself down over the years. Feel the feelings and pain that these experiences have caused you. Realize now that you can release each of these burdens, one by one, as you forgive yourself. Extend forgiveness in saying the following:

> *For the ways I have let myself down through action or inaction, out of weakness, fear, or confusion, I now extend to myself complete and total love and forgiveness. I forgive myself. I forgive myself. I forgive myself.*

6

Releasing Addictions

*There is a candle in your heart, ready to be
kindled.*
There is a void in your soul, ready to be filled.
You feel it, don't you?[1]

—RUMI

We all use the word "addiction" very casually. In casual conversation, it can apply to any self-indulgent habit. When we say we're "addicted" to our favorite TV show or buying beautiful shoes, everyone knows what we mean. As a result, there are a lot of misconceptions about what an addiction is and what it isn't.

From a medical standpoint, an addiction is characterized by compulsive engagement in a rewarding stimulus, despite adverse consequences. Psychologically, it is uncontrollably craving, seeking, and engaging in a certain behavior (including use of a substance) on which we have become dependent and which results in impairment or distress. In layman's terms, it's when we repeatedly seek out something that feels good despite it being bad for us. From a spiritual perspective, an addiction is one of the consequences of living a life out of sync with one's soul.

Fulfilled

In a letter exchange with Alcoholics Anonymous founder Bill Wilson, the renowned psychiatrist Carl Jung equated addiction with a spiritual thirst for wholeness.[2] Living out of sync with your true nature makes life a constant struggle. When it becomes too hard to sustain the illusion, people turn to addictions to stay occupied and thereby escape what they are truly feeling deep inside their soul. Or sometimes they may feel numb, which occurs when we are feeling something so strongly (even if we don't admit to ourselves) that our capacity to feel becomes overwhelmed and we therefore stop feeling anything altogether. Once a pattern of avoiding difficult feelings takes hold, it is a sure way to create a self-perpetuating cycle of frustration and pain.

For the purposes of this book, we are going to consider addiction to be anything outside of ourselves that we crave, seek out, and feel dependent on for happiness and a sense of wholeness, despite it being bad for us on some level. Often with an addiction, the more of it that you get, the emptier you feel. While sometimes an addiction is truly debilitating and life-wrecking, other times it can be harmful in the long term but not incapacitating in the short term, such as cigarette smoking. Some people may even wonder, how bad can this addiction really be if the substance or behavior is legal and doesn't interfere with one's ability to hold down a job, have a relationship, or pay off credit card bills?

Many of the patients I've seen lead me to believe that addictions to psychological or behavioral urges can be every bit as damaging and difficult to break as substance addictions. For this reason, I group addictions into three categories:

Substance Addictions: Nicotine, stimulants (cocaine, amphetamines, methamphetamines, caffeine, tobacco, etc.), depressants (alcohol, benzodiazepines, barbiturates, opiates, heroin), cannabis, inhalants, sugar,[3] chocolate.[4]

Behavioral Addictions: Gambling, eating, sex, pornography, video games, work, watching TV, Internet, shopping, sleep, exercise, hoarding, and/or high-risk behavior.

Psychological Addictions: Status, power, money, fame, achievement, attention, approval, chaos, drama, and/or falling in love.

Once addictions take hold, they can be all encompassing, will satiate you only temporarily, if at all, and will leave you feeling empty after the initial high wears off. Breaking the addiction only treats the symptom, not the root cause. Sometimes this is enough. Yet to free yourself completely, you have to dig deeper and uncover the implicit core beliefs about yourself and the world that led to the addiction in the first place.

One of the most common beliefs that drives addiction is the assumption that, since you feel so empty inside, happiness, peace, and fulfillment must come from the outside. This belief creates the illusion that you will finally be happy and at peace if you can smoke a joint, have great sex, lose weight, make more money, find your soulmate, achieve something important, or create another specific outcome.

All my life I looked for ways to fill my inner emptiness, to finally feel whole, complete, and happy. In my early thirties, I appeared on the surface to have everything going for me. Below the surface, I knew only too well that something was missing and I berated myself for being dissatisfied. What was wrong with me? Why did my easy smile not reflect what was going on inside? Faking my way through the day as a "happy person," I felt like an imposter.

For a fleeting moment, now and then, I got a taste of the happiness I longed for in my parents' pride when I became a doctor, the laughter I shared with good friends, or the discovery of new wonders as I studied neuroscience or traveled the world. In those moments, I sometimes let myself believe that I had found it—the life I deserved. And then it slipped away, evaporating as surely as the morning dew.

No matter how wonderful those interludes, I always returned to feeling empty and alone, looking for the next creative way to fill my inner void. Over time I began to wonder if the emptiness could ever be filled.

As the years went by, I heard many patients ask the same question: "By societal standards, I have it all! So why am I not happy?" The reason is because they, like myself, felt inauthentic and disconnected from who they truly were. Feeling empty inside, they looked for the source of happiness on the outside—in one of myriad addictions so prevalent in our society.

We often seek out addictions to relieve our pain or to remain in denial about what is missing in our lives. But the very pain we seek to mask is often our soul's clue to what's missing. Unfortunately, addictions mask the true self even more. Even those that heighten experience or light the fuse of adrenaline only offer a temporary escape from emptiness.

If a diversion was the best we could do, then turning to addictions as a last resort would make sense. But we can do better than that. We can find fulfillment by living an authentic life. So an addiction is nothing but a lie that takes us farther and farther from the truth of who we are.

THE ROOT OF ADDICTION

There are many theories of what causes addiction. Classical psychiatry argues that an addiction is an attempt to self-medicate psychological issues, such as unresolved conflicts, childhood traumas, social unease, and general dissatisfaction with life. From a biological point of view, people with a genetic predisposition become addicted far more easily than everyone else. Some believe that addictions are curable, while proponents of Alcoholics Anonymous (AA) believe that once an addict, always an addict. Most would agree that addictions are influenced by complex physical, emotional, social, and genetic elements.[5]

Addictions can take many forms, and very often they start with a therapeutically prescribed medication. That was the case with my patient Luke. Luke came to me after having been prescribed Valium, a sedative and antianxiety medication, by his gastroenterologist to help him deal with very complex and long-standing stomach pains. Many medical tests had been run and many medications tried, but to no avail. The gastroenterologist then turned to Valium as a last resort to help Luke. Perhaps by reducing Luke's anxiety, his stomach pain would improve as well. Amazingly, the Valium worked and Luke finally had some relief after literally years of pain and discomfort.

The problem is that Luke started to need more and more of the Valium to have the same effect. His doctor increased his dose. Luke then started having withdrawal symptoms every day when the medication wore off, which affected his work performance and necessitated an even higher dose of medication. The only way Luke knew to "medicate" his withdrawal was by taking more Valium. This continued until neither Luke nor his doctor knew what to do next. Luke had become addicted to his Valium in order to keep his stomach pain at bay.

I have seen similar presentations with patients becoming addicted to opiates, or pain pills. The opioid epidemic killed more than thirty-three thousand people in the United States in 2015, leading public health officials to call it the worst drug crisis in American history.[6] One of my patients wrote the following poem when her older brother, Ethan, fell victim to opiate overdose:

Drugs aren't cool,
Drugs aren't fun,
I used to have two brothers,
Now I have one.

These simple words powerfully encapsulate the tragic effects of drug overdose on those left behind. Ethan had become addicted to a pain pill called oxycodone after taking it recreationally with his friends. He never anticipated the uncontrollable cravings and debilitating physical and psychological withdrawal. Ethan spiraled further into addiction, cycling in and out of multiple rehabs. Despite years of effort to break free from the hold opiates had over his life, Ethan sadly became one of the tragic statistics. The saddest day in my patient's life was the day Ethan was found dead in their family home from an opiate overdose. My patient and her family continue to grieve Ethan's death to this day.

Prolonged and repeated exposure to any addictive drug literally changes the brain's pleasure pathway, the mesolimbic dopamine system (MDS). When that happens, the messages sent to the frontal lobes of the brain, where choices and decisions are made, change. They become abnormal. Instead of warning the person to stop doing something dangerous, they take away their impulse control, so the person feels like they can't stop. The person is then dependent on the substance to diminish their cravings. The original pleasure brought on by the substance has been all but lost. Rather than bringing pleasure, now the substance only diminishes the pain and withdrawal. What once felt good evolves into despair punctuated by temporary relief from the pain.

ADDICTIONS AND ALONENESS

Addictions can be compounded by the fact that in our society we are taught that we are inevitably alone. We believe that we are separate from everybody and everything, as opposed to part of the great interconnected web of life. As a result, the most common cause of addiction is a deep desire to love and be loved. Addiction psychologist Dr. Rosemary Brown considers addiction to be a form of emotional dependency. "Most of us never learn how to meet our own emotional needs," she says. We are socialized to seek approval from parents and others rather than cultivate self-knowledge and self-fulfillment.[7]

In this way, addictions often replace our basic human needs for connection, attachment, and love. As soon as we are born, we become "addicted" to our caretaker. We need them. We crave them. We cry in their absence. We seek them out at all costs. All our lives thereafter, we seek to replace this primary attachment with other attachments. It is our nature.

Rather than doing away with dependency completely, the basic strategy should be to choose good, healthy addictions/attachments (i.e., supportive, loving relationships) that enable you to grow, strive, and live authentically rather than destructive, unhealthy addictions/attachments that dominate your life and undermine your sense of your own power.

Exercise: Identifying Your Addictions

For this stream-of-consciousness writing exercise, set your stopwatch to five minutes and write without stopping on the topic Identifying Your Addictions. Don't censor or judge what emerges! Remember to practice self-compassion through this exercise.

Questions for Reflection

1. When in life have you felt empty and alone? Try to be as concrete and descriptive as possible.

2. How do you fill that feeling of emptiness? Do you try to replace it with other feelings? Do you turn to a certain activity, such as eating, drinking, smoking, exercising, or seeking out a friend or family member?

3. Do you turn to addictions of any sort? If so, which ones?

4. In what parts of your life do you look outside yourself for happiness?

ADDICTION TO DRUGS

Tamar knew her deepest longing was for love. But when she couldn't find it, she filled the void with heroin. No amount of heroin ever made her feel that blissful for long. The quick return to the emptiness of life was a misery.

Fulfilled

According to Tamar's mother, Rachel, she had been a very happy baby from the moment she was born. She loved being held and rarely cried. When either of her parents were around, her face lit up with joy.

Rachel had met Tamar's father while volunteering on a kibbutz near Haifa, Israel, after she had graduated from college. The day she arrived on the kibbutz, she was greeted by one of the dynamic leaders, a man named Eli. Dark eyed and passionate, Eli had just returned from military service. He showed her around the kibbutz, telling her stories of skirmishes in the desert. It wasn't long before the two of them fell in love and married.

When Rachel became pregnant with Tamar, the couple moved to New York to be near her parents. Eli liked many things about America and expected to make a life in the city, but he never really fit in. Back home he was a promising young leader. In New York he was a foreigner with a strange accent who didn't understand the local ways of doing things. For her own part, Rachel found motherhood to be more of a strain than she expected.

With Eli and Rachel both feeling out of sync with themselves, the marriage suffered. Occasional disagreements became shouting matches. All the good will between them drained away. When Eli started going by the pub every night after work and coming home drunk, things got even worse. Rachel lived in fear of his temper. He would fly into a rage over nothing. Once he even threatened to hit her. At other times he would pick up and shake baby Tamar. Everybody encouraged Rachel to leave Eli. After a year of mayhem, Rachel finally summoned the courage, packed up her things, took baby Tamar, and moved into her parents' house.

Eli was outraged. In his world, divorce was not an option. If the marriage had been stressful, the divorce proceedings were a nightmare. Ongoing trauma and instability came to define Tamar's second year of life. Yelling threats, Eli would bang on the door of Rachel's parents' apartment, swearing he would break it down, or crying that he'd kill himself if they didn't take him back. When she refused, he would punch holes in the wall and trash her apartment.

The turning point came just before Tamar's second birthday. Despite a restraining order, Eli came to Rachel's apartment and calmly asked to talk. He petted Tamar's head and gave her a new stuffed animal. His manner seemed to be conciliatory.

Rachel almost dared to hope that he would ask for her forgiveness and go back to being the charming, passionate man she'd met at the kibbutz. But Eli was dreaming, too. For him, this moment of calm could only lead to his and Rachel's ultimate reconciliation. He presented his proposal: Rachel and Tamar would move to Israel with him to start a new life. The past would be forgotten. He said he had forgiven Rachel for everything.

When Rachel said no, Eli was devastated. His hopes crushed, he flew into a rage. If she wouldn't give him back his family, he would have to take it, he said. Eli picked Tamar up from her playpen and stormed out of the house, cursing Rachel as he left.

Rachel immediately called the police and her parents. All of them convened at Eli's house. Eli barricaded himself inside with Tamar and refused to respond to the SWAT team at the door.

When they called out to him over speakers, Eli went onto the second-story balcony, holding Tamar in a soft pink baby blanket. From there, he shouted at the SWAT team, telling them to mind their own business, that this was a private matter.

When they threatened to come up, Eli was alarmed. He dangled two-year-old Tamar out over the edge of the balcony. Her blanket fell free and tumbled all the way to the grass. "If you come any closer," Eli warned them, "I swear to God, I'll drop her."

Tamar, of course, doesn't remember any of this; she was two years old. She heard the story from her grandparents and her mother. But our early years are the most formative years of our lives. We form our impressions of the world without yet being able to speak, to ask questions, to clarify things.

How that one afternoon affected both Tamar and Rachel, Tamar can't possibly know. Her mother can only relate that thereafter Tamar was no longer a happy child. When she cried, it was more like a howl or a scream than tears. She was hard to console.

When I met her twenty-one years later, Tamar was still looking for consolation. For more than a decade, she thought she'd found it in heroin. It helped her deal with difficult feelings about growing up with a violent, absent father and a terrified mother.

Tamar was one of the first patients I treated as a psychiatry resident. She presented with an addiction to heroin that she'd had since she was thirteen years old. She told me she had come to a turning point. It was time to change her life.

In treatment, Tamar stopped the heroin. To help with the physical withdrawal, I prescribed her a medication called buprenorphine, which acts similarly to heroin but in a more controlled and less addictive manner. Rather than taking a drug recreationally to get high, Tamar was taking this medication therapeutically, as prescribed by her doctor (me) in the context of weekly therapy. All the connotations had changed.

Without the heroin, Tamar had a deep void to fill. Her hunger for connection was palpable. The craving for love that had propelled her addiction was back, looking for new sources to meet its need. Understandably, she became "addicted" to the therapy. Replacing an unhealthy, destructive addiction with a healthy, constructive addiction (like therapy) is often an important and positive first step in treatment.

As I often say, love heals. In this case, a series of supportive and nurturing relationships—first with me, then with her family, then with a community of like-minded individuals at Narcotics Anonymous—enabled Tamar to let go of her illusory, unsatisfying relationship to heroin. In the next stage, she would learn to transfer that love back to herself, thereby taking back her own power.

I treated Tamar in the last two years of my psychiatry residency, during which she stopped using heroin and received her high school equivalency degree. Five years later, Tamar reached out to me again to restart treatment, this time to better understand the root of her long-standing anxiety. In those interceding five years, she had remained off heroin and had gradually weaned herself off buprenorphine, which she said was even more difficult than stopping heroin. She had never experienced more physical pain in her life. But she did it. She then pursued further training as an emergency medical technician (EMT), did exceptionally well at her job and eventually became a paramedic.

As a paramedic, she works in a New York City ambulance, responding to emergency calls all over the city. She tells me she finds the job fulfilling because every day she is able to help people with physical and psychological problems in a meaningful way. She proudly told me that she has saved the lives of two people who wanted to commit suicide but didn't because she intervened. She has a particular empathy for individuals dependent on drugs—probably a quarter of the calls she gets.

It is now seven years since Tamar stopped heroin and four years since she stopped buprenorphine. While Tamar is doing so much better in all aspects of her life, she says she is still healing. Every year she feels healthier and stronger, as though a chronic disease process is still reversing itself. It was not until one year after she stopped buprenorphine that she finally felt like herself again. She still has dreams about using heroin. On rare occasions, she still has cravings. But she is in a different place now. Whenever she feels the void that drugs used to fill, she knows now how to fill it in constructive and healthy ways.

Fulfilled

An effective first step in the treatment of addiction is replacing an unhealthy addiction (like heroin) with a healthy addiction (like therapy or a constructive relationship or meaningful work). Truth be told, even a healthy addiction can become unhealthy if it begins to control you, rather than the other way around. That being said, the most potent treatment for addiction is cultivating love inside yourself. When we look to anything other than our own hearts for love, we may find it only temporarily. Healing requires a concerted effort to stop searching for external happiness and let love fill your heart. The exercises that follow will help you to facilitate this process.

Exercise: Filling Your Heart with Love[8]

We could go to all sorts of places, including beautiful mountaintops, oceans, or spiritual retreats to find peace, happiness, fulfillment, and a sustained feeling of love. But what if these feelings were available to you simply by tapping into the intuitive intelligence of your heart? Rather than going away to a beautiful place, you can find that beautiful place within yourself and discover the sanctuary of peace and love awaiting within.

This exercise is designed to help you connect with your heart. Many of the exercises in this book focus on your thoughts, but this one is not about asking questions. Instead, it is about connecting to feelings of love, appreciation, care, and compassion—and maintaining these states. Connecting to these feelings is one of the most powerful ways of filling the inner emptiness that often leads to addiction.

As you tap into your heart, you renew yourself on a physical, mental, emotional, and spiritual level. This sense of renewal creates a deep feeling of fulfillment, especially if it is sustained. Your life begins to take on a new energy. Quieting the mind and sustaining a solid connection with your heart for at least five minutes per day activates the heart's power to heal. This is not a process that you can force but rather an easy-does-it approach that you can relax into and cultivate over time. When you are ready, sit in a comfortable position and begin.

1. Find a quiet place, close your eyes and begin to relax by slowly focusing on your breath. Close your eyes and take several slow deep breaths:
   - Inhale through your nose for the count of two.
   - Hold your breath for the count of four.
   - Exhale through your nose for the count of eight.
   - Repeat for five breath cycles.

2. Now pretend that you are breathing slowly through your heart. With each inhalation, imagine your heart expanding as it fills with love and white light. As you hold your breath, focus on the love, kindness, and compassion as it spreads from your heart to the rest of your body. With each exhalation, imagine your heart contracting as it releases negative energy and dark light. Repeat this for at least ten breaths. Do this at least three times per day for one week. I encourage you to journal about your experience with this exercise.

ADDICTION TO RAGE

Drugs were not Marcella's addiction. She had never taken an illegal substance in her life. As the high-powered owner of a successful chain of coffee shops across Italy, Marcella had a widespread reputation as a dragon slayer. The week that I met her, she had sliced-and-diced three unwitting sales representatives trying to sell her products she didn't want or need. Her temper was legendary. When things didn't go her way, she often lost her objectivity in a torrent of words and emotions. Rage had taken control of Marcella's life and gone from being a maladaptive, impulsive behavior to an addiction over which she felt powerless.

Similar to any other addiction, Marcella's rage provided her with a temporary "high" followed by a feeling of remorse and emptiness. Impulsive explosions became a way of life for Marcella. Emotional tension would build up inside her if she had not "exploded" in a while (like the feeling of withdrawal in a drug addict), leading her to crave, seek out, and even provoke opportunities for her next rage attack. Her impulsive aggression was almost always disproportionate to the provocation. Employees did not last long under her tutelage. She had few friends who could tolerate her outbursts. Her devoted husband of many years was seen as either a saint or a fool, depending on whom you asked.

Marcella sought treatment for anger management, and she soon began to realize that the person most harmed by her rage addiction was herself. Her work suffered. Her relationships suffered. People called her "toxic." This was more than merely a maladaptive behavior—Marcella had become a slave to her impulses, constantly discharging her anger at everybody around her. Each rage attack gave Marcella a natural high that temporarily filled her inner void and made her feel powerful. But the feeling of emptiness would soon return, sinking Marcella into a mix of shame, regret, and depression.

The work of therapy involved helping Marcella channel her frustrations in more constructive ways, such as writing, putting her feelings into words, and communicating small frustrations daily in order to prevent larger explosions. At the same time, we worked to help Marcella build her frustration tolerance with relaxation exercises, stress management, and eventually, a daily meditation practice. With these tools, Marcella learned to communicate frustrations to others without losing control and was finally able to kick her rage addiction. As she healed, what surprised Marcella most was how much more energy she began to have during the day. She had not realized how much her daily rage attacks drained and exhausted her and how much more productive she could be once her rage was under control.

ADDICTION TO WORK

Like Marcella, Jay was a business dynamo. A thirty-five-year-old Afro-Caribbean man, Jay was an expert at developing new companies and then selling them to larger companies. He was fantastic at what he did, with four prior successes under his belt and many millions of dollars in the bank to show for it. Jay came to see me because his wife threatened to leave him if he didn't stop working ninety hours a week.

As a busy CEO herself, Amy had been supportive of Jay at first. She knew that start-ups required arduous work hours. But five years later, she felt estranged from her husband, whom she saw for a few hours per week if she was lucky. When they did spend time together, Amy felt like she was competing with Jay's cell phone for his attention. Somebody always needed Jay at work, and Jay felt compelled to respond to every text message immediately. Work had become Jay's life. Jay was a workaholic.

Jay was just coming home at 6:00 a.m., after working at the office all night, as Amy was leaving for work. He gave her a bleary-eyed kiss on the cheek, and she realized it was the first physical contact they'd had all month! "Okay, that's enough," she said. "I love you, but this isn't working."

When Amy reached that breaking point, it sent pangs of fear through Jay. In his last relationship, he'd spent so much time at work that his girlfriend found somebody else. The experience had been deeply wounding, but Jay loved Amy even more. Losing her would have devastated him.

The truth was, as much as he was absent from Amy's life, he was also absent from his own. Work was important to him, but love was also a part of his implicit core values. By continuing to run on the business treadmill year after year, it was as if he were living someone else's life—someone who valued work more than love.

As Jay and I sought to understand the underlying motivations for Jay's addiction to work, we discovered an important thing. His father had been a workaholic, too. As a child, Jay had sworn he would never fall into that trap. What he didn't count on was the constant gnawing feeling in the pit of his stomach that no matter what he accomplished, it was never enough. In essence, he was never enough.

Paradoxically, the more successful Jay became and the more money he made, the emptier and more depressed he felt inside. He mistakenly thought that success, money, achievement, and the beautiful woman he married would make him feel whole, loved, and complete. His plan had failed, and now the woman he loved was threatening to leave him.

In order to move past this addiction, it was essential that Jay acknowledge the self-sabotaging implicit core beliefs that were running his life without him knowing it. Together we identified the following:

- If I get more money, I will be happier.
- If I am more successful, I will be more worthy as a human being.
- I am lovable only if I am super-successful; anything less is a failure.
- If I get approval from the CEO, I will know that I am worthy.

I often asked Jay the question "What do you most deeply want?" He was very lucky, as he had earned the financial means to be able to ask such a question and live accordingly. After working together with me for a year, Jay ultimately decided to leave the job at his start-up company in order to save his marriage and reclaim his life.

Shortly thereafter, he and Amy took their first vacation in five years. Jay then grew a long beard and entered "pre-retirement," which he told me was a period of not working. He was going to study interesting things, take up meditation, and think about his next life project, which he hinted may be starting a family with Amy. He no longer felt driven by the fear that once defined his every day. This, Jay told me, was his most authentic self.

ADDICTION TO ALCOHOL

When you can barely cope with faking your life, exploring who you really are can seem like a luxury. Steve found it particularly hard to spend time with himself. He had devoted a lot of time to creating a false front to protect himself, yet he still felt vulnerable.

At the slightest sign of stress, Steve poured himself another scotch. It was always going to be the last, but somehow it never was. It was just the first of many. When he got out of rehab for the fourth time, Steve swore he would make it stick. A counselor at the rehab clinic had given him my name, so he called to set up an appointment.

Months in rehab had left his used car business in tatters. His cousin had been managing it so poorly while Steve was away that the business was barely making enough to function. The day we met, Steve discovered that his cousin had used ten thousand dollars of the operating capital they had left to pay off a gambling debt.

"This kind of thing always happens!" Steve exclaimed. "I need a partner to run this business, but every time I find one, I get ripped off, one way or another. You just can't find honest people out there."

As we began to explore his predicament in therapy, we found that Steve was not only drawing in dishonest business partners, but also dishonest friends and romantic partners as well. Steve's life was illustrating the spiritual principle we discussed earlier: you don't draw into your life who you want; you draw in who you *are*. As you grow and change, the people you draw into your life will change as well.

As Steve progressed in therapy, he gradually realized that he had not been honest with himself or others. In the darkest depths of his alcoholism, Steve would resort to lying, cheating, and stealing. He lied about why he didn't show up to work in the mornings. He cheated on girlfriends left and right. He even stole from family members when his booze money ran low. In the intimate and nonthreatening environment that we created together in the therapy room, Steve was able to look at himself honestly in a way he never had before. As this occurred, Steve began to take small but tangible steps toward becoming more honest with himself and the other people in his life. As he began to live more authentically and honestly, he started drawing more stable, honest, and trustworthy people into his life as well.

THE BEST TREATMENT

Often, at the root of an addiction is the implicit core belief that we are alone in a cruel, punishing world. We try to fill the void by looking outside ourselves, desperately hoping to latch on to somebody or something that will make us whole. While addictions may fill this emptiness temporarily, complete healing and fulfillment entail removing the blocks inside ourselves that are cutting us off from love. Loneliness is the plaintive cry of addiction. Freeing oneself from addiction takes more than quitting drugs or letting go of rage or giving up scotch for good. It involves finding a way to love yourself.

Addiction is one of the few areas of medicine where one of the most effective treatment modalities is spiritually based and involves invoking the assistance of a Higher Power. There are the twelve-step programs like Alcoholics Anonymous, Narcotics Anonymous, Overeaters Anonymous, Gamblers Anonymous, and Sex and Love Addicts Anonymous, among other such programs. In the following exercise, I have adapted the first three steps of a twelve-step program. You're invited to use this exercise for any addiction that you may be ready to work toward releasing today.

Exercise: Surrendering Your Addictions

For this exercise, identify an addiction you would like to release. This can be a substance addiction, behavioral addiction, or psychological addiction. Think about why you would like to release this particular addiction and how your life would change if it were no longer in your life. How did this addiction begin and what adaptive value did it serve in your life? What damage has this addiction caused you? Are you ready to part with it now?

If your answer is no, I invite you to journal about your resistance to letting go of this addiction. Releasing an addiction is a huge step, and one must be personally and emotionally ready before taking such a step. It is important to identify and explore your resistance if you are not yet ready. Give yourself the time and space to become ready, or enlist the help of a friend, family member, or professional to help you get there.

Step One: Be Honest with Yourself and Others

In this step, you admit to yourself and at least one person close to you that you have a problem. In AA, this is the step that goes something like "Hi. My name is Bill and I'm an alcoholic." For the sake of this exercise, you can use any language that resonates with you to communicate the following:

I,_____, admit on this date of _____ that I have an addiction to _____ that I would like to release, once and for all.

Sharing your desire to release your addiction with somebody you trust serves many purposes. First, it breaks the silence and solidifies your honesty. Oftentimes, our addictions are our "dirty little secrets." As long as nobody knows, we can remain in denial. Telling somebody you trust takes courage and strengthens your resolve to truly release this self-destructive habit. Second, it makes you accountable to somebody other than yourself, thereby creating a supportive partnership with somebody with whom you will have to be honest. Third, it ensures you have support in this process and that you do not have to do this alone. For individuals who would prefer not tell somebody they personally know, I recommend finding a twelve-step group near you for the specific addiction you are working to release.

Step Two: Admit Limited Control over Addiction

Depending on where you are in the process of overcoming your addiction, you may or may not feel that we have limited control over this addiction. For some people, willpower and insight may indeed be enough to stop smoking, stop using alcohol or drugs, or stop a destructive habit or behavior. If you are such a person, then executing step one above may be all you need.

However, if the addiction returns or if you find yourself relapsing despite maximizing your willpower, you are probably at the point where you recognize your limited control over your addiction. When it comes to addiction, willpower is often not enough.

To execute step two, you can use any language that resonates with you to communicate the following:

I, _____, having identified my addiction to _____ that I would like to release once and for all, admit my limited control over this addiction. My willpower alone is not enough to overcome this addiction. This addiction is greater than me, and I no longer want to overcome it alone.

Step Three: Surrender Addiction to a Higher Power, As You Understand It

If you have gotten to the point where you feel powerless to overcome this addiction alone, you may be ready to welcome in some help from above. You do not need to be religious or believe in God for this step to work. Your Higher Power may be

God, the Universe, Mother Nature, love itself, or whatever ineffable guiding force may exist in this world that helps people overcome life challenges. Since twelve-step programs are consistently found to be among the most widespread and effective treatments for addiction around the world (in the United States, there are approximately 1.3 million active members of AA alone, meeting in around fifty-seven thousand weekly meetings)[9] there's obviously Someone or Something somewhere helping all the souls who surrender their addictions to Him, Her, or It. If faith does not appeal to you, do this step because the science supports it.

To execute step three, use any language that resonates with you to communicate the following:

Given that I, _____, have admitted my powerlessness over my addiction to _____, I now open myself up to the possibility that Something greater than myself can restore me to a state of balance, peace, love, and/or sobriety. On this date of _____, I surrender my addiction over to this Higher Power and ask for His, Her, or Its help in ridding me of this addiction, once and for all.

Having requested assistance from a Higher Power, be open to how help and guidance may manifest in your life to help you overcome this addiction.

7

Transforming Fear

We fear our highest possibilities. We are generally afraid to become that which we can glimpse in our most perfect moments, under conditions of great courage. We enjoy and even thrill to godlike possibilities we see in ourselves in such peak moments. And yet we simultaneously shiver with weakness, awe, and fear before these very same possibilities.

—ABRAHAM MASLOW

"I haven't slept in days!"

After her beloved mother died suddenly in a car accident, Christina would lie awake all night long. Night after night, Christina dreaded the hour when she would find herself in bed anticipating yet another sleepless night followed by yet another day of exhaustion. She tried to fight off her insomnia with over-the-counter sleep medications, but nothing worked. Two years went by without relief.

Eventually, with a stronger sleep medication prescribed by a sleep specialist,

Christina began to sleep fitfully. But the lack of quality sleep was already interfering with all aspects of her life, and she was about to get fired from her job at a fast-paced marketing agency. So, she sought me out for help.

Our conversations soon revealed that the true reason for her lack of sleep was a silent, yet crippling, anxiety. Her mother's death had stirred something much deeper, an existential fear of death that all of us share.

Freud believed that the fear of death was not about death, per se, but about something missing from our lives.[1] He thought fear of death was a mask for other distinct yet related fears, such as uncertainty ("What will happen when I die?"), helplessness ("How can I ever solve this situation?"), regret ("How could I have lived this way?"), loneliness ("Why must I die alone?"), or shame ("How can I bear the exposure of death?"). Existential psychiatrist and author Irvin Yalom believed that the people who have the most "unlived life" fear death the most ("I have so much left to do! How could I have wasted so much of my life?!").

In my work with Christina, we began by focusing on two questions:

"What is missing from your life?"

"How can you begin to live your life more fully and authentically?"

These questions brought us closer to the core of Christina's anxiety. It would be impossible for any of us to live our lives fully in a state of constant sleep deprivation. Christina's insomnia further fueled her anxiety, which only worsened her insomnia. She became inadvertently stuck in a self-perpetuating downward spiral from which she did not know how to escape.

By exploring these existential questions together, Christina and I began to zero in on the essential part of Christina's life that was not being fully lived. I believe that it was *that* part of her keeping her awake at night. Her mother's death had made the inevitability of death more real—and far more personal. Now a part of her soul was saying, "I can't die yet. I haven't lived!"

In my initial evaluation with patients, I am always looking for their souls to emerge. Our soul is the blueprint we bring into this world of how we are meant to grow, change, evolve, transform, and meaningfully contribute to humankind over the course of our lives. Some call it our "divine essence," that which connects us to something greater than ourselves, to each other, and to who we really are. Once we learn to hear the whisper of our soul and follow its secret longings, it will guide us to a life of meaning and fulfillment … and sounder sleep. Opening ourselves to our soul's deepest longings is a powerful catalyst for growth, healing, and transformation.

For Christina that meant listening to the voice inside that knew what it wanted to do in life but had been blocked by her career choices. She had taken a job in marketing because it was practical, available, and paid the bills. But in her heart Christina had always wanted to become a writer. When she finally began to confront her own death anxiety, she realized that the act of writing also provided her with a metaphorical sense of immortality. When she heard that part of her soul speaking to her through her insomnia, she began to take small but tangible steps toward making her dream come true.

For Christina, following her dream was a risk. So she started with a simple morning writing practice without any promises about where that risk would lead. With each passing day, Christina felt more connected with the part of herself she had lost many years ago—her love of language, her passion for writing, her deeply emotional core essence. She studied literature in college and graduated with honors. Where had that passion gone? Writing became an important part of Christina's healing journey. Slowly but surely Christina began to sleep a little more soundly through the night. To her surprise, she soon found a job as a staff writer at a health journal. Two years later, she left that job to write her first book.

By taking a risk, confronting her fears, and following her dream, Christina began to live her life more fully. When she did, she had no more need for symptoms of insomnia warning her about what is missing in her life. Her death anxiety gradually abated.

WHAT WE REALLY FEAR

This famous quote by author and spiritual educator Marianne Williamson echoed true for Christina as she gained the courage to undergo these powerful changes in her life:

> *Our deepest fear is not that we are inadequate. Our deepest fear is that we are powerful beyond measure. It is our light, not our darkness, that most frightens us.*
>
> *We ask ourselves, "Who am I to be brilliant, gorgeous, talented, fabulous?" Actually, who are you not to be? You are a child of God. Your playing small does not serve the world. There is nothing enlightened about shrinking so that other people won't feel insecure around you. We are all meant to shine, as children do. We were born to make manifest the glory of God that is within us.*
>
> *It's not just in some of us; it's in everyone. And as we let our own light shine, we unconsciously give other people permission to do the same. As we are liberated from our own fear, our presence automatically liberates others.*[2]

A Course in Miracles, an inspired text about spiritual transformation written by Columbia University psychologist Helen Schucman, makes it clear that, for every decision we make, we have a choice of whether to align with fear or love. The opposite of love is not hate or indifference—it is fear. Just like turning on a lightbulb eradicates the darkness in a room, feeling love can eradicate the feelings of fear inside us. In contrast, defensiveness and fear block our capacity to feel love fully and completely—for other people, for ourselves, and for life. Fear keeps our hearts small. Feeling love creates a space of vulnerability, which may be uncomfortable if we think of love as a limited commodity. We fear, for example, that if we extend ourselves and really love someone, they may eventually leave us and we may feel abandoned and devastated. Thus we feel more fear than love, which keeps our hearts small and closed. When we "fall in love," as quickly as we may open our hearts in these instances, we may also feel fear. We may close up and build a wall of self-protection around ourselves to avoid the seemingly inevitable devastation that may ensue. Since true love eradicates fear, personal growth entails learning how to gradually come into alignment with love more often, and as a result, with fear less often.[3]

However, when we have learned to live in fear because of a difficult childhood or extremely challenging life circumstances, it can be difficult to release fear and align with love. It often requires consistent and deliberate baby steps, each of which may feel like a big risk. Risks are enlivening, exhilarating, and at times, terrifying, but they enable us to expand our sense of who we are. Choosing a challenge like this and meeting it creates a strong sense of empowerment that makes it easier for us to face our fears, whatever they may be.

Exercise: Seeing the Innocence

To put this idea into practice, let us focus on making a small perceptual shift in our lives. As I wrote above, all actions are driven either by fear or by love. Since all human beings at the deepest level ultimately want to be loved, heard, and understood, any action driven by fear can also be seen as an appeal for love. Sometimes these appeals for love come in harsh, angry, and heartless ways. The more ferocious the roar, the greater the fear and desperation for love.

For this stream-of-consciousness writing exercise, look back to an instance when somebody treated you in a way that didn't feel good. Now set your stopwatch to five minutes and write continuously on the topic Seeing the Innocence.

Questions for Reflection

1. In what way this did person hurt you?

2. How did you understand and explain this person's behavior at the time?

3. Now see this person as a scared little boy or girl who desperately wants love and simply doesn't know how to get it. How might this person have been driven by fear and appealing for love?

4. How does revisiting this interaction change your perception of it?

Next time somebody treats you in a way that does not feel good, instead of getting angry at this person, practice making the perceptual shift of seeing the innocence in their action. Being able to reframe a situation in this way can be a powerful tool for forgiveness, letting go and opening your heart. However, being able to reframe a situation and have more compassion for another person does *not* mean that you should therefore allow this person to mistreat you, violate your boundaries, or compromise your safety in any way.

THE EVOLUTION OF FEAR

Ultimately, fear is the reason we are all still alive today. If early human beings had not been afraid when they saw a tiger or a blazing forest fire, we might have disappeared from the face of the earth millennia ago. Fear is one of our most invaluable survival instincts. When you think about it, it's amazing that our bodies have a built-in warning system to let us know when we are—or even might be—in danger! It is far better to panic and run for the hills than to find ourselves on the menu as the midafternoon snack for a hungry alligator!

Fear, by definition, is our response to danger, real or perceived. When the danger is perceived rather than real, stress and anxiety result. In *Why Zebras Don't Get Ulcers*, Stanford biology and neuroscience professor Dr. Robert Sapolsky reminds us that in more dangerous times, human beings needed fear to signal the stress response. The hallmark of the stress response is mobilizing our energy stores away from the body's "rest and digest" functions (stimulated by the parasympathetic nervous system) and into the body's "fight or flight" functions (stimulated by the sympathetic nervous system).[4] Activating the sympathetic nervous system fuels all the critical muscles of your body so that you can effectively outrun the saber-toothed tiger chasing you. Your heart rate, blood pressure, and breathing rate also speed up. While short-term increases in these parameters are adaptive when outrunning a tiger or dealing with any emergency, the overactivation of this response (like if your blood pressure spikes every time you're stuck in traffic) is a heart attack waiting to happen. This is why with long-term chronic stress, your immune system's ability to fight off infections is compromised, gastrointestinal symptoms like diarrhea and constipation abound, females are less likely to ovulate and carry pregnancies to term, and males begin to have trouble with erections and secrete less testosterone. When in constant "stress" mode, your body has little time to worry about digestion, reproduction, and fighting off colds.[5]

And then there is the effect of chronic stress on your brain! While short-term stress heightens cognitive function (like enhancing your focus to ace your math test), long-term stress can actually overtax your poor aching brain and kill neurons in the part of the brain responsible for learning and memory called the hippocampus.[6] We naturally lose some brain cells as we age, and chronic stress basically speeds up the aging process.

Heart disease, irritable bowel syndrome, fibromyalgia, certain autoimmune conditions, some forms of dementia, and other illnesses linked to chronic stress do not befall zebras, baboons, or other animals in the wild. And we as human beings may develop these chronic illnesses partly because our bodies aren't designed for the constant stresses of a modern-day life. Rather, we seem more built for the kind of short-term stress faced by a zebra—like outrunning a predator. Today, "danger" is not usually physical but emotional and psychological: fear of failing at work or school, fear of being intimate with somebody, fear of a conflict with a friend or loved one, fear of death, or fear of never finding a life partner, to name a few.

Most fears—whether physical, emotional, or psychological—can be divided into five categories.[7] The first category is fear of death—as in the case of Christina—which arouses a primary existential anxiety in most human beings. The second category is fear of losing one's bodily integrity, such as through disability, aging, illness, or injury of any kind, as in a car accident. The third category is fear of losing one's autonomy, as via imprisonment, immobilization, paralysis, and the like. Interestingly, some fears of commitment in relationships fall into this category. While there is significant overlap between the second and third category, the former focuses specifically on deterioration or damage to the physical body, while the latter focuses on loss of one's freedom, self-sufficiency, and sense of control in life. The fourth category is fear of separation, such as loneliness, abandonment, or loss of connectedness. This stems from a fear of becoming a non-person—not wanted, respected, or valued by somebody else. The fifth category is fear of ego dissolution, or the shattering of one's constructed sense of lovability, capability, and worthiness. This includes humiliation, shame, or any other mechanism of profound self-disapproval that threatens the loss of integrity of the self.

Over the centuries, certain fears have been passed down through our genetic memory. Through the hard-won lessons learned by our ancestors, many of us have inborn fears of heights, angry faces, glaring lights, and loud noises. But as individuals we also accumulate more fears as we encounter difficult, painful, or traumatic life experiences. In an effort to protect us, our bodies learn to warn us of new "dangers" based on past trauma. We are unconsciously conditioned to react with fear to things that remind us of those traumatic events, whether the associations are valid or not.

THE DEFENSE OF FEARLESSNESS

Daryl was a twenty-eight-year-old professional bodybuilder with a Herculean six-foot-four-inch, three-hundred-pound body. For as long as he could remember, Daryl thrived on "living on the edge." He loved nothing more than racing cars, riding motorcycles, skydiving, base jumping—anything to keep his adrenaline pumping. On the surface, Daryl was absolutely fearless. He told me time and again that he did not fear death.

But I was suspicious, because if he truly did not fear death, he would not have had to repeatedly remind me of it. More likely, he was as terrified of death as Christina but dealt with his fear in the exact opposite way: by confronting it head-on with countless death-defying activities. This defense against one's fear is unconscious and called "counterphobia." What is feared—in Daryl's case, death—is denied and disavowed, just like Carl Jung's "shadow." As far as Daryl was concerned, fear of death was the farthest thing from his conscious mind. His unconscious was a different story.

Daryl was conflicted. On a conscious level, getting as close to death as possible filled his life with excitement and passion. The closer he came to death, the more alive he felt. But on an unconscious level, he was terrified, using death-defying stunts to deny the terror he felt deep inside. When a conflict exists between the conscious and unconscious mind, we may develop a symptom.

In time, Daryl's body couldn't keep up. While doing dead lifts, Daryl threw out his back. It was a disappointment, but Daryl recovered quickly and went back to his old habits, only to pull his back out again, this time much more seriously. He was told by his doctors to stop his workouts and allow his body to heal. Some therapists might interpret Daryl's back injury as a symptom he unconsciously created to resolve the conflict between his conscious mind (I don't fear death!) and his unconscious mind (I'm terrified of death!). The result of the symptom: Daryl was paralyzed from engaging in any more death-defying acts!

Daryl was devastated. Not only was his self-image closely linked to his ability to perform incredible feats, but he had devoted himself to high-energy activities so completely that he didn't know what to do with his time now that he had to stop. His unconscious solution to this problem came as a surprise, even to him.

For reasons beyond his awareness, Daryl started going to bars late at night and picking fights. This was a completely foreign behavior to Daryl—he had many friends, was well liked by his peers, and was not a violent or angry person by nature. So what in the world was driving this unusual aggressive behavior? As Daryl and I explored this, we discovered that what he was ultimately craving in these bar fights was the adrenaline rush. He felt this rush when he pushed himself beyond his limits with dead lifts or jumped out of planes. Not being able to get his adrenaline rush through workouts anymore, he succumbed to provoking bar fights without even knowing why! He was exhibiting the unmistakable signs of an adrenaline junkie.

The pattern had developed in the most innocent way. When Daryl was only ten years old, his mother died from a heart attack. His father was so heartbroken that he repeatedly attempted suicide. Even as a boy, it was Daryl who "saved him." It was understood that Daryl's job from then on was to keep his father alive. If there is any activity that will rev up your adrenaline, it's pulling your father back from the brink of death again and again and again. Daryl lived in a constant state of stress, fearing that one day his efforts would not be enough to save his dad. With so many people grateful for his efforts and the love of his father to show for it, Daryl was rightly proud of his ability to defy death. It had started so young that it felt like his birthright.

With a strong physique and a determination to live that role to the fullest, Daryl naturally gravitated toward extreme sports. What better way to thrive at the place he felt he belonged—at the brink of death? It's no surprise that it felt right.

While his back was healing, the risks of bar fights gave him a modest but sufficient rush of adrenaline to get him by. It all came crashing down when he got arrested.

Handcuffed to a metal chair at the police station, Daryl was forced to take a look at what he'd been doing. He felt guilty and ashamed of himself. This adrenaline addiction had driven him down a road he had never meant to take. He had become *a violent offender!* The very idea made him wince. That's not who he was! Not only did Daryl have to face his own embarrassment about being arrested, but his arrest meant he had to call his wife, Marla, to bail him out.

From the very beginning, Daryl had always been the rock in their relationship. His wife had married a strong, confident, death-defying man. He was terrified of her reaction. Would she leave him? Could she ever look him in the eyes again?

To his surprise, Marla was immediately loving and empathetic despite her shock. In fact, months later she confided in Daryl that she "loved him even more." She had always loved and admired the strong man he presented to the world, but now his vulnerability had allowed her to feel closer to him. Letting down his guard to reveal himself in all his human vulnerability to the woman he loved was not humiliating after all. Instead it strengthened his marriage.

In this situation, Daryl's soul correction involved kicking his adrenaline addiction. Lack of a high-adrenaline activity led Daryl to feel empty, a feeling so painful and dark that he looked for any possible way to fill this inner void. At first going into this space was so uncomfortable that Daryl needed to retreat immediately—he could not even talk about it. Throughout his therapy work, Daryl slowly and gently allowed his void to emerge while developing tools to tolerate his emotions, like a loving-kindness meditation Daryl began to do daily. Over time Daryl felt less need to escape his void because he was able to transform his fear into something constructive through the use of loving-kindness.

A devoted athlete, Daryl still engages in competitive activities that push his body to the limit—boot camps, triathlon training, rowing, hiking, hot yoga, and extreme sports. The difference is that now, if he puts them on hold for any reason, he is able to tolerate his inner void rather than turning to bar fights or any other destructive activity for this adrenaline rush. As he gradually became more in touch with his true self, he was also able to build a more intimate bond with his wife.

Exercise: Loving-Kindness Meditation

This twenty-five-hundred-year-old Buddhist practice is a powerful tool for filling one's inner emptiness and transforming one's fears and worries by cultivating an attitude of unconditional loving-kindness.[8]

1. Find a relaxed position, whether sitting or lying down.

2. Focus your attention on the area around your heart.

3. Now imagine that you are breathing in and out through your heart. With each inhale, your heart expands as it fills with fresh air. With each exhale, your heart contracts.

4. Now close your eyes and take several slow deep breaths through your heart:
   - Inhale through your nose for the count of two.
   - Hold your breath for the count of four.
   - Exhale through your nose for the count of eight.
   - Repeat for five breaths.

5. For the next three to five minutes, repeat inwardly to yourself the following four phrases:

> *May I be free of worry and fear.*
> *May I be happy.*
> *May I be free from suffering.*
> *May I be at peace.*

6. After each repetition, bring your attention back to your heart center and take a breath through your heart as above.

Throughout this week, repeat these phrases to yourself every time you feel empty, sad, fearful, or alone. As you do, connect to your heart center and imagine these words opening your heart more and more as you read each line.

FEAR OF BEING ALONE

In contrast to Daryl and Christina, who came to me with the underlying existential anxiety of fear of death, Lahari, a beautiful twenty-three-year-old medical student from Ghana, was plagued by fears of separation, alienation, and aloneness. When she came to my office, she, like many women I treat and like myself in years past, was afraid she would never meet her soulmate. Unlike most young people in New York City these days, Lahari felt ready to settle down, get married, and have a baby at a relatively young age. In Ghana, women are often married with children by their early twenties. Lahari said she felt a loneliness in her heart and soul that only her soulmate could fill.

Together we worked to allay her fears of never meeting the right man. She worried that she might one day find herself living alone after it was too late for her to have a family. If that were to happen, she wondered if life would have any meaning for her. In her worst moments, this downward spiral of "catastrophizing" and self-defeating thoughts led Lahari to feel like life was no longer worth living.

When women come to me in search of their soulmates, I tell them about the two distinct yet not mutually exclusive approaches to meeting the right person. The first approach is purely rational, best summarized as "it's a numbers game." You meet as many people as possible and go on as many dates as you can, and eventually, chances are you'll meet your soulmate. The more people you meet, the greater the odds of finding "the One." Obviously, this is highly oversimplified, as most people with whom I would be having this conversation come to therapy not because they haven't met enough people, but because, for one reason or another, relationships have not worked out with the people they have met. Nevertheless, many people employ the first approach for years before deciding to explore the second approach.

The second approach is more psychological and spiritual. This approach is artfully delineated in Katherine Woodward Thomas's book, *Calling in "The One."* To draw in your soulmate, you work on yourself to clear out the emotional, psychological, spiritual, and sometimes physical blockages that exist within you that keep your soulmate from coming into your life. As you work through your resistances, blockages, fears, and conflicts about being in a committed relationship, the chances of a relationship working out become much higher. Obviously, the two approaches are not mutually exclusive but actually quite complementary.

People who adopt the second approach and begin to work on clearing out their so-called blockages often begin to notice different kinds of partners appearing in their lives. Every person you draw into your life is a mirror of yourself in some way. This is true not only of romantic relationships, but also of friendships and business relationships. If you keep drawing the same exact kind of person into your life over and over, it means that you have not yet learned the lesson that precisely this kind of person is supposed to teach you.

As I wrote about earlier, I kept drawing in one emotionally unavailable man after another before I finally realized that the problem was not with the men. On some level, I too was emotionally unavailable. These men were mirrors for this important truth I had not yet faced about myself.

My patient Lahari soon started dating a man who looked very promising. He always said the right things. More than any other man she had ever met, Danilo was romantic and attentive. She loved the sense of being wooed. Beyond that, Danilo felt like family from the start. She could not quite place it, but something in his manner made her very comfortable thinking of him as her partner for life. She began to wonder if Danilo was the soulmate she had been dreaming of. Maybe he was the one to end her fear of being alone all her life.

As the months went by, however, Lahari and I began to notice that, for all his attentiveness and charm, Danilo cared most about Danilo. When Lahari's needs conflicted with his, he always put his own needs first, without apology. The connection Lahari thought she had felt with him was shaken.

Finally, we saw that when it really came down to it, Danilo was quite narcissistic. If he felt like family, it might have been less because of a soul connection and more because Lahari's father had also been narcissistic. As a child, she had grown accustomed to her father putting his own needs first while charming her into thinking her small needs didn't matter as much as his. But Lahari knew better now. Eventually, Lahari ended her relationship with Danilo. She had no intention of spending the rest of her life bound to a narcissist.

In the aftermath, I worked with her to keep her soul's intention clear. Lahari's relationship with Danilo helped her to become clearer about what she was looking for in a soulmate: somebody who was romantic, charming, charismatic, handsome, fun (all qualities Danilo had) but who was also generous, loving, empathic, vulnerable, and capable of putting Lahari's needs on par with his own.

About a year later, Lahari went with her medical school friends to a birthday party for a man named Gerald. Lahari had once met Gerald several years prior and thought he was very nice. But since he was a little older and not in the medical field himself, Lahari did not think there was relationship potential. Now, with more clarity in what she was looking for in a partner, Lahari let herself be drawn in by Gerald's warm and endearing smile. A kindhearted archeologist who came to love her very deeply, Gerald was far more capable of seeing Lahari for who she was and aligning with the truest needs of her heart. Despite her fears, she had found a man to be her soulmate after all. Although Gerald had come into Lahari's life before, she had not been in the place to recognize him as her soulmate until she had done the necessary work on herself and gotten clear about exactly what she was looking for in a soulmate. At the time of this writing, she remains happily married to him three years later.

As with Lahari, fear is often our guide to the soul correction we need to make. Lahari's fear of being alone enabled her to access her soul's deep desire for a life partner and use that desire to grow as a person and transform herself. In this way, Lahari's fear served as an impetus for her spiritual and psychological transformation. Aligning with your soul and cultivating authenticity are often key components to overcoming fear. Having the courage to overcome your fear, in turn, emboldens your soul. The truth is that together, your mind and soul are truer, bigger, and stronger than even your darkest fear.

Exercise: Release Your Fears

As you go through the exercise that follows, you may want to journal about your experience and what comes up for you. Some questions for reflection are provided throughout the exercise.

1. Choose a Fear to Release

It sometimes helps to start with easy ones ("I am afraid I'll be late for my early meeting tomorrow" or "I'm afraid this dress makes me look fat").

After you've had some success releasing the smaller fears, you can move to larger ones ("I'm a failure," "I'll never meet my soulmate," "I won't make enough money this year to support my family," etc.).

2. Identify Your Triggers

Too often we figuratively shut our eyes and turn away from our fears, hoping to avoid them. It doesn't help. We still feel them anyway. But turning away like that does keep us from questioning whether they're legitimate or not.

You can find a hint in the triggers. What happens to provoke your fear? If you can identify the triggers, you can anticipate the fear, so you won't be thrown off as much by it.

Maybe one of your current goals is to meet a life partner. Two triggers that could set off your fear of failure might be "When I go online, I come up empty, never connecting with anyone" and "My self-consciousness about my own flaws or vulnerabilities makes me fear that no one will want me." If instead you have a fear of commitment, your trigger might be "When someone starts wanting to get serious, I suddenly start daydreaming about leaving."

Notice where your resistance lies. How can you use your fear to grow as a person and expand your current limitations? How can you work it through with the man or woman who comes into your life?

3. Reframe Your Fear as a Soul Correction

Ask yourself how your response to this fear can benefit your soul. Will it push you to develop more courage or confidence? Will it make you go outside your comfort zone and give up habits that have been blocking your happiness? How can you transform this fear instead of casting yourself as its victim?

4. Center Yourself

To deactivate fear, breathe deeply, close your eyes, and repeat: "I am not my fear. I am so much more." To center yourself further, repeat the Loving-Kindness Meditation exercise on page 123.

Connect to the love inside you. Feel your soul expand.

This connection to your deepest self will make you strong in the face of even the darkest fears. This inner connection is your true self and your most reliable friend. Trust it. Rely on it. Breathe it in.

8

Harnessing Personal Power

In the depth of winter, I finally learned that
within me there lay an invincible summer.

—ALBERT CAMUS

As soon as I confronted some of my fears and began to live from a place of personal power, everything around me shifted. My life took on a very different quality. Instead of relying on other people to help and rescue me if things went wrong, I began to rely on myself.

It was a new experience. I had imagined that the people who appeared to go through life without the constraints of niggling worries and fears were extraordinarily strong and powerful. But I slowly began to see that this was wrong. If you face it bit by bit, life is not so overwhelming that it requires some kind of superhuman strength to get it right. Regular strength and courage work just fine.

You can navigate life successfully, with your eyes wide open—fully aware that we will face challenges. You don't have to know every answer, anticipate every problem, or make sure you stay in complete control at all times. Sometimes you will fall. You'll experience self-doubt. You'll feel sorry for yourself.

You won't always get it right, but that's okay. In fact, that's how it is for everyone because we are human.

Patients sometimes come to me upset because an issue they believed they had worked through years ago has suddenly and unexpectedly resurfaced in their life. "I thought I had worked through that insecurity!" Or that problem. Or that mind-set. Or that relationship issue. The resurfacing of old challenges is not an indicator of failure, or weakness, or not having worked hard enough in therapy or in life. In fact, it is the natural order of things. Challenges will and do resurface and cycle through our lives. That's why some therapists call psychotherapy "cyclo-therapy." It's not the absence of challenges that signals progress; it is being able to handle those same challenges with greater ease and fortitude. Accessing your personal power is what enables you to do that. In this chapter, we'll explore four steps necessary to accessing your personal power: relinquishing victim mentality, cultivating faith and forgiveness, rising above indecision, and owning your thoughts and feelings.

While we sometimes feel hopeless and trapped, we all have personal power and have always had it. But some of us don't claim it. The power to change our lives is already in our own hands. As Freud famously said, "Most people do not really want freedom, because freedom involves responsibility, and most people are afraid of responsibility."

RELINQUISH VICTIM MENTALITY

Taking responsibility for one's life is the key to soul alignment and, ultimately, fulfillment. However, rather than acknowledge our role in creating our own lives, sometimes it seems much easier to blame our problems on a difficult childhood or an unjust world. I do not at all mean to imply that a difficult childhood doesn't present challenges to overcome or that there are not real problems in the world that truly victimize the people they afflict. Violence, genocide, war, discrimination, poverty, homelessness, hunger, domestic abuse, rape, human sex trafficking, natural disasters, and global warming are just a few of the very real and impactful human problems that require widespread change at the social and global level.

Still, it is not uncommon for some of us to relish the feeling of righteous indignation that comes from being a victim. Over time, our grip on this role can grow so tight that we come to identify with it. For example, it becomes familiar to say "this always happens to me" when faced with adversity. In a similar manner to how we can become confused thinking that our false self is actually who we are, we can become equally confused thinking that we are primarily victims of our circumstances rather than creators of our destiny.

The idea of playing the victim is as old as time. Just look at the story of Genesis. Adam said, "I didn't do it. She told me to do it." Eve said, "I didn't do it. The snake told me to do it." This is was the moment that humanity jumped onto the wheel of blame, which has been turning ever since.[1] Taking on a victim mentality is one of the primary ways we as human beings give away our power to others. But who knows better what you really need other than you? When you give that power away, you're choosing to let someone else have a say in your life even though they know less about your needs than you do.

There are certainly situations in life where it's common to feel victimized— the death of a spouse, the loss of a job, or a natural disaster destroying one's home. But being a victim of a calamity or even suffering a tremendous hardship are very different from adopting a victim mentality. While we frequently cannot control the life challenges and circumstances that befall us, we do have control over how we view these things and the mentality we adopt moving forward. A victim mentality keeps people stuck in a toxic, self-righteous state of pain and indignation.

On the flip side, taking accountability for how we respond to these problems and becoming involved as an agent of change in our own lives, as well as socially and globally, can be incredibly empowering. Our response is certainly a way of harnessing one's personal power, as is relinquishing victim mentality to the degree that one's personal circumstances allow. One recent and powerful example of this is Nobel Peace laureate Malala Yousafzai, the young woman from Pakistan who was shot for going to school and speaking out on behalf of girls' education in her community. After months of recovery from severe bullet wounds, she turned her adversity into powerful advocacy for girls' education around the world, raising awareness and resources as well as influencing policy-makers and the media to push for change globally.

In contrast to Malala, if anyone had ideal circumstances for feeling empowered, it was Joanna, a twenty-seven-year-old college graduate living in New York City. With a hefty trust fund she inherited from her family's oil business, she had the money to do absolutely anything she wanted yet could not summon the will to do anything.

Desperate to feel any sense of power or authority in her own life, Joanna resorted to judging others by imagining herself as being superior to everybody around her: this one didn't dress very well; that one was not very smart; another one was unattractive or had a bad personality. But her temporary fantasies of grandiosity could not override the nagging sense of defeat, anxiety, and self-doubt that were gobbling up her life.

Kabbalah teaches of a concept called "bread of shame," which is akin to the feeling of shame from receiving something we did not earn.[2] The saying "there's no free lunch" is never more true than when it comes to our psychology as human beings. For something to have value for us, we must work for it and earn it. For Joanna, too many things were handed to her on a silver platter without her having to lift a finger. This undermined and immobilized Joanna into a state of entitlement.

Entitlement is actually one of the most disempowering mentalities one can adopt. Feeling entitled to "the finer things in life," for instance, makes one not appreciate those things when they are present and sorely feel their lack when they are absent. Joanna suffered from both entitlement and bread of shame, which together undermined and immobilized her, leading her to feel depressed, confused, and always looking for somebody to blame or put down.

All day long Joanna sat in her mother's exquisitely decorated Park Avenue apartment feeling sorry for herself. She had graduated five years prior from one of the top liberal arts colleges in the nation. Rather than doing what most of her classmates did—looking for a job, taking a year off to do something different, or applying to graduate school—Joanna moved back in with her mother and never left. In the narrative she had constructed for her life, Joanna was "screwed up" because of a difficult childhood. Her mother was emotionally distant, self-absorbed, and trapped in a lifetime of victim mentality herself. Joanna's father was equally aloof, having had numerous affairs with other women, some even younger than Joanna! In a twisted attempt at vindication, Joanna's mother always told Joanna about her father's affairs, which at once broke Joanna's heart and filled her with rage—both at her father for having the affairs and at her mother for telling her about it. In Joanna's self-constructed narrative of her life, not only had her wealthy parents taught her bad values, but she had no role models of happiness.

When her older sister, with whom Joanna was once very close, moved to India three years ago to join the Hare Krishna movement, Joanna's grief was so extreme that she nearly became a recluse. She took her sister's "abandoning the family" as a sign that their childhood experiences were impossible to survive; she would either have to continue to live out her miserable life or figure out her own escape plan.

In order to move forward, Joanna had to process her turbulent childhood memories. Sadness, anger, fear, and resentment poured out of her in our sessions. Joanna had built a fortress around herself with her victim mentality. Nothing could reach her behind those walls, because the one who has been wronged is invincible. No one can accuse the victims of anything. They are righteous. Untouchable. And utterly helpless.

Slowly, Joanna began to realize that the more she blamed others, the more despair and hopelessness she felt. Every time she cast herself as the victim, she denied her own power. It was a self-sustaining loop, going nowhere.

That's why the moments of real breakthrough felt so remarkable. At those times, Joanna was able to temporarily set aside her blame and experience what was underneath it for the very first time: the deep grief she felt for the loss of her sister (with whom she no longer had contact), the anguished longing for good parents and a happy childhood. For the first time in her life, Joanna began to experience her unexpressed grief. Tears poured out of Joanna from the moment she sat down in my therapy chair to the moment she left. Day after day. Week after week. I was struck by how authentic her emotions felt now, as opposed to our early sessions where her feelings of entitlement and indignation had felt like impressions of someone else.

As heartbreaking as it was for Joanna to feel that pain, processing her pain gave her a new kind of strength. She no longer felt alone in her pain. And she'd felt the worst of it—the tears that would not stop for weeks on end. She had survived this. That was clear evidence that she was not weak, but strong; not a victim, but a survivor.

At the end of one of our emotional sessions, Joanna declared: "I'm done complaining. I'm not going to keep blaming my parents for screwing up. I want to finally start living my own life!" Joanna had made this proclamation before. Many times. But somehow, this time was different.

Change did not happen overnight. There was a period of experimentation as Joanna began to slowly step into her newfound power. It had, of course, been there all along, but it took her time to discover it and learn how to wield it.

For a long time, it felt strange for Joanna to make bold decisions on her own behalf without checking with anyone else. It was especially difficult to set boundaries with her mother.

Joanna's family had always encouraged her to follow in their footsteps, building a life of luxury, status, and travel. But this was without any real sense of individual purpose. To live a truly fulfilled and purposeful life, one must cultivate a work ethic consistent with productivity, accomplishment, and meaning. Living with purpose is difficult without this, especially if you are burdened by bread of shame. As an important step in harnessing her personal power and relinquishing her bread of shame, last year Joanna claimed her life for herself and decided to apply to graduate school to become an architect.

Although none of us can change what happened in the past, we can be responsible for how we see ourselves in the present and what we choose to do with our lives. This recognition is an important part of relinquishing victim mentality and beginning to take responsibility for a fulfilled life.

Exercise: What Stops Me from Harnessing My Personal Power

For this stream-of-consciousness writing exercise, set your stopwatch to five minutes and write continuously on What Stops Me from Harnessing My Personal Power using the guiding questions below. As with life, let your writing take you where it may.

Questions for Reflection

1. Where in my life do I see myself as a victim?

2. What would it mean to stop thinking of myself as a victim? How would I feel?

3. What would it mean to take full responsibility for all aspects of my life and not blame anybody else for anything that happens to me?

FAITH AND FORGIVENESS

Yolanda's story could not have been any more different from Joanna's. Yolanda did not have a trust fund. She was everything but entitled. From the age of fourteen, she worked full-time at the McDonald's down the street from her Harlem apartment in order to help take care of her two younger brothers after her father went to jail for selling drugs. Her mother was dependent on cocaine and her older brother was in prison for murder. She was sexually abused by her uncle when she was five years old, raped by her cousin at eleven, and got pregnant by her boyfriend at the age of fourteen.

When I was a psychiatry resident, Yolanda came to see me at the age of eighteen for anxiety. As she recounted her life story to me, I couldn't imagine how anybody with her set of circumstances could *not* be anxious! Yet as I got to know her, I realized that this woman who had been to hell and back in her short lifetime had a deep and enduring sense of inner peace. I wondered where it came from.

As I got to know her, I realized that her sense of peace came from her faith. A born-again Christian since the age of sixteen, Yolanda had an amazing sense of strength about her that made her quite charismatic and immediately likable. She had a sharp wit, easy smile, and calm demeanor. She would often say, "Yeah, life is hard, but God takes care of me." Yolanda was a deeply spiritual woman and saw evidence of God's work in all aspects of her life. She went to church every Sunday and frequently attended Bible study classes during the week. Her faith was what allowed Yolanda to get through all the situations in her life where many people would have called her a victim. When she would become overwhelmed or anxious, she would pray to God. In fact, it was while she was praying that she "got the message" to go see a psychiatrist for help with her anxiety. For Yolanda, and many others with challenging or difficult life circumstances, maintaining a strong sense of faith and being part of a supportive spiritual community was their way of harnessing their personal power.

Yolanda and Joanna, two very different young ladies with radically different life histories, learned to harness their personal power through wholly different means. Although Yolanda is the one who many may view as a "victim" after hearing her life story, it was actually Joanna who had to relinquish victim mentality (and entitlement) in order to harness her personal power. Life circumstances had forced Yolanda to harness her personal power long ago by embracing her faith and surrendering to a Higher Power.

Yolanda's capacity to harness her personal power through her faith is similar to that of my friend Jean-Baptiste, with whom I worked in Rwanda in 2009. Jean-Baptiste is a spiritual man who works in peace building, reconciliation, and trauma healing in Rwanda. He comes from a Tutsi family. His neighbors—a family with many children who would all come over to Jean-Baptiste's home for dinner—were Hutus. When the Rwandan genocide occurred in 1994, the Hutus began killing the Tutsis in what felt like a situation of "kill or be killed." Tragically, Jean-Baptiste's neighbor, a young boy named Paul who used to come over to his home and be fed by his mother almost every day, violently and brutally killed Jean-Baptiste's mother.

Understandably, Jean-Baptiste was horrified and enraged with Paul, who was put in jail as soon as the genocide ended. For fourteen years, Jean-Baptiste harbored pain, rage, resentment, and a desire for retribution in his heart. In the course of these fourteen years, Jean-Baptiste began to lead a national forgiveness program across the country of Rwanda, in which he inspired individuals to use the power of faith and God to find within themselves the courage, strength, and power to forgive the perpetrators of the genocide and move forward with their lives.

Fourteen years after the genocide, Jean-Baptiste went to visit Paul at the Rwandan jail. Paul thought Jean-Baptiste had come to kill him for killing his mother. Instead, Jean-Baptiste forgave Paul then and there, which Jean-Baptiste describes as the most liberating moment in his whole life. He could finally let go of all the pain and anger he had been carrying inside of him. A powerful example of harnessing one's personal power through faith, this story signifies to me the strength of the human spirit to overcome any obstacles that enter its path. Aristotle's words echo the wisdom of Jean-Baptiste: "Anybody can become angry—that is easy. But to be angry with the right person, to the right degree, at the right time, for the right purpose, and in the right way—that is not within everybody's power and that is not easy."

As Jean-Baptiste's incredible story shows, one of the most powerful ways of harnessing personal power is through the act of releasing anger in the service of forgiveness. Atrocity, betrayal, injustice, malice, abuse, recklessness, and slights not only cause us pain, but they hurt our pride. They feel intensely personal, and it's hard to let them go. But if we don't let them go, they stay stuck in the recesses of our minds and hearts for years, draining our energy without our even knowing it. My friend Jean-Baptiste is proof that in the core of our hearts, we have the power to move beyond the most difficult atrocities we have ever faced and forgive the perpetrators.

People choose to hold on to past grievances for a number of reasons. It gives them a sense of righteous indignation. They get a lot of energy from maintaining victim mentality. They feel the perpetrator does not *deserve* to be forgiven. These are just three of the many reasons people can hold on to grievances all the way to the grave. But the paradox is: the person who most benefits from forgiveness is *not* the person being forgiven. The person who will most benefit from forgiveness is *you*! When you are able to truly forgive somebody, you can finally let go of the anger, hurt, resentment, grudge, sadness, and vengeance that you have been carrying around in your heart, sometimes for years. As Christian theologian Lewis B. Smedes wrote, "When we genuinely forgive, we set a prisoner free and then discover that the prisoner we set free was us."[3]

Forgiveness does not mean that you were not hurt or that the act you are forgiving was acceptable. It means that you have chosen to move forward and heal yourself. From this perspective, forgiveness is a predominantly selfish act, and one in which we should engage as much as possible! Holding grudges is exhausting. You're letting perpetrators live rent-free in your heart and mind, thereby continuing to let them hurt you. Forgiveness is simply the most energy-efficient option we have in looking out for ourselves, and the one most conducive to health, well-being, and fulfillment. It's far from easy, and is more like an ongoing disciplined spiritual practice, like meditation, rather than an event or one-time occurrence. This is why when Jesus's disciple Peter came to him and asked, "Lord, how many times should I forgive my brother when he sins against me?" Jesus's reply was "Not seven times, but seventy times seven times." The wounds we carry, especially deep wounds, often require more than one attempt at forgiveness before we can truly release the pain we carry in our hearts and souls and be healed.

Exercise: The Art of Forgiveness

This is one of the longer exercises in the book. Please commit thirty to sixty minutes to it. Forgiveness is not something that happens overnight for most people. It often takes commitment, intention, perspective, and an expansion of the heart. This can only be achieved honestly, organically, and over time. Forgiveness cannot be forced, and efforts at forced forgiveness will only lead to confusion, repression, and denial—the counterfeits of forgiveness.

Please keep in mind that you may have experienced a transgression that you were absolutely powerless to change, and/or to which you did not contribute in any way. One such example is sexual abuse or molestation during childhood, although there are many others.

Forgiveness involves first accepting and honoring your own hurt feelings, anger, and indignation. Often, this very hurt and anger are our best teachers.

Before engaging in forgiveness, it is important to mobilize your hurt and anger in the service of yourself—to establish a sense of safety and boundaries so that the transgression does not occur again, insomuch as we can prevent it.

Therefore, before we are able to forgive others, we first need to forgive ourselves for our role in what transpired, if we had any role in it at all. From this space, we are ready to begin the process.

In this exercise, we will lay down the foundation to begin the complex yet empowering process that has the potential to lighten our lives and heal our souls.

1. Intention

Begin this process by setting the intention to forgive somebody who has hurt you. You can set this intention, even if you are not yet ready to forgive. As author Louise Hay wrote, "We may not know how to forgive, and we may not want to forgive; but the very fact we say we are willing to forgive begins the healing practice."

2. Ask for Help

This step is optional. If you are somebody who believes in a Higher Power, asking for help from that Higher Power with this process can also be quite helpful: "Dear God, please help me find in myself the strength, courage, and compassion to forgive _____ for _____."

3. Honor Your Anger

In your journal, write why you are angry at the person you wish to forgive. Describe the boundary violation you experienced, or loss of personal safety that resulted from his or her transgression. Describe the anger, hurt, and resentment you experienced.

4. Take Responsibility, If Relevant

In your journal, identify whether you had a role in the transgression that transpired. How, if at all, did you contribute to what occurred? What part of the transgression, if any, can you take personal responsibility for? What did you learn from this experience? How will you do things differently in the future?

5. Restore Your Own Well-Being

Now make a list of the actions you can take or commitments you can make to yourself to restore your sense of well-being, safety, and balance. What steps in self-care can you take to show yourself the support you need to begin, slowly but surely, the forgiveness process?

6. Open Your Heart

Forgiveness is impossible without broadening your perspective and expanding your heart. Hopefully, the above exercises have helped you expand your perspective a little. Now to expand your heart, let's return to the exercise in chapter 6 titled "Filling Your Heart with Love" (see page 102).

Before you repeat this exercise, remind yourself of your intention to forgive the person you wish to forgive. As you do this meditation over time with intention, you will feel less anger and resentment toward this person. One day you may be able to release these feelings from your heart completely, at which point you will be ready to truly forgive.

7. Release the Hurt

If you're truly committed to forgiving somebody, I recommend you repeat the steps above at least once a week. As your heart expands, you will become ready to finally release the anger, hurt, and resentment. Only you will know when you are finally ready to release the difficult feelings you have been carrying in your heart. If you find after you've tried this exercise for several weeks that you are unable to release these emotions, that's okay. You can take a break for some time and come to back to the exercise when you feel ready.

Harnessing Personal Power

RISE ABOVE INDECISION

Every important choice we make in these areas is an act of self-definition—we are what we choose. Psychologist and psychoanalyst Eric Erikson said that two of the most important areas of striving in life involve love and work. Often people come to me for therapy because they are struggling to make a choice in one or both of these areas.

In John Gardner's novel *Grendel*, a wise man encapsulates the mystery of life in four inspired words: "Things fade, alternatives exclude."[4] The first profound proposition—everything fades—will be explored in chapter 12, Immortality. The second—alternatives exclude—encapsulates the meaning of this section: that every decision we make is a kind of renunciation. Choosing one thing closes the door to others. In a society with nonstop media telling us we ought to "have it all," it has never been more difficult to deliberately cut off some of our options.

An inability to make important life choices prevents people from moving forward with their lives. Very often, people avoid making a decision out of an understandable fear of losing something. The trouble is, not making a decision is a decision, too! And, at a certain point, making a choice—any choice—is more liberating than being plagued by the relentless anxiety of indecision.

While Eduardo, a fifty-five-year-old Peruvian bartender, was working with me in therapy, he found himself facing the difficult decision of whether to leave his marriage or end his affair.

As far back as Eduardo could remember, he always had women "on the side." Even before he was married, he had never been monogamous. If nothing else, he would hire a call girl. Over the years, Eduardo began to realize that he was not just relieving his boredom, but he had become a slave to his impulses.

If a relative slighted him at a family gathering or he experienced financial stresses in his business, Eduardo felt an immediate need to go have sex, which restored his sense of power, potency, and prowess, at least temporarily. If he ignored the urge, it became stronger until he could think of nothing else. It was no longer a simple sexual desire; it was a compulsion. Through sex, Eduardo replaced his feelings of inferiority, lack, or failure with a temporary sense of power, control, and grandiosity.

Eduardo was an expert at compartmentalizing different aspects of himself. There was Husband Eduardo, Lover Eduardo, Bartender Eduardo, Son Eduardo, Friend Eduardo, et cetera. "Husband Eduardo" and "Lover Eduardo" were virtual strangers who wouldn't even recognize each other on the street. What one of them felt ("I love my wife") was a matter of indifference to the other ("I can't wait to see Beth").

An important part of Eduardo's healing would be to create a safe space where the different parts of Eduardo could meet, discuss their values, and combine their efforts in making choices in Eduardo's best interest. When we did this during therapy, a very interesting thing began to happen. As we began to "decompartmentalize" Eduardo in my therapy room, he began to recognize the deep feelings of love he had for Beth, one of the women he had been seeing. It is possible that the safe space of therapy enabled Eduardo to feel loved and accepted as he was without having to put on one of his many masks. This, in turn, enabled Eduardo to love and be loved by another person, in this case Beth, in a way he never thought possible.

People don't always have affairs to find another person. Sometimes they hope to live another version of themselves—one they don't feel empowered to live within their marriage.

Eduardo liked the version of himself he was around Beth. He showed Beth more parts of himself than he had ever shown to another romantic partner. Beth was good at seeing and accepting Eduardo for all that he was. This soul connection was a new and exhilarating feeling for him.

But when Eduardo began seriously thinking about leaving his wife to begin a life with Beth, it filled him with more anxiety than he had ever known. The very notion of leaving his marriage filled Eduardo with incapacitating fear and guilt. Eduardo was terrified of either decision: losing his family or losing the beautiful connection he had with Beth. For one year, Eduardo floundered between two terrible choices he simply could not reconcile. It was the most stressful year of his life.

After a great deal of soul searching, Eduardo was able to rise above his own indecision and make a choice. Although he loved his intense, passionate connection with Beth, he realized his family was more important to him. He decided to walk away from the love he had found with Beth and make a commitment to improving his relationship with his wife. As he opened up to his wife in new ways, she reciprocated, and Eduardo began to discover a part of his wife he'd never known existed, a part he loved very much. By claiming his own power, he transformed his life. Instead of remaining a slave to sexual compulsion, Eduardo took responsibility for his choices and began to craft the life he wanted. As Rabbi Noah Weinberg said, "People often avoid making decisions out of fear of making a mistake. Actually the failure to make decisions is one of life's biggest mistakes."

Like Eduardo, Veronica found herself caught in a web of indecision. At the age of thirty-five, she came to see me with anxiety over her relationship difficulties. Always looking like she just stepped out of a glamour magazine, she was married to a rich and powerful real estate mogul who liked to drink and carouse and would, at times, lose his temper and scream uncontrollably at Veronica. She very much wanted to leave the marriage on the one hand, but at the same time she desperately wanted to have a child with this man, as she felt that her childbearing years were passing her by.

Before we started working together, Veronica had once gone to a psychic, something she told me about at our very first session. The psychic had told Veronica that one of her greatest life challenges would be to extricate herself from the role of being somebody's "step stool" and instead step into her full power, which, as the psychic said, was akin to the energy of Queen Elizabeth.

As I got to know Veronica better, I was struck by the accuracy of the psychic's chosen metaphor illustrating Veronica's soul correction.

My beautiful, elegant but scared patient was indeed letting herself be used as a step stool by many people in her life, including her husband. It is a role she learned as a little girl with an overly controlling mother who had such high expectations for her children that she enrolled Veronica in piano lessons at the age of two! Always having to be the "good girl" to get her demanding mother's approval, Veronica learned to constantly walk on eggshells and let herself be stepped on or else risk her mother's sinister wrath. Leaving her mother's home in Georgia, she came to New York City to extricate herself from a life of proverbial servitude, only to marry a man just like her mother!

A large part of my work with Veronica involved helping her with this particular soul correction. In our sessions, I would often ask her to tap into the Queen Elizabeth part of her. I would say, "What would Queen Elizabeth do in this situation?" In response to these questions, Veronica never skipped a beat. She answered these questions with more confidence and certainty than any other questions I asked. And her answers resonated with strength and confidence (her Queen Elizabeth side) rather than fear and worry (her "step stool" side). When I would ask Veronica the same question without any reference to Queen Elizabeth, her answers came with more trepidation and uncertainty.

By tapping into Queen Elizabeth, Veronica was able to connect to her soul and get clear guidance as to how to handle any situation that came her way. When I asked Veronica one day what Queen Elizabeth would tell her to do about her marriage, she quickly and confidently answered that she should have a child with this man and then, if things did not work out, leave the marriage. By invoking the spirit of Queen Elizabeth, Veronica finally had clarity on a question she had been wavering on for many months.

One could argue that perhaps a much better outcome for Veronica would have been to leave her marriage, find a better man, and have children with him. This may very well have been an overall better outcome. Or maybe it wouldn't. We don't know, because that is not the decision that Veronica felt was right for her at the time. Veronica ultimately did have a child with her husband and, after three more years together, decided to leave her marriage. As we continue our work together today, we frequently invoke the spirit of Queen Elizabeth to help Veronica tap into her strength, own her power, and make sense of the difficult decisions in her life.

OWN YOUR THOUGHTS AND FEELINGS

We discussed previously that thoughts are a very powerful form of energy. The Buddha said, "You are what you think. All that you are arises from your thoughts. With your thoughts you make your world."

In *Man's Search for Meaning*, Viennese psychiatrist Dr. Viktor Frankl talks about being in the concentration camps in World War II. One of the most startling things he observed was that what people thought determined whether or not they survived. The external circumstances were the same for everybody, but the thoughts people dwelled on were quite different. Frankl watched as many prisoners became sick with malaria, while others remained healthy. Some deliberately ran into electric wires to electrocute themselves to death, while others chose to remain alive. The conditions, as we know today, were so horrific, that it would be understandable for every prisoner to suffer miserably. Yet Frankl tells us from firsthand experience that some were able to remain amazingly cheerful and positive much of the time. While in the camps, Frankl observed hundreds of fellow prisoners and came to this powerful and poignant realization:

> *The experiences of camp life show that man does have a choice of action. There were enough examples, often of a heroic nature, which proved that apathy could be overcome, irritability suppressed. Man can preserve a*

vestige of spiritual freedom, of independence of mind, even in such terrible conditions of psychic and physical stress. We who lived in concentration camps can remember the men who walked through the huts comforting others, giving away their last piece of bread. They may have been few in number, but they offer sufficient proof that everything can be taken from a man but one thing: the last of the human freedoms—to choose one's attitude in any given set of circumstances, to choose one's own way....Fundamentally, therefore, any man can, even under such circumstances, decide what shall become of him—mentally and spiritually. He may retain his human dignity even in a concentration camp....It is this spiritual freedom—which cannot be taken away—that makes life meaningful and purposeful.[5]

This powerful recognition suggests that the real source of stress in our lives is internal, not external. Our stress is based on how we choose to see the world and respond to it. Whether we react with fear to any given situation depends on how fearful we are in the first place. For a fearful person, the world is a terrifying place. For an angry person, it is teeming with frustration. For a guilty person, sin and evil lie around every corner. Frequently, what we hold on to in our minds colors our entire world.[6]

Most of our lives are created by automatic thoughts to which we are completely unconscious. This is why becoming aware of the automatic thoughts that take us down the wrong roads is so important. Our conscious and unconscious minds are accustomed to working together. We learn new things—like riding a bicycle—consciously, but with practice, we can do them automatically.

We can depend on the same cooperation between our conscious and unconscious minds when we decide to change any of our unconscious tendencies, such as seeing ourselves as victims in a dangerous world. Our minds are inherently far more powerful than we realize—powerful enough to create our life experience.

While it seems that our thoughts are out of our conscious control, learning to be mindful of what we are thinking is an important part of soul alignment.

Human emotions can easily be hijacked by negative thoughts. As Aaron Beck, the founder of cognitive behavioral therapy, discovered in the early 1960s, streams of negative thoughts can flow through our minds whether we consciously decide to think negatively or not.[7] When we make that a habit, our lives suffer. Memories of intense emotions also operate unconsciously to influence our thoughts.

When we feel something without knowing why, it is often a reaction in our unconscious mind. Feelings can be triggered faster than our mind can intercept them.[8] Our perceptions race directly to the emotional center of our brains (the amygdala) without passing through the rational decision-making area. As a result, we often feel things we don't want to feel or, sometimes, don't even agree with! Even after we come to a new way of seeing things, old ways of thinking can pop into our minds. We can feel swept away by emotional patterns that we've recognized were faulty long ago. If we jump to the conclusion that we haven't really changed, it's because it takes time to shift things in the unconscious mind even after we've consciously had new insights.

In his classic book *The Emotional Brain*, Joseph LeDoux, a pioneer in the study of the neuroscience of emotion, reminds us that "Evolutionary programming sets the emotional ball rolling, but from then on we are very much in the driver's seat."[9]

CULTIVATING MINDFULNESS

Most of us are not aware of what goes on in our minds and bodies when we have a thought or feeling. Mindfulness, the practice of focusing our awareness on our thoughts, emotions, and sensations, enables us to be aware of a thought, emotion, or sensation without identifying with it. Moreover, mindfulness has been shown to positively change the structure of the brain itself.[10] Too often we assume that just because we feel or think something strongly, it must be true. The practice of mindfulness challenges this age-old assumption and enables us to see both thoughts and emotions as fleeting events. Thoughts are not facts. And certainly neither are emotions. Making that slight shift in perception is the first step, however small, to freeing our mind and liberating our soul. If our thoughts and feelings are mental weather patterns, mindfulness is our figurative umbrella.

Jon Kabat-Zinn, a pioneer in the study of mindfulness, says that mindfulness is not a special state of mind; "it's rather that you can bring awareness to any state you happen to be in."[11]

Rather than providing a way to avoid a feeling of confusion, uncertainty, fear, or stress, the transformative power of mindfulness lies in finding a connection to whatever you're feeling. When you are attentive to whatever is going on inside you, you are in a far better position to make good decisions in your life. This enables you to take control over your inner world rather than vice versa. Cultivating the practice of mindfulness puts you more in touch with yourself, gives you deeper insight into how you are really feeling, and enables you to come at the world from a place of greater authenticity. As Harvard-trained UCLA psychiatrist, author, and mindfulness expert Dr. Daniel Siegel explains:

> *Mindfulness is a form of mental activity that trains the mind to become aware of awareness itself and to pay attention to one's own intention. As researchers have defined it, mindfulness requires paying attention to the present moment from a stance that is nonjudgmental and nonreactive. It teaches self-observation...At the heart of this process, I believe, is a form of internal "tuning in" to oneself that enables people to become "their own best friend."*[12]

An exploratory process like mindfulness provides relief to the mind and body by making frightening thoughts conscious, thereby neutralizing their gravity. Simply becoming aware of a feeling and describing it ("name it to tame it") can transform it into a different form of energy. Because feelings are inherently "messy," primitive, and intangible, putting them into language is not always easy to do. Giving language to these experiences is one way of making available the energy that we have kept locked away behind walls or cordoned off from our lives. Language is a powerful way of liberating the energy behind our emotions. This frees us to live more dynamic, fulfilling lives.

Knowing this gives us a greater incentive than ever for learning to be mindful of what we think and feel. This skill improves with practice and is well worth learning. In a recent study in the *Journal of Positive Psychology*, Dr. Natasha Odou and Dr. Jay Brinker found that the best ways to handle negative emotions is to write about them while holding a compassionate stance toward yourself. You achieve this stance by feeling love for yourself, forgiving yourself of any perceived wrongs, and coming from an overall place of positive self-regard. Even after only ten minutes of sustaining this stance, people in their study significantly improved their moods by learning to process their negative emotions in this way, instead of avoiding them.[13]

To be clear, the goal of mindfulness is not to eliminate negative emotions, but to become more aware of them, accept them as a part of who we are, and in the process, gain more control over them. Mahatma Gandhi espoused the virtues of mindfulness when he said, "I will not let anyone walk through my mind with their dirty feet." Many scientific studies have shown that mindfulness decreases rumination[14] and increases our control over negative emotions.[15] Similar to embracing our shadow side, we would often disavow and avoid our difficult emotions rather than embrace them as a part of our authentic selves.

Scientists are now coming to understand that, in our optimal state, human beings need emotional diversity. In the *Journal of Experimental Psychology*, researchers reported measuring participants' positive emotions (gratitude, amusement, awe) and negative ones (anxiety, anger, sadness). When they tested the degree of the emotions, as well as their variety and abundance ("emodiversity"), greater emodiversity was linked to less use of medication, fewer doctor visits, and decreased hospital stays, medical bills, and overall health care costs. Experiencing a full range of emotions had a positive effect on diet, exercise, and overall health as well—more so than an attempt to feel only positive emotions.[16] The lesson is clear: it is important to learn to feel, tolerate, and listen to all of our emotions.

Exercise: Mindfulness Meditation

Through this exercise, you can begin to cultivate a mindfulness practice. First begin with just five minutes per day and gradually increase the duration of your practice if you can. Many experienced meditators say that they meditate an average of twenty minutes twice per day. This can be a goal of your practice, if you so choose, though even five minutes per day over time will make a noticeable difference.

This exercise is about exploring and becoming more mindful of your relationship with your thoughts. As you've done with some previous exercises, remove any distractions from your environment so you can fully surrender to the process. Put on comfortable clothing and go to your favorite place in your home or a beautiful place in nature. You may want to light some candles and incense, or put on some relaxing music to help create a peaceful atmosphere for yourself. Keep a journal nearby so you can write about your experiences afterward.

Read these directions completely before starting this meditation. When you are ready, sit in a comfortable position, then begin:

1. Close your eyes and take several slow deep breaths:
    - Inhale through your nose for the count of two.
    - Hold your breath for the count of four.
    - Exhale through your nose for the count of eight.
    - Repeat for five breath cycles.

2. Now, begin to breathe naturally and focus on your breath without trying to control it. As you do, thoughts will eventually begin to enter your mind.

3. When a thought enters your mind, label it. For instance, if a thought enters about what you have to do later today, you will say to yourself in your mind, "I'm having a thought about what I have to do later today." If a thought enters your mind about what you will have for dinner tonight, label that thought accordingly. Don't judge any of the thoughts that come to you; simply label them.

4. Now imagine a cloud floating by in front of you. As the cloud is floating by, imagine physically taking your thought out of your mind and placing it on the cloud. Then watch your thought float away.

5. Now return your attention to your normal breathing. Continue to breathe until the next thought enters your mind. Label this thought and then place it on a cloud and watch it float away.

6. Repeat this process for the next five minutes. Try to do this for five full minutes to allow yourself to experience mindfulness.

Our thoughts can be our best friends, spurring us to care about people and the world, helping us achieve goals and motivating us to rise to challenges. When we lose control of our thoughts through worry, fear, or obsession, though, they can become our worst enemies. Labeling our thoughts separates us from them and reminds us that *we are not our thoughts* and *just because we have a thought doesn't make it true*. This is easy to forget. By placing our thoughts on a cloud and watching them float away, we recognize that we are in control of our thoughts at all times, rather than the other way around. Through this simple meditation, we can change our relationship to our thoughts over time.

After completing this exercise, begin to allow yourself to notice where your thoughts go throughout the day and make a note about what's happening. Here are a few things to look for:

1. What do you think about when you are doing a mundane task that doesn't take much thought, such as washing the dishes or taking out the garbage?

2. Can you notice an inner pattern or dialogue of negative thoughts that take you away from being present and in the moment? Are there specific activities, experiences, or people that trigger these patterns or inner dialogues?

3. How often in a given day do you feel anxious or worried?

4. How often in a given day did you feel happy, joyful, determined, optimistic, or empowered?

After you have gone through your day mindful of these things, take some time to write in your journal about your thoughts, feelings, and experiences with this exercise. Over time you may notice some patterns and shifts in your relationship to your thoughts and you will be able to separate yourself from them more readily.

When it comes down to it, no one can face our challenges for us. You are the only one who can carry out your soul corrections. By harnessing your personal power through relinquishing victim mentality, cultivating faith and forgiveness, rising above indecision, and owning your thoughts and feelings though practices like mindfulness, you will be able to grow stronger, take more responsibility for your life, and reveal your true potential.

PART III

Part of Something Greater

FROM: I am disconnected and alone.

TO: I am interconnected with everybody and everything.

When we try to pick out anything by itself, we
find it hitched to everything else in the Universe.

—JOHN MUIR

9

Synchronicity

*I am open to the guidance of synchronicity, and
do not let expectations hinder my path.*

—The Dalai Lama

In the depth of winter in Moscow when I was four years old, my father bundled me up and carried me through snowy streets on our way home from the *Organizatsiya Viz Immigratsii i Registratsii* (otherwise known as OVIR, the Organization of Visas, Immigration, and Registration), his heart swelling with pride. He had just applied for visas for the whole family. We were going to America!

Little did we know that the Russian government would be in upheaval and soon Leonid Brezhnev, the then-current general secretary of the Communist Party, would fall ill and die. Each of the next two general secretaries would die within about a year of taking office. Soon Mikhail Gorbachev would replace them, restructuring the country with *perestroika* and granting us the new freedoms of *glasnost*. But by then we were well on our way to America, thanks to an amazing act of synchronicity.

For a while it looked like the Soviet government wouldn't let us leave. The bureaucracy had always been cumbersome and prone to suspicion, but with so much regime change and death, the lumbering system nearly came to a halt. No matter how many times my parents made the trek to OVIR, for two and a half years there was no sign of our visas.

In late November 1981, my grandfather Yefim decided to ask my beloved grandmother Bronya for help. Since she had died ten years earlier, he thought she might have some influence on the other side. On Friday afternoon, when he replaced the flowers on her grave as usual, he explained the matter and left it in her hands. Standing at his side, my father heard his prayer. A week later, a letter from the government appeared in our mailbox. Our visas had been approved.

It was December of 1981. At the time, the Russian government did not allow anyone to immigrate directly to America, so we had to say we were immigrating to Israel. A Viennese organization, Rav Tov (translated as either "the Good Rabbi" or "Great Goodness"), helped people immigrate to America rather than Israel, which was in keeping with my parents' original dream of one day moving to America. Once my parents received the call from OVIR that our visas were ready, we had thirty days to leave, but we wanted to get out as soon as possible lest they change their mind, so we left in ten.

Since my father didn't yet speak fluent English, he sent Rav Tov a telegram with only three words: PLEASE MEET ME. The rest is history. Since January 1982, we have been living happily in America.

BEAUTIFULLY ILLOGICAL MOMENTS

Carl Jung coined the term "synchronicity" to describe experiences like my grandfather's answered prayer. Two seemingly unconnected events (e.g., my grandfather's prayer, and then my family obtaining our visas) take on particular meaning for an individual experiencing them (i.e., "my grandmother must have helped us from the other side" or "God must have heard our prayers").

Synchronicity

By their very nature, synchronicities require our active participation. They are not something we just passively watch and by which we remain unaffected. On the contrary, we co-create the meaning and relevance we imbue on what could otherwise be dismissed as a random series of events.

Synchronicity may present itself as a meaningful coincidence, a feeling of déjà vu, a powerful dream, a strong intuition, an unexpected thought, or even a curious breakthrough after sending a request out into the afterlife. Most of us have experienced synchronicity in some way, shape, or form. Jung believed that these are not mere coincidences, but meaningful occurrences that reveal a deep underlying order in the universe.

In his book *Synchronicity*, Jung describes a famous story about a gold-green scarabaeid beetle appearing at his therapy office window at the exact moment that one of his patients was describing her dream of a golden scarab. He opened the window, caught the insect in midair, and presented it to his patient, saying, "Here is your scarab." This beautifully illogical moment resulted in a breakthrough for this woman who had been blocking her own progress with a wall of logic.

Even though the synchronicity was a reflection of Jung's patient's inner landscape, it was simultaneously a synchronistic reflection of what was taking place within Jung. For Jung to be hearing a patient's dream of a golden scarab and to have a golden scarab fly into his office was an externalized, synchronistic reflection of an important process that was happening inside of him. It is noteworthy that a synchronistic event can collectively reflect and be mutually shared by more than one person in both similar and singularly unique ways. For Jung and his patient, the shared synchronistic event was a living experience of being connected to something greater than oneself.[1]

A skeptic would argue that this was merely a coincidence, with no inherent meaning aside from that ascribed to it by Jung and his patient. In their search for meaning, Jung and his patient created a "magical" message of a meaning by combining a series of random events. Jung would say that what made this a synchronicity was not the co-occurrence of these two events, but precisely the *subjective meaning* ascribed to this co-occurrence. The relatives of that gold-green beetle were no doubt arriving at windows all over town without setting off any emotional breakthroughs in anybody else. It's not the objective events themselves, but what we make of them that counts.

Another powerful synchronicity occurred between Sigmund Freud, the preeminent founder of psychoanalysis, and Carl Jung, who was twenty-five years Freud's junior and being groomed by Freud to take over the psychoanalytic society Freud founded. Despite Jung's spiritual leanings, Freud strongly dissuaded Jung from publicly sharing his spiritual interests and theories, for fear that their subjective, unscientific nature would undermine the field of psychoanalysis. As Freud and Jung sat together in Freud's library discussing this matter, Freud told Jung not to pursue his interest in the occult. Jung, understandably, felt patronized, angry, and misunderstood by Freud.

Suddenly, Jung and Freud heard a loud creak from out of nowhere, to which Jung replied, "This is an example of exactly what I'm talking about! Moreover, it's going to happen again." Then, suddenly, another loud creak occurred from out of nowhere, startling both Jung and Freud!

It was after this peculiar occurrence that Freud decided to withhold the leadership title he was planning to give Jung, leading Jung to feel abandoned and confused. This foreshadowed Jung's nervous breakdown, during which time Jung wrote his famous *The Red Book*, an opportunity for him to individuate from Freud by integrating psychoanalytic tenets with the principles of spirituality.[2]

The scientist in Freud, however, had to understand what was causing the unexpected and mysterious noises in his library. So Freud decided to sit there until the noise occurred again, at which time he deduced that the heat in the library was drying out the oak bookshelves and causing them to creak![3]

The coinciding of this fairly normal mechanical phenomenon with the precise moment (or two) of Freud and Jung's disagreement is precisely what turned this coincidence into a meaningful synchronicity. From this perspective, there is nothing mystical or divine about the origin of synchronicity, although it nevertheless affirms a wondrous appreciation for the creative capacities of each person to order his or her own internal and external world.[4]

Earlier in the book, we talked about how our internal world can create our external reality. Was the heat-induced breakage of the wooden bookshelves an external manifestation of the breakage in the relationship between Freud and Jung?

Mysterious coincidences are intriguing. As human beings with a powerful need for meaning in our life, we are constantly looking for patterns and explanations. When something amazing, yet inexplicable, happens, we can't help but wonder why. It's in our nature.

Exercise: Exploring Synchronicity

For this stream-of-consciousness writing exercise, set your stopwatch to five minutes and write without stopping on the topic of Synchronicity. The Questions for Reflection are included as guideposts. As before, let your writing take you where it may.

Questions for Reflection

1. Have you experienced synchronicity? Describe the event or situation.

2. How did you make sense of this experience?

3. Did this experience make you see the world differently? If so, how?

WARNING SIGNS

When my friend Don received his three-number locker combination for his medical school locker, he was intrigued to see that it was the date of his girl-friend's birthday. For him, this sign was confirmation that he was with the right person at this point in his life. He took this synchronicity to mean that the Universe was in support of his relationship. Synchronistic moments like this can feel like grace, as they induce in us the feeling that we are right where we are supposed to be. So how do we know when to make subjective meaning of a synchronous experience or "sign" versus dismissing it as mere coincidence or randomness?

Mental and emotional stability is a necessary prerequisite for a healthy experience of synchronicity. Prior to connecting to something greater than oneself, it is important to first be stably grounded in the here and now. While working in the psychiatric emergency room at Bellevue Hospital, I saw many patients who had ended up there because they had given too much credence to signs. Many received what to them were clear and irrefutable signs that they are Jesus Christ or God or the Prophet Mohammed. Relying too heavily on signs without being stably grounded in the here and now can alienate us from reality and, in its most extreme forms, reflect a state of psychosis.

In his book *The Three Christs of Ypsilanti*, social psychologist Milton Rokeach tells of three men institutionalized at the Ypsilanti State Hospital in Michigan in the 1960s. All of them believed they were Jesus Christ. Rokeach came up with an inspired intervention: he introduced them to one another. If a man who thought he was Jesus Christ met another Jesus Christ—and then *another!*—surely, the stark reality would convince him that he was not Jesus Christ at all. But the men and their psychoses outwitted Rokeach. Initially they argued over who was the most holy and nearly came to blows, but ultimately each one found his own explanation for the presence of two other Christs. (The other two were clearly mental patients, or dead, or animated by machines.) In the end, Rokeach wrote: "While I failed to cure the three Christs of their delusions, they had succeeded in curing me of mine—of my God-like delusion that I could change them..."[5]

As Bertrand Russell wrote in his book *Power*, "Every man would like to be God if it were possible; some few find it difficult to admit the impossibility."[6] It's even said to be an occupational hazard for doctors. "What's the difference between a doctor and God?" the old joke goes. "God doesn't think he's a doctor."

Aside from mental and emotional stability, it's important to note that those who embrace spirituality too suddenly may be prone to draw quick conclusions about perceived synchronicities. This is why engaging with spiritual knowledge and receiving spiritual guidance requires maturity, discernment, patience, practice, and discipline.

One of my young patients, Yehuda, had a genetic predisposition to bipolar disorder, which can sometimes present with delusions and psychosis. At an early age, he fervently embraced the study of Kabbalah. The more Yehuda studied, the more signs he began to receive. Billboards started speaking directly to him. Radio messages felt to him like personal directives from God. Before long, he was not eating or sleeping, but was staying up all night to study Kabbalah, enrapt in interpreting all the signs he was receiving.

When people spend the day looking for signs and making decisions based on special instructions given to them from invisible powers, it can be a dangerous form of externalizing one's power.

Even those with mental and emotional stability can be prone to certain biases around synchronicity. These biases include confirmation bias, or the tendency to look for and find confirming evidence for what you already believe and ignore the disconfirming evidence. You remember the hits, you forget the misses. There is also hindsight bias, otherwise known as Monday-morning quarterbacking, in which one makes connections to explain things with perfect clarity—after they happen. And then there is self-justification bias, in which we convince ourselves, after the fact, that what we did was the best thing we could have done. We carefully screen subsequent data and filter out all contradictory information related to our decision, leaving only evidence in support of the choice we made.[7]

People's perception that random events are signs meant especially for them is known in psychiatry as *ideas of reference*. Whereas synchronicity can provide a powerful sense of meaning, guidance, and connection for somebody who is generally mentally healthy and grounded in reality, ideas of reference can be maladaptive, destabilizing, and paranoia-inducing in individuals who are not mentally healthy at baseline.

As Western-trained doctors and therapists, we are taught to listen for ideas of reference and other versions of "magical thinking" as signs of psychopathology.[8] Yet sometimes it's surprisingly hard to know where to draw the line. Many magical beliefs have become so commonplace that we don't think to question them. Where is the line between a psychotic patient and a religious leader, when both claim to be receiving signs from above? Generations of children have wondered, why is Santa imaginary but God isn't?

The most widely reprinted editorial in any English-language newspaper appeared on September 21, 1897, in the *New York Sun*. This editorial, written by war correspondent Francis P. Church, was a response to a letter he received from a little girl named Virginia O'Hanlon:

> *Dear Editor: I am 8 years old. Some of my little friends say there is no Santa Claus. Papa says, "If you see it in The Sun, it's so." Please tell me the truth; is there a Santa Claus?*

Addressing issues of hope, faith, and idealism, Church's thoughtful response rose way above Virginia's innocent question:

> *Virginia, your little friends are wrong. They have been affected by the skepticism of a skeptical age... They think that nothing can be which is not comprehensible by their little minds. All minds, Virginia, whether they be men's or children's, are little... as compared to the boundless world about him, as measured by the intelligence capacity of grasping the whole of truth and knowledge.*
>
> *Yes, Virginia, there is a Santa Claus. He exists as certainly as love and generosity and devotion exist, and you know that they abound and give to your life its highest beauty and joy... You may tear apart the baby's rattle and see what makes the noise inside, but there is a veil covering the unseen world which not the strongest man, nor even the united strength of all the strongest men that ever lived, could tear apart... It is all real! Ah, Virginia, in all this world, there is nothing else real and abiding.*[9]

SEEING WHAT WE WANT TO SEE

As human beings, it may bother us on a deep level to think that things could happen for no particular reason at all. Dr. John Allen Paulos, professor of mathematics at Temple University and the author of *Irreligion*, says that a meaningless coincidence may make us feel a loss of control. By finding a reason or a pattern where none exists, we make a strange event logical and, therefore, less frightening. "Believing in fate, or even conspiracy, can sometimes be more comforting than facing the fact that sometimes things just happen."

For Dr. Paulos, startling coincidences are indeed marvelous—not because an affectionate Universe is sending us an emoticon, but because of the little appreciated wonders of mathematics. He tells the story of a boy whose mother was tragically killed while he was still young. As family and friends gathered outside at the memorial service, the boy stepped up to the lectern to give a heartfelt eulogy. Just as he said the word "mother," a sparrow flew down from the sky and landed on his head. People in the audience gasped. The boy gently took the bird in his hands, then set it free.[10]

As you can imagine, many of the friends and family who were there at that moment will remember it for the rest of their lives. "What are the odds of something like that happening?" they might ask. "One in a million." Quite good, actually. Persi Diaconis, a Stanford statistician whose career has been devoted to the study of coincidence, points out that "the really unusual day would be one where nothing unusual happens." There are 319 million people in this country. That means that in America alone a one-in-a-million coincidence happens 319 times every day.[11]

That being said, when remarkable coincidences do happen we are inevitably astounded. One of my favorite instances of synchronicity happened to my dear friend Yvette. A psychiatrist like myself, Yvette's attitude toward synchronicity can be best described as skeptical, but open-minded. Whenever an interesting coincidence occurred in her life, Yvette would call to tell me and jokingly say, "It must be a sign!"

As Yvette was walking to work one day, a book flew through the air and landed on the sidewalk right in front of her. Yvette looked around. She could only guess that somebody had thrown the book out their window.

Not being one to pick up random books on New York City sidewalks, Yvette's first inclination was to ignore it. Then she saw that book was *Calling in "The One": 7 Weeks to Attract the Love of Your Life* by Katherine Woodward Thomas. Many years ago, Yvette and I had referred to this rich book of timeless wisdom as our "Soulmate Bible." Yvette had done the exercises in the book right before she met her soulmate, the man to whom she has been happily married for many years. How and why this book seemed to literally fall out of the sky and land at her feet, Yvette had no idea.

That same day, Yvette had a first-time appointment with a new patient. A spiritual young woman named Candace came to see Yvette because she felt like she was never going to find her life partner. At the end of their session, Yvette told Candace about the synchronicity that occurred on her way to work and offered Candace the book. Candace accepted. At her next session with Yvette, Candace said she had read the book and felt like it "changed her life."

Although this is a sweet anecdote, it certainly does not provide irrefutable evidence of God or a greater overarching purpose to our existence. Yet if somebody is open to spiritual experiences and guidance from the Universe, experiences of this nature can create a sense of awe that makes them wonder if perhaps there is something greater out there after all.

In some cases, people turn to synchronicity after they've exhausted other avenues of trying to "make things happen." Be it searching for a soulmate, a new job, or a home, American culture promotes grit, perseverance, and a never-say-die attitude in what is often cast as a dog-eat-dog, survival-of-the-fittest world. While this type of messaging and encouragement can be motivating for some, it eclipses the idea that there is something larger at work and that things come to fruition by a combination of our hard work and a divine hand orchestrating things.

The power of synchronicity was recently made evident in the life of one of my best friends from high school, Masum, who epitomized hard work and "making things happen." With an interdisciplinary PhD from Harvard, Masum had published extensively on topics like education, social justice, feminism, and the arts. For the past twenty years, she had held several fascinating and prestigious jobs focusing on social justice through the arts.

Fulfilled

At this point in her life, Masum was ready for a career transition but was not 100 percent sure what this transition would entail. She thought perhaps she would like to work in philanthropy. But a career transition proved more challenging than anticipated. Despite her impeccable credentials and extensive work experience, Masum could not find a job she loved. In searching for the right job, Masum did everything and more—hiring a job coach, retooling her résumé, optimizing her social media profiles, reflecting on her goals and skills, building networks in her field, and restrategizing continuously month after month when job postings and offers did not materialize.

Having known her a long time, I encouraged her to be open to synchronicity. I invited her to visualize leaders in her area of expertise approaching her with the perfect job for her, saying that they were looking for the right person to "carry the baton" and inquiring whether she might be that person. She had tried so many methods over the past year; why not try this for a month or so as an experiment? In trying so hard to find the right job, she had lost sight of the possibility that someone might approach her. Doing the visualization repeatedly would serve as a reminder that synchronicity was at play alongside her efforts.

About two weeks after she began her visualization, she received an e-mail from a literary agent in London. This woman had found Masum's writing online and loved it! She was looking for the right person to write a book on feminism and the arts; would Masum be interested in being that person?

Despite meditating regularly on something just like this happening, Masum could not believe it. She was absolutely stunned to encounter a job offer in this way after thousands of hours of combing through job postings, crafting and submitting applications, and meetings over coffee for networking.

In shifting her internal core belief from "everything I achieve only comes about through hard work" to "the Universe has my back and will position me in the right job that is going to use my talents for the greatest good," Masum was offered an unexpected new job opportunity. By surrendering to something greater than herself, Masum embraced a spiritual principle that would serve her for the rest of her life. This spiritual principle is beautifully encapsulated in the words of author and educator Anita Moorjani:

> *I'm at my strongest when I'm able to let go,*
> *when I suspend my beliefs as well as disbeliefs,*
> *and leave myself open to all possibilities. That*
> *also seems to be when I'm able to experience the*
> *most internal clarity and synchronicities.*
>
> —ANITA MOORJANI

Exercise: Harnessing the Power of Prayer and Surrender

In this exercise, we will harness the power of prayer and surrender by turning some of our worries over to something greater than ourselves, whether to God, a Higher Power, the Universe, Mother Nature, or whatever resonates most with you.

For this exercise, you will need either a stack of Post-it sticky notes or a piece of paper. If you're using the latter, cut the piece of paper into four rectangles. On each Post-it or rectangle, write down one worry you presently have. Aim to write four worries in total.

You may have worries about your relationship, finances, health, friendships, family, and/or spiritual life. You may worry that you will fail an upcoming exam, be stuck in a lifetime of debt, never find your life partner, among many other things.

Once you have four worries written down, take one of them at a time and say the following simple prayer. I use the word "Universe" below, but please fill in whatever your title is for something greater than yourself:

Dear Universe:

*I surrender this worry over to you. Please resolve this worry
in the right way in the right time for the greatest good of
all involved.*

Once you have surrendered your worries over to something greater than
yourself, tear up the piece of paper or Post-it note and put it in the nearest garbage
can. Now repeat this process with each of your pieces of paper, one at a time.

For the next week, stop worrying about the four things you have just surrendered. You have given the Universe a clear directive through your prayers to
help you with what pains you most, and to show you that the ineffable "something greater than yourself" has your back. If you need proof that help is on the
way, ask for proof. The Universe can respond to your directives, but only if you
ask clearly and succinctly. Once you've asked, begin looking for positive signs
and synchronicities in your life indicating that a resolution is on its way.

Make a note in your calendar or planner to revisit this exercise in exactly
one week. Now go through each of your four worries and answer the following
questions in your journal:

1. Have you received any help, guidance, clarity, or insight this week in
   resolving these concerns?

2. How did the help, guidance, clarity, or insight manifest in your life?

SEEING THE MAGIC

With our consuming desire to make sense of things, God is a handy stand-in
for those moments when we don't have a clue. As Dr. Paulos points out in his

book *Irreligion*, there are also a lot of people who believe "God exists simply because He says He does in a much extolled tome that He allegedly inspired."[12]

Yet sometimes, the strange synchronicities of life make us wonder: Is there perhaps something more than coincidences, like special signs of reassurance sent from on high? Filmmaker Woody Allen joked, "If only God would give me a clear sign. Like making a large deposit in my name at a Swiss bank."

Like answered prayers, surrendering to synchronicity often brings people the same kind of reassurance that Someone or Something—be it the Universe, God, a loving energy, divinity, Mother Nature—is present in their lives.

One of my patients, Manuel, told me of two instances in his life where he had felt so depressed and hopeless that he contemplated ending his life. Those were the only two times in his life that he had prayed. Both times he felt "lifted" out of his suicidal state shortly thereafter. Manuel concluded that these experiences were evidence of a Higher Power.

When Barbara, another of my patients, prayed for a change in herself, it had an almost instantaneous result. After an argument with her mother one day, she became so overcome with anger that she was unable to focus on anything else for weeks. Recognizing how destructive this negative emotion was, Barbara prayed to God to give her the strength and compassion to forgive her mother. Minutes later, she felt her anger finally lift.

Were these cases of divine intervention? Or had Manuel and Barbara finally harnessed their personal power by the very act of prayer and the intention of lifting themselves out of depression and forgiveness, respectively?

Through our minds, we can make the banal into something magical and, likewise, something magical into something banal. Through our minds, we create our reality and thereby co-create the unfolding of our lives.

Although powerful experiences of synchronicity can make us feel connected to something greater than ourselves, at times our prayers may appear to go unanswered. I can personally attest that I experienced many unanswered prayers in the midst of my soulmate search. When I met Scott toward the end of my psychiatry residency, I was convinced beyond a shadow of a doubt that he was my soulmate. He felt so uncannily familiar. I was immediately drawn to him without knowing why. Since I had never had an experience like it before, I assumed it must be meaningful.

Once I cast Scott as my soulmate in my mind, he became the perfect person onto whom I could project all my hopes, wishes, and dreams. It was easy to do, because I didn't really know him.

As soon as we started dating, I fell hard and fast. He was everything I'd hoped for: charming and attentive, brilliant and interesting, masculine yet sensitive. Daydreams about our wedding, our children, and our long happy life together started sneaking into my mind.

The pivotal moment came when I learned that he was dating not one, but *several* other women! It was abundantly clear that Scott had no interest in committing to me or anyone else. It was a blow. The wise thing to do would have been to accept the evidence that this man was not for me and move on. But I had never been good at taking "no" for an answer. That same determined, persistent part of me that would will my way through life when the going got tough rose to the occasion now. Not knowing what to do but determined to change the course of events, I closed my eyes to the facts and prayed with all my might.

A few days later, I had the craziest experience in an ice cream store. Just as I was leaving the store with a scoop of lemon sorbet, a young woman I had never seen before came up to me with her young child. "I'm a psychic," she said. "Can I give you a message?"

Seeing no harm in it, I said, "Sure."

"You met your soulmate the other day. His name is Scott. God wants you to know that he has heard your prayers. Everything *will* work out for you." With that, she left the ice cream store, never to be seen again.

I was dumbfounded. What in the world just happened? Who was this woman? And how did she know Scott's name?

There was only one answer I wanted to entertain. "God must have heard my prayers and taken time out of His busy day to send this psychic to the ice cream store to reassure me that things will work out with Scott." Whatever cognitive bias I used to convince myself of this, I left the ice cream store that day with a big smile on my face.

But things did not work out with Scott. For a long time afterward, I tried to make sense of this strange experience.

When I look back at things now, I realize that the psychic never actually said "things will work out *with Scott*." She merely said that things would *work out*. And ultimately they have, very much so. But I can't say I didn't feel somehow duped or abandoned by God at what I perceived to be an uncanny promise, delivered through a mysterious psychic, which never came to pass.

Only when I finally took off my rose-colored glasses was I able to see that I had been head over heels in love—not with Scott, but with my own projections and fantasies about him. With the benefit of hindsight, I know now that I was enjoying a wonderful romantic relationship...with myself.

In fact, I realize now that I had been praying for the wrong thing all along. As Wayne Dyer wrote, "Rather than praying to God or a saint for a miracle, pray for the miracle of an inner awakening, which will never leave you." In retrospect, what I should have been praying for was "the greatest good for all involved" or "the ability to grow and change in such a way as to have a truly ful-filling relationship with the right person at the right time," and not just "please make it work with Scott!"

EXPANDING OUR CONSCIOUSNESS

The mysteries of synchronicity—answered prayers, rightfully unanswered prayers, books landing at our feet, locker combinations that remind us of someone we love, immediate dispensations of compassion by request—often lead us to see the world we live in a little differently. We have the choice of whether to view all of these life experiences as random coincidences or as expressions of what Carl Jung called the *unus mundus*, which is Latin for "the one world," or the profound interconnectedness of all things.[13]

Revealing its designs through events in the outer world as interpreted through our inner mental landscape, the *unus mundus* actualizes itself in time through synchronistic clues encoded within the fabric of experience itself. In this way, synchronicities have the potential to transform us, awaken us and alter us from within. Rich in meaning, a synchronistic event can affect and deepen our state of awareness and perception. The inherently revelatory nature of synchronicity underlies the realization that we are playing an active, participatory, and hence, co-creative role in the unfolding of our lives, and therefore the world. In this way, synchronicities can and do expand our consciousness.

10

Consciousness

*The Universe begins to look more and more
like a great thought than like a great machine.
The mind no longer appears to be an accidental
intruder into the realm of matter... we ought
rather hail it as the creator and governor of the
realm of matter.*

—Sir James Jeans,
British physicist and mathematician

PHYSICS, PARTICLES, AND WAVES

In the 1600s, Christiaan Huygens and Isaac Newton proposed competing theories for light's behavior. Huygens proposed that light behaves as a wave propagating through the medium of ether. Newton, in contrast, proposed that light behaves as a particle. Because of Newton's prestige and the fact that nobody could prove the existence of Huygens's ether, Newton's theory was dominant for more than a century.

If Newton was right and light was indeed composed of particles, then firing a straight line of light through a single slit should produce a pattern corresponding to the size and shape of the slit on the receiving screen. However, when this "single-slit experiment" was performed, the pattern on the screen was spread out far beyond the size and shape of the slit. This phenomenon is known as diffraction and results from wave interference patterns. The smaller the slit, the greater the spread. Particles don't show diffraction. Waves do. Was Newton wrong after all?

Now, if you fire light through two parallel slits at the same time, as Thomas Young did in his famous "double-slit experiment," in addition to seeing even more pronounced diffraction, you see the light moving through both slits at the same time. No physical particle can be in two places at once, further confirming that light must indeed be a wave and not a particle.

Researchers then did something very interesting: they added a detector next to each of the two slits to watch the photons as they passed. Amazingly, with the detectors present, each photon was found to pass through only one slit (as would a classical particle), and not through both slits (as would a wave). Moreover, the diffraction was gone. So, with the detectors present, light behaved as a particle. With the detectors absent, light behaved as a wave. Because the researchers could not believe their findings, they assumed it must be a problem with their technique and so they performed the experiment repeatedly. To their amazement, they always ended up with the same result.

This unexpected finding, now known as wave-particle duality, radically changed how we see the nature of reality and is one of the fundamental tenets of quantum theory: light functions as both a particle and a wave, depending on how the experiment is conducted and how observations are made.[1]

At first it didn't make sense that something could be a wave, fluid and boundless, and at precisely the same time, be a particle, solid and discrete. As Albert Einstein wrote, "We are faced with a new kind of difficulty. We have two contradictory pictures of reality; separately neither of them fully explains the phenomena of light, but together they do."[2]

With this striking discovery, the question then became: Is light the only thing that functions as both a particle and a wave, or is wave-particle duality a property that can be applied to all matter? This question was tackled by the bold young physicist Louis de Broglie in his PhD dissertation, for which he was awarded the Nobel Prize in 1929 (the only time a Nobel Prize was awarded for a PhD dissertation!). The de Broglie hypothesis showed that wave-particle duality was not merely an aberrant behavior of light, but rather was a fundamental principle exhibited by all physical matter.[3]

SO WHAT?

So why am I telling you about waves, particles, and quantum physics in a book about connecting to your soul and finding fulfillment?

Because the implications are so profound that they turn our understanding of reality on its head and offer a new perspective on the meaning of fulfillment.

What findings like the wave-particle duality *actually mean* for our lives is a key debate at the heart of quantum physics.[4] One of the most widely taught interpretations of quantum mechanics is known as the Copenhagen interpretation. Devised in the 1920s by physicists Niels Bohr and Werner Heisenberg, this interpretation states that our consciousness—or the act of our observing and measuring something—takes physical reality out of its infinite potential of probabilities (the wave function) in which it existed prior to our observation and brings it into the proverbial "here and now" (the particle). This feature is known as wave-function collapse.

For example, when we are not looking at a cloud, the cloud suddenly turns into energy waves. But the moment we look at it, the wave collapses into material particles like electrons, protons, and neutrons, forming atoms and thereby producing the physical cloud we observe. If we turn our gaze away again, the atomic and subatomic particles instantly transform into unseen waves. In other words, the very act of our observation brings the cloud into existence.

In essence, our consciousness "collapses" a wave into a particle, which creates the physical matter we know of as our universe. Werner Heisenberg wrote in *Physics and Philosophy*, "In classical physics science started from the belief—or should one say from the illusion?—that we could describe the world or at least parts of the world without any reference to ourselves."[5] This interpretation of quantum physics describes the way in which our perception creates our reality and, in essence, how *our consciousness creates our world.*

IT'S ALL ABOUT CONSCIOUSNESS

In a July 2005 essay in the journal *Nature*, Johns Hopkins physics professor Richard C. Henry concluded that the universe is not purely physical, as Newton's ideas would lead us to believe. In quantum physics, a particle exists in a state of infinite potential (all possibilities all at once) as a wave until a person observes it. Our act of observation forces the quantum particle to "choose" a single state of being. Without our observation, the particle is free to return to a state of infinite potential as a wave. This means that every time we observe something, we transform it. Through the act of observation, we are constantly transforming the world of waves that surrounds us into a physical world of matter that we can see, hear, taste, touch, and smell.[6]

This discovery is one of the most profound revolutions of twentieth-century physics. But it is so utterly different from our assumptions about how the world works that it is hard for even the greatest scientists and physicists to accept. Theoretical physicists Werner Heisenberg, Niels Bohr, and Max Planck tried to explain what this meant for our daily lives, but the idea that we actually create our own reality was far too unsettling for many people. When one of the great physicists, Eugene Wigner, stated definitively that the very laws of physics themselves could not be formulated in a fully consistent way without including human consciousness as a part of the phenomenon, conventional scientists were appalled.[7] However, such discord is an expected and necessary part of the scientific dialogue that moves our world along.

If we accept the Copenhagen interpretation of quantum physics, then it follows that the content of our mind—our consciousness—is the ultimate reality. Taken to its logical conclusion, this means that nothing exists without our consciousness. Only the conscious mind can give shape and form to the dandelions in the meadow or this book in your hand.[8] Without consciousness, even the moon does not exist in a definite state. Einstein struggled with this idea throughout his life: "I like to think that the moon is there even if I'm not looking at it."[9]

How is it that anything can be concrete and tangible one moment, but then escape back into the state of infinite potential as soon as we shift our gaze? Since we obviously cannot observe everything at all times, how do physical entities like the moon maintain their continuity? When I am no longer looking at something but my friend is, how we do reconcile our separate "creations" of reality? While you are sleeping, who is watching you to make sure you continue to exist as a physical reality? And how did life start at the very beginning, where there were no physicists and no sentient beings to observe the formation of galaxies and stars?

The Dalai Lama encapsulates our difficulty in reconciling these paradoxes in saying, "The West really has much knowledge about matter, yet Western knowledge on consciousness seems very limited. It is at the beginner's stage. Without a deep knowledge of consciousness, even a full knowledge of matter is questionable."[10]

Although we do not yet fully understand the nature of consciousness, quantum physics has shown that we make conscious and unconscious choices every minute that literally bring the world into existence. It gives all the more credence to our potential to create our own reality through our thoughts, emotions, and intentions.

THE LAW OF ATTRACTION

Popularized by Rhonda Byrne's book and movie *The Secret,* the "law of attraction" is a universal principle that describes the way in which our thoughts create our reality. We are what we think, consciously and unconsciously. In other words, what we attract into our lives reflects the contents of our mind.[11]

When we put out thoughts of lack and emptiness, we attract more of exactly that: lack and emptiness. When we shift instead to thoughts of sharing and giving, we get the same energy coming back to us.[12] When we complain that we never have enough time, then we will attract precisely that: the state of never having enough time. When we put out thoughts of gratitude into the world, we attract more gratitude.

According to the Law of Attraction, by changing your thoughts, you can change what shows up in your life. Many psychological theories, like Aaron Beck's cognitive behavioral therapy (CBT), are based on a similar premise: by changing your thoughts, you can change your feelings and behaviors which, in essence, changes what shows up in your life.

According to the Law of Attraction, if you would like more financial abundance to show up in your life, you need to begin thinking thoughts of financial abundance rather than of financial lack. You are even encouraged to start envisioning scenarios that signal financial abundance to you: opening your mailbox to find paychecks for large sums of money, being offered a higher-paying job, eating dinner at a nice restaurant, or whatever financial abundance means to you. The trick is that rather than thinking thoughts about *wanting* those things, you are encouraged to think thoughts about *already having* those things.

Because thoughts of *wanting* are actually thoughts of lack. We want what we don't have. According to the Law of Attraction, such thoughts would attract more lack. In contrast, thoughts of *already having* are thoughts of abundance, which would attract more abundance. The way to manifest something in your life, therefore, is to think thoughts of already having it in your life.

While the Law of Attraction is a powerful tool for manifesting what you want in life by changing your thoughts, there are many caveats. First, practicing the Law of Attraction does not mean that you should begin to live in a permanent state of delusion or self-deception, believing that you have something you do not. While changing your thinking is a powerful tool for drawing what you want into your life, it is a not a replacement for taking the actions necessary to accomplish and attain those very things. Nor should you blame yourself and your misguided thinking if, despite your best efforts, you cannot manifest what you want via the Law of Attraction. There are many reasons why the Law of Attraction may not work, including:

1. What you asked for is not in the highest and greatest good of all involved (which may be for a number of reasons, including that the timing is not yet right for it to manifest).

2. You were not clear about what you asked for.

3. You didn't really believe that you could have what you asked for (meaning your conscious mind was saying one thing but your unconscious mind was saying the opposite, which is a common problem).

4. You weren't able to receive it when the Universe was trying to give it to you (often because you had too fixed an idea of exactly how your desired outcome should manifest).

Fulfilled

My patient Alana, a powerful, capable, and spiritual thirty-year-old Dominican woman, felt stuck in her life. Although doing well in her job and happily married to Hank since the age of twenty, Alana had a self-sabotaging behavior—compulsive shopping—that was ruining her life and beginning to ruin her marriage. Both she and Hank grew up in poor families. For Hank, this resulted in a strong work ethic that, together with his talent, intelligence, and charisma, got him many promotions at work and a nice six-figure income as a corporate executive by the age of thirty-five. As the head of counseling and clinical services at a local drug rehabilitation center, Alana also did very well at her job and felt fulfilled in helping people on a daily basis. Given their circumstances, Hank and Alana should have been doing well financially, except for Alana's shopping compulsion.

Whenever Alana felt overwhelmed, she would go to Saks, Bloomingdale's, or online and get the latest and newest handbag, pair of shoes, or pretty dress. For a few hours thereafter, her stress abated and she felt better. But the feeling of emptiness always returned, and she would again turn to "retail therapy" the next day. And the next day. And the next. This resulted in many thousands of dollars in credit card debt and a very upset husband! Hank always wanted Alana to feel good, have nice clothes, and buy everything she ever wanted, but not to the point where they no longer had the money to pay their taxes! Hank was overwhelmed and he encouraged Alana to seek help, which is how she found me.

As Alana and I began to explore her compulsive shopping together in therapy, we realized that her feelings of emptiness and subsequent need to fill it through shopping came from deep long-standing feelings of inadequacy. Always feeling "less than" in comparison to her peers, she was able to make up for her secret belief that she was not good enough with "retail therapy." It didn't change her basic sense of inadequacy, but wearing nice clothes at least allowed her to look like her peers. "Fake it till you make it," she always said.

Alana and I used a number of different approaches to help Alana address her feelings in a positive and constructive way while gaining more control over her compulsive need to shop. This included attending Debtors Anonymous meetings (an offshoot of Alcoholics Anonymous for individuals with shopping addictions), limiting Alana's access to credit cards (cash only!), and beginning to address the long-standing feelings of inadequacy at the core of her compulsive shopping habits. These tools were successful in beginning to change Alana's behavior and improve her marriage. Yet the most successful tool came as a surprise to all of us.

Because Hank and Alana are both spiritual people, I thought they might benefit from learning about the age-old Law of Attraction. After one of our sessions, I recommended they watch the popular movie *The Secret*. I thought this could be helpful to them as a couple, but I certainly did not expect what was to come.

At our next session, Alana announced that she and Hank watched *The Secret*, tried out some of the strategies, and were having unbelievable, unexpected results. They were hooked! Hank had "manifested" an unexpected check for a large sum of money within a week, as well as an invitation to watch a boxing match at his neighbor's home, which he would have been unable to watch because they did not have cable. Part of the formula of the Law of Attraction is getting clear about exactly what you want, and Hank had asked for precisely these two things. Imagine his surprise when they actually happened!

Seeing Hank's success, Alana decided to start to experiment with the Law of Attraction herself. By this time, her shopping habits were under relatively better control, so she began to focus on three other goals: passing a licensing exam at work, getting a higher paying job at a top teaching hospital in the city, and losing thirty-five pounds. She had tried to lose weight many times before but had never been successful. Somehow the Law of Attraction seemed to change this. Alana came to our next session in sweatpants—she was off to a workout right after. She had also started juicing to aid in the weight loss process.

To help use the universal spiritual principle of the Law of Attraction to manifest a higher paying job, I recommended that Alana read Marianne Williamson's *The Law of Divine Compensation: On Work, Money and Miracles*, which begins by saying, "From a metaphysical perspective, every experience begins with a thought, and our experience changes when we change the thought."[13] So Alana began working hard to change her thoughts, through verbal and written affirmations, about financial abundance in her life. She set concrete goals on what she wanted to accomplish: a fifty percent salary increase by year's end.

Not only did Alana meet her weight loss goal by December 30, she had landed a new job at a top teaching hospital that paid exactly fifty percent more than her previous job! She also passed her licensing exam that September.

In helping patients change their lives, I cannot always know what will create the greatest impetus for change. It is different for every person, which is why I do not believe in a one-size-fits-all approach. While the more standard strategies helped Alana grow, change, and improve her life up to a point, my most effective intervention was recommending that she and Hank watch *The Secret* and implement the Law of Attraction in their own lives.

Exercise: Practicing the Law of Attraction

In this exercise, we will explore an adaptation of the age-old Law of Attraction. There are three steps to putting this law into action:

1. Ask
2. Believe
3. Co-create/Receive

For the sake of this exercise, let's start with asking for something relatively small and work your way up to bigger and more important things.

1. Ask

To begin, get clear about one thing you would like to change in your life. For instance: Tomorrow I would like there to be a readily available parking spot for me when I get to work. Or, I'd like to have a positive interaction with my difficult boss tomorrow. Or, by the end of the week, I'd like to hear from a good friend I have not heard from in a while. Or, this month, I'd like my efforts at work to be noticed by my superiors.

Get as clear as possible about what you would like to happen, as well as the time frame in which you would like it to happen. Through your thoughts, ask for exactly what you want. You do not have to ask over and over. Just ask once. Jack Canfield, coauthor of the Chicken Soup for the Soul series, said that "most of us have never allowed ourselves to want what we truly want, because we can't see how it's going to manifest."[14] In this process, you do not need to know how it's going to manifest. All you have to do is ask, believe, and take whatever steps you can to make it happen. How it will *actually* manifest is up to the Universe.

2. Believe

Believing is the hardest part for most people. To experiment with the Law of Attraction, you must, at least for the brief period of this exercise, eradicate your doubts, and believe (in your thoughts) and feel (in your heart and body) that what you've asked for is *already* yours. If you have trouble actually believing it, begin by make-believing. Act as if you have it already. As you make-believe, you may start to truly believe.

Since thoughts are a powerful form of energy and "like attracts like," you are changing your thoughts to draw into your life exactly what you want. Begin to feel exactly what you will feel once your request arrives. Feel and believe it with your heart, mind, body, and soul. Invoke your five senses to experience exactly what you will feel like when you receive what you have requested: What will it look like? Feel like? Sound like? Smell like? Taste like? You may invoke the mantra "I am receiving now. I am receiving _____ now." Then feel it as though you have already received it.

3. Co-create/Receive

In this process, you do not have to figure out *how* what you have asked for will manifest in your life. Leave that to God, the Universe, Mother Nature, or whatever Higher Power you wish to invoke. Depending on what you've asked for, the amount of concerted action you must take to co-create it will vary. For smaller things, like manifesting a parking spot or hearing from a friend you have not heard from in a while, asking and believing may be enough. For larger things, like manifesting a new job or life partner, you must take action consistent with the future you desire and avoid, to the best of your ability, actions that are inconsistent with that future. If you would like to manifest a new job, start networking, applying for jobs online, and telling trusted friends and colleagues your intention. If you would like to manifest a new life partner, tell the people you are close with of your intention and begin to keep your eyes and ears open for how this person may show up in your life.

In implementing the Law of Attraction, be open to different and unexpected ways in which your desired wish may manifest. Often, the Universe may be trying to help us, guide us, and give us what we want, but we just don't see it. This reminds me of the story of a man who asked God for help while caught in a terrible storm. Being a man of faith, he knew that God would save him. As the storm progressed, his neighbors offered him a ride out of town, but he turned them down because he had faith that God would save him. When the water rose, a man in a canoe paddled up to his house and offered to take him, but the man turned him down, saying, "No thanks, God will save me." As the floodwaters rose, a police motorboat came by and yelled for him to hop aboard, after which a helicopter dropped a rope ladder and offered to pull him up. The man's response was always the same. "No thank you! Please save yourself! I know God will save me!" Needless to say, the man drowned. When approaching heaven, the man stood before God and asked, "I put all of my faith in You. Why didn't You come and save me?" God replied, "Son, I sent you a car. I sent you a canoe. I sent you a motorboat. I sent you a helicopter. What more were you looking for?"

This famous story is a reminder to be mindful of how your prayers or wishes may be answered. It may be a bit different from what you expect, and the answer to your prayers may be right in front of your eyes without your ever realizing it. That being said, once you receive what you wish for, acknowledge and be grateful for what you received and begin the process anew with something else. As you put out gratitude into the world, the Law of Attraction will bring you more of exactly that: more feelings of gratitude.

The Law of Attraction can have powerful and enduring consequences, as evidenced by my patient Alana and her husband Hank. That being said, the steps must be followed consistently if the results are to be consistent as well. Having accomplished all her goals, Alana then stopped her daily affirmations and stopped using the Law of Attraction. She thought that she was done. The Law of Attraction had served its purpose.

Not surprisingly, her old thought patterns and behaviors returned, and she gained the weight back over the next six months. This is an important illustration that healthy thought patterns and behaviors require consistent and disciplined practice. Just like some people need to take a blood pressure medication daily to keep their blood pressure in check, it is equally important to have daily disciplined practice of positive and constructive thinking to keep the negative thoughts at bay. Though this process, Alana learned this important lesson and is now taking up the Law of Attraction exercises again in order to lose weight, this time hopefully for good.

PHYSICISTS AND MYSTICS

The emerging view of consciousness—and our ability to affect our reality by changing our thoughts—gives us a deeper understanding of the science of spirituality. The pioneers of quantum physics—Werner Heisenberg, Niels Bohr, Erwin Schrödinger, and Wolfgang Pauli—were the first to recognize the spiritual implications of their work.

In *The Tao of Physics: An Exploration of the Parallels between Modern Physics and Eastern Mysticism*, physicist Fritjof Capra described his early struggle to reconcile theoretical physics with Eastern mysticism. As far back as the 1970s he discussed the ideas of mysticism with physicist Werner Heisenberg in Munich. While developing quantum theory, Heisenberg had gone to India to lecture. There he spent long hours discussing Indian philosophy with Rabindranath Tagore, the Bengali polymath who was the first non-European to win the Nobel Prize in literature. This discussion helped Heisenberg to recognize that there was in fact a whole culture believing very similar ideas. Heisenberg said that this was a great help for him. Niels Bohr had a similar experience when he went to China.[15]

Erwin Schrödinger, the Austrian physicist who won the Nobel Prize for his seminal work in quantum theory, also had a long-standing interest in Eastern religions.[16] Although he was an atheist, the Vedanta philosophy of Hinduism appealed to him, especially the idea that our individual consciousness is a manifestation of a universal consciousness.[17]

Wolfgang Pauli worked closely with psychiatrist Carl Jung in studying psychoanalysis, archetypes, and Kabbalah. Pauli could hardly deny the effects of invisible interconnectedness. He had such a reputation for breaking experimental equipment simply by standing in its vicinity that his colleagues lovingly called it "The Pauli Effect." The events were inexplicable examples of synchronicity and enlivened the dynamic collaboration between Pauli and Jung.

It is not surprising that these physicists turned to mystical texts for insight into the strange subatomic world they had discovered. Were they perhaps uncomfortable with the implications of these new ideas, and thereby looking toward spiritual texts to anchor these strange new discoveries in a cultural context? Or did their predilection toward spirituality and mysticism precede and foreshadow their interest in the mysterious world of quantum physics?

CONSCIOUSNESS, THE BRAIN, AND THE INFINITE FIELD

Newton and Descartes considered us to be the observers of reality rather than its creators. In contrast, the quantum pioneers discussed above believed that our act of observation, namely our consciousness, creates reality and therefore is central. But what exactly is this sublime and mysterious thing we call consciousness? Where is it located and how can we observe, study, and understand it?

According to the "old" ideas of consciousness, the brain is a discrete organ and the home of the mind, which is largely driven by chemistry—the communication of cells and the coding of DNA. This is what is taught in medical schools, so most doctors share this belief and use the words *brain* and *mind* interchangeably. In this paradigm, the human being is a survival machine largely powered by chemicals and genetic coding. These processes, including the DNA mutations that fuel evolution, are ultimately random as opposed to somehow "guided."

The "new" ideas of consciousness are that communication between cells, organs, and organ systems does not occur in the visible realm of Newton, but in the subatomic world of Bohr and Heisenberg. Cells and DNA communicate not only physically (i.e., through particles), but also energetically, through frequency and interference patterns (i.e., through waves). The brain is not the creator of consciousness, but a filter allowing us to experience a limited aspect of consciousness here and now in the physical world. Just as there are light frequencies the human brain cannot see and sound frequencies the human brain cannot hear, there are also aspects of consciousness that the human brain cannot perceive. The brain records the world through pulsating waves, by resonating with everything around it. In this way, consciousness is not just a bunch of physical processes, but energetic processes that transcend the physical realm.[18]

The brain certainly plays a role in shaping our conscious experiences, but this is different from saying that the brain *creates* consciousness. Philosophy professor David Chalmers coined the term "the hard problem of consciousness" to describe the difficulty in understanding how something nonmaterial like consciousness could arise from something physical and material, like the human brain.

Scientists such as Walter Schempp and systems theorist Ervin László believe that human memory does not reside in our brain at all, but is instead kept in an infinite storehouse of consciousness that connects all human beings.[19] Some scientists have gone so far as to suggest that all higher-level cognitive processes, including intuition and creativity, arise from our interaction with this field.[20]

This is a belief shared by many spiritual healers, mystics, shamans, and yogis. Some hypothesize that among the information contained in this field is a blueprint of all the ideas, stories, technologies, great works of art, medical breakthroughs, innovations, inventions, and imagination from the past, present, and future. According to this theory, every great idea came from this all-pervasive field. Some individuals are gifted with an exceptional capacity to tap into this field of information, which can result in rarely seen talents and abilities.

One such example is Srinivasa Ramanujan, a self-taught math prodigy from India with almost no formal math education who is considered to be the most innately brilliant mathematician who ever lived. In his short lifetime of thirty-three years, he independently compiled nearly thirty-nine hundred mathematical works and was "discovered" and sponsored by a British mathematician, Godfrey Harold "G. H." Hardy, to study and work at Cambridge. How did a man with no formal math training independently compile thirty-nine hundred mathematical works? A spiritual man deeply committed to his Hindu faith, Ramanujan said he would receive visions of scrolls of complex mathematical content unfolding before his eyes. In this way, he believed that mathematical equations represented the thoughts of God.[21] Ramanujan, therefore, believed himself to be a channel or conduit for inspired information in the form of mathematical knowledge.

Although Ramanujan's talents were indeed exceptional and may represent a particularly powerful example of tapping into "the field," it has long been recognized that strangers in distant parts of the world have simultaneously made some of our most important discoveries in science and beyond. This phenomenon is so widely acknowledged by the scientific community that it has been named *multiple discovery.* Oxygen, calculus, evolution, the existence of black holes and the stratosphere, and personal computers were all discovered by scientists working independently of each other. Did two people simultaneously tap into this mysterious storehouse of wisdom, knowledge, and information at precisely the same time? Or is the mechanism of multiple discovery far less mysterious? Given that new discoveries arise from thinking about old concepts in new and innovative ways, it's not surprising that multiple individuals can draw similar inferences from the same set of existing facts. Mysterious or not, multiple discovery is not an aberrant historical event but a common pattern in science.[22] Likewise, in business, it is widely assumed that the next big idea is out there, waiting to be discovered. The first one who does it becomes a multimillionaire.

The idea of tapping into "the field" for creativity and inspiration is never more present than in the world of art. Artistic creativity can be seen as an act of listening and receiving, rather than creating. When a painter is painting or a writer is writing, for instance, he or she may begin with a plan, but the plan is soon surrendered to the artwork's own plan, whereby "the brush takes the next stroke" or "the book writes itself." In dance, writing, sculpture, filmmaking, and any other work of art, the artist is the channel for the creative process rather than its sole and independent creator. The ideas and inspiration for works of art exist just a bit beneath the surface of our consciousness. If we know how to listen, we can tune in and receive the necessary guidance for a higher level of creativity. As artist Julia Cameron writes in *The Artist's Way*,[23]

> *Be alert: there is a second voice, a higher harmonic, adding to and augmenting your inner creative voice. The voice frequently shows itself as synchronicity. You will hear the dialogue you need, find the right song for the sequence, see the exact paint color you almost had in mind, and so forth. You will have the experience of finding things—books, seminars, tossed-out stuff—that happen to fit with what you are doing.*
>
> *Learn to accept the possibility that the Universe is helping you with what you are doing.*

In this way, all forms of creativity—whether mathematical, artistic, scientific, or otherwise—may involve connecting to an infinite storehouse of ideas, wisdom, knowledge, and information. Like Julia Cameron's quote suggests, people connect to this field in many different ways, including recognizing the synchronicity of their lives. Others connect through meditation, intuitive flashes, dreams, premonitions, sometimes even telepathic connections and visits from the dead, which we'll explore later. This type of connection is not something reserved for the chosen few, but something we can all cultivate and experience if we so choose.

DREAM A LITTLE DREAM

One powerful way of connecting to "the field" is through our dreams. Dreams have been used by people of various cultures throughout the centuries for healing, guidance, and answers to life's difficult questions. Sigmund Freud believed our dreams represented our unconscious wishes, conflicts, and desires. Carl Jung believed dreams were messages from our unconscious of what we need to do as human beings to attain wholeness. Ancient Egyptians believed that dreams were like oracles, bringing messages from the gods. They thought that the best way to receive divine revelation was through dreaming and thus they would induce (or "incubate") dreams. Dream incubation is a practiced technique of learning to "plant a seed" in the mind right before you go to sleep, in order to receive guidance or solve a problem through your dreams. Ancient Egyptians would go to sanctuaries and sleep on special "dream beds" in hope of receiving advice, comfort, or healing from the gods.[24]

In ancient Greece, dreams were used in a similar way to confer healing. A person with an illness would go to sleep in a designated temple, where the Greek God Asklepios would appear in a visionary dream to perform a symbolic operation. The person would awaken either healed, or prescribed a specific treatment that would lead to healing.[25] To this day, Native American dream quests involve young boys going out alone to the wilderness as a rite of passage into manhood. Among the Ojibwa tribe of the Great Lakes, for example, a young boy prepares himself a ritual nest, where he remains and fasts until he receives an anticipated dream. In the dream, his particular gift or ability is revealed to him by a representative of the spirit world. This is the gift or ability he will use to serve his community thereafter.[26]

The benefits of dream incubation are not limited to ancient civilizations or indigenous cultures. It is something that each of us can use to help us solve creative, emotional, or personal problems in our lives. In a study at Harvard Medical School, Dr. Deirdre Barrett had her students focus on a problem, such as an unsolved homework assignment or another objective problem, before going to sleep each night for a week. She found that it was certainly possible to come up with novel solutions in dreams that were both satisfactory to the dreamer and rated as objectively solving the problem by an outside observer. In her study, two-thirds of participants had dreams that addressed their chosen problem, and one-third reached some form of solution within their dreams.[27] Others have found this type of bedtime dream incubation effective in solving problems of a more subjective, personal nature.[28]

In Barrett's book *The Committee of Sleep*, she describes her study of prominent artists and scientists who draw inspiration from their dreams. While most of these dreams occur spontaneously, a small proportion of the respondents discovered informal versions of dream incubation on their own. They reported giving themselves successful pre-sleep suggestions for everything from seeing finished artwork in their dreams, to developing plots or characters for a novel, to asking dreams to solve computing and mechanical design problems.[29]

In the following exercise, we will utilize the technique of dream incubation or "programming your dreams" to obtain clarity and guidance about a personal or professional issue or problem.

Exercise: Tapping into the Field through Your Dreams

Dreams often speak to us in symbols. As such, the guidance you receive through them, whether obvious or subtle, often speaks directly to the heart of the issue you are asking about.

When working with dreams, it helps to keep paper and pen handy to record information as you awaken. It's extremely common to forget dream content once you get out of bed. Keeping pen and paper at the bedside ensures that you can record your dream impressions immediately upon waking, thus not losing pertinent information or answers to memory. It has also been shown that the more often we record our dreams, the more we remember them.

1. Before you go to sleep tonight, write down one question you would like some guidance on in your life. If your question easily lends itself to an image, hold it in your mind and let it be one of the last things you envision before falling asleep. If it's a personal problem, you might envision the person with whom you have the conflict. If you're an artist, you might envision a blank canvas. If you're a scientist, you might envision the device you're working on that's half assembled or a mathematical proof you've been trying to solve.

2. Deeply feel your intent to receive guidance and connect with your sense of trust that this will happen. Go to sleep with full confidence that you will in fact receive an answer by morning.

3. Immediately upon awakening, record every aspect of your dream(s) that you can. Include all action, experience, sights, sounds, colors, and very importantly, all the feelings involved.

4. Peruse your recorded dream for any symbols that jump out as being obvious. The more literal the better. Did you receive an answer to your question?

5. If an immediate answer does not reveal itself, get up and go about preparing for your day. Allow at least one hour before returning to your recorded dream to try again to ascertain an inherent answer within it. While at times the guidance is immediately obvious upon awakening, I sometimes find that allowing a bit of time between recording the dream and interpreting the guidance helps.

6. If you do not feel you have received guidance through your dream, repeat the above steps for at least two more nights. Receiving guidance through dreams becomes easier with practice.

Receiving answers through dreams is a wonderful way to get to the nuts and bolts of a personal issue. If you get into the habit of taking a few moments prior to sleep to "incubate" your dreaming process, you'll be amazed at all that your dreams may reveal. All you need to do is to pay attention and listen. After a few weeks of asking questions prior to sleep and recording any dreams remembered upon waking, you'll be successfully receiving guidance through dreams on a regular basis. In this way, dreams are a powerful way of tapping into the infinite field of consciousness.

EGO VERSUS SOUL CONSCIOUSNESS

But let's be clear that not all knowledge, information, guidance, creativity, and invention that arises from the infinite field of consciousness is "good" or has a positive impact on humanity. For instance, inventions like guns, weapons, and the nuclear bomb have only added to world violence, warfare, and our ability to hurt and kill one another. With respect to dreams, Babylonians and Assyrians divided dreams into "good," which were sent by the gods, and "bad," sent by demons. Hebrews also differentiated between good dreams (from God) and bad dreams (from evil spirits).[30]

Along with the force of creativity at the heart of our consciousness is another unseen influential force of consciousness in the world. It is the dark and destructive adversarial force of negativity, often acting in direct opposition to the creative force. Every single one of us has this force within us. Some call it ego. Some call it the adversary. Some call it Satan, or the evil inclination. Some call it our inner darkness. For every one of us, this force manifests in different

196

ways: as anger, negativity, addictions, cynicism, victim mentality, pessimism, inauthenticity, hatred, jealousy, pride, violence, and destruction. These are all negative extensions of the ego. Overcoming this very force in our lives forms many of our soul corrections. This force of consciousness is real, powerful, and will "attack" us where we are most vulnerable. When we know something is bad for us, this negative consciousness makes us do it anyway. When we know something is positive, this force rejects it or makes us procrastinate.

Part of each of our soul corrections is overcoming the adversarial force within us. Another way to say this is that we must transform our ego consciousness into soul consciousness.[31] In chapter 4, we did an exercise on the Proactive Formula, a four-step process to enable us to transform your ego-based, reactive responses to soul-based, proactive ones. In this lifetime, each of us has the free will to resist our ego, transcend it, and become aligned with our soul. As we transform our ego-consciousness, layer by layer, piece by piece, our lives gradually improve. Each time we transform a measure of ego, it's like flipping on a light switch: darkness is replaced by newfound light. Just like a filament creates resistance in a bulb to produce light, our resistance of the negative force within us creates the light or positive energy that we radiate into the world.

RESONATING WITH OUR WORLD

Einstein's famous equation, $E=mc^2$, scientifically equates that matter and energy are two forms of the same universal substrate of which we are all composed. All matter is also energy, so every living thing emits a subtle energy that results in an information exchange at the quantum level. All our bodily functions— thinking, eating, sleeping, dreaming, living, growing, and breathing— participate in this exchange with the energy field of which we are all a part. The mechanisms of this energy exchange are resonance and wave interference.

When two systems or entities vibrate at the same frequency, they are said to be in resonance. When two systems are in resonance, the total energy of the system is greater than the sum of its parts. The system with the higher vibrational frequency at the outset causes the other systems to sync up or *entrain* with it. In this way, we are always entraining with the rhythms, frequencies, and vibrations of the world around us, although we are not aware of it most of the time.

Everything in our world is essentially composed of energy waves, complete with phase, amplitude, and frequency. Everything in nature has its own unique or characteristic resonance or signature vibration. Moreover, *everything is a vibration*. All matter is also energy. All particles are also waves. They are two forms of the same universal substrate. Our sensory systems, especially our eyes and ears by way of the brain, process information through the frequencies of vibrating waves. This could be electromagnetic radiation presenting as light visible to the human eye, or sound waves traveling through air and striking our eardrums.

Our brain interacts with the world around us by resonating or getting in sync with it. As we do, we create wave interference patterns. Stanford University professor and neuroscientist Karl Pribram was one of the leading thinkers about the language of wave interference at the subatomic level:

> *When we observe the world…we do so on a much deeper level than the sticks-and-stones world "out there." Our brain primarily talks to itself and to the rest of the body not with words or images, or even bits or chemical impulses, but in the language of wave interference: the language of phase, amplitude, and frequency—the "spectral domain." We perceive an object by "resonating" with it, getting "in sync" with it. To know the world is literally to be on its wavelength.*[32]

Our internal vibrations, pulses, or frequencies are inseparable from those of the outside world. In fact, our internal rhythms will speed up or slow down to match a stronger external rhythm. This is why we may start to feel relaxed around certain people, tense around others, connected to some, and completely disconnected from others. In essence, we are vibrating systems and we are literally resonating with our world at all times. We know our world by resonating with it.

Some people, like psychiatrist David Hawkins, MD, PhD, have suggested that just like everything else in the universe, every human being has a characteristic resonance or signature vibration that changes as a function of everything we do, including the thoughts we think and the emotions we feel. Certain emotions—like shame, guilt, apathy, grief, and fear—decrease our vibration, while other emotions—like acceptance, love, joy, and peace—increase our vibration. Dr. Hawkins equates increases in vibrational frequency to a literal and metaphorical elevation in human consciousness—the thoughts, emotions, perceptions, attitudes, world views, and spiritual beliefs that make us who we are.[33]

Research at the HeartMath Institute is being done to explain the way in which different body systems communicate with one another through the vibrational processes of resonance and entrainment. It turns out that the heart is the most powerful biological oscillator within the body, with an electromagnetic field that is at least five thousand times greater than that produced by the brain. Many people think that the brain rules the heart, but research suggests that it is actually the other way around. Because the heart has the most powerful resonance, the rest of the body systems can be pulled into entrainment with it.[34]

At the moments when we enter a flow state or feel in harmony with something else—a glorious sunset, inspiring music, or another human being—we are coming into sync with ourselves. Not only are we more relaxed and at peace at such moments, but the entrained state increases our ability to perform well and offers numerous health benefits. People can develop their ability to maintain entrainment by sustaining sincere, heart-focused states such as appreciation and love. Many people have been able to cultivate this through the discipline of regular meditation. Research indicates that energetic information contained in the heart's field isn't detected only by our brains and bodies but can also be registered by the people around us, which is how we connect or resonate with people on an energetic level that occurs outside of our conscious awareness.[35]

Exercise: Raising Your Vibration by Sending Loving-Kindness to Others

One way of increasing our own vibrational energy and positivity is by sending love to others. This is a practice that can significantly improve the quality of your relationships over time, simply by sending unconditional love to or praying for the people in your life for a few minutes per day.

In chapter 7, Transforming Fear, we used the twenty-five-hundred-year-old Buddhist practice of loving-kindness to fill one's inner emptiness. In this exercise, you will use the loving-kindness meditation to send positive energy to somebody in your life. It could be somebody you love dearly or somebody with whom you have a more challenging relationship that you would like to improve. In either case, repeating this exercise daily can create profound positive changes in that relationship due to our inherent interconnectedness.

1. Find a relaxed position, whether sitting or lying down.

2. Focus your attention now on the area around your heart.

3. Now imagine that you are breathing in and out through your heart. With each inhale, your heart expands as it fills with fresh air. With each exhale, your heart contracts.

4. Now close your eyes and take several slow deep breaths through your heart in the following way:
    - Inhale through your nose for the count of two.
    - Hold your breath for the count of four.
    - Exhale through your nose for the count of eight.
    - Repeat for five breaths.

5. Now picture the person to whom you would like to send loving-kindness and repeat inwardly to yourself the following four phrases:

    May you be free of worry and fear.
    May you be happy.
    May you be free from suffering.
    May you be at peace.

6. Repeat these words to yourself for at least three minutes while focusing on this person. To enhance the power of this meditation, you can imagine this person bathed in a white light as you repeat these words.

11

Interconnectedness

Learn how to see. Realize that everything connects to everything else.

—LEONARDO DA VINCI

"Something bad is going to happen!"

Suzanne had always had premonitions. From an early age, she knew when something bad would happen. A tingling feeling would start in her chest, then spread to her arms, down her torso to her legs until her whole body tingled with anxious anticipation. Along with it came a premonition of some fearful thing about to happen to someone she knew: a car accident, an unexpected death, a disaster of some kind. The tingling wouldn't relent until she got word that her fears were confirmed—usually within twenty-four hours.

"I don't want to know when something bad is going to happen!" she told me when she sought therapy for this unusual symptom. "I just want to live my life like everybody else!" Suzanne believed she had inherited this "psychic" gift from her mother, who always magically knew when something was wrong with one of her four children. When Suzanne got into a car accident in college, her mom had an intense chest pain that signaled to her something was wrong with Suzanne. Before Suzanne could even reach her mom and tell her what happened, Mom was on a plane to visit Suzanne. Suzanne's grandmother and great-grandmother both had the same "premonitions."

Some psychiatrists may view Suzanne's premonitions as repressed fears, inner conflicts, or unconscious wishes or fantasies. They may argue that Suzanne constructed her premonitions after something bad happened as she retrospectively searched her mind for any possible "omen" that could have foreshadowed the event. Dr. Lenore Terr, a psychiatrist specializing in post-traumatic stress disorder, has shown repeatedly that in times of crisis and calamity, human beings are excellent at recalling omens, premonitions, and signs foreshadowing the event. She believes we recall these "predictors" only after the fact in an effort to give us some control and power at times when we feel out of control and powerless.[1] Thus, premonitions may be just retrospective rationalizations.

While Suzanne and I explored these possibilities together, we both believed there was more going on here. Perhaps Suzanne and the women of her family had a particularly gifted sense of intuition? What if this intuitive sense that Suzanne had come to know as a burden could have a positive side she had not yet discovered or acknowledged?

As I got to know Suzanne, I learned that her disturbing premonitions—which was the original reason she had come to see me—were just the tip of the iceberg. Suzanne's heightened intuition and enhanced perception manifested in all aspects of her life. She would often know things about other people that they never told her and she had no way of knowing, like what they did for a living, or the name of their child, or where they were born. She didn't know how she knew this—she just knew. She frequently knew how the people close to her were feeling, to the point where if somebody was distressed or in physical pain, she would feel the same feeling or sensation.

Whenever she was around somebody who was angry, she would feel drained and need to leave the room. She found crowds and big parties intolerable and shopping malls overstimulating, often having to depart soon after she arrived because she felt panic, anxiety, or pain in some part of her body. She could not be around bright lights or loud sounds for long periods of time. Suzanne was like a sponge, absorbing information and energy from other people and her surroundings at all times and processing this information more deeply and thoroughly than your average person.

Dr. Judith Orloff, a highly intuitive psychiatrist and author, calls people like Suzanne intuitive empaths.[2] Intuitive empathy is the ability to sense what's going on in others both physically and emotionally as if it were happening to oneself. It involves energetically merging with others and, for the moment, seeing and experiencing life (both positive and negative) through their eyes and sensing the world through their feelings.

For intuitive empaths, the idea of boundaries is particularly important, because it can be difficult for empaths to know where their experience ends and another's experience begins. Is the sadness they're feeling theirs or their mother's? Is the pain in their chest theirs or their sister's? Tania Singer, director at the Max Planck Institute for Human Cognitive and Brain Sciences in Leipzig, Germany, uses the term "emotional contagion" to describe shared empathy where the distinction between self and other becomes blurred.[3]

The effect of empathy and sensitivity on quality of life has been a topic of great interest among physicians, therapists, parents, and academics alike. In their 2005 paper in the journal *Development and Psychopathology*, researchers Ellis and Boyce classified children as either "dandelions" or "orchids." Dandelions make up about 80 percent of children; they are generally resilient and have the capacity to survive, even thrive, in whatever circumstances they encounter, provided their environment isn't excessively harsh. In contrast, orchids make up the remaining 20 percent of children and are highly sensitive to their environment, especially the quality of parenting they receive growing up. In difficult environments, orchids do poorly, while in supportive environments, they actually fare *better* than dandelions, with the potential to become "a flower of unusual delicacy and beauty."[4]

Another term for the "orchids," coined by psychologist Elaine Aron, PhD, is "highly sensitive person" (HSP). In addition to the traits discussed above, HSPs are aware of subtleties in their environment, are highly affected by others' moods, and have a rich and complex inner life. In brain imaging studies, they show stronger activation of brain regions associated with attention, awareness, and empathy.[5]

My patient Suzanne was very much an orchid. In difficult, overstimulating, energy-draining environments, Suzanne floundered. In supportive environments, she flourished, as evidenced by her excelling in school and having an exceptionally successful writing career.

In my work with Suzanne, I first helped her to become aware of how other people and her environment affect her. Having always had a strong people-pleasing side, Suzanne would often endure difficult people and environments to the point where she felt completely drained. She was especially sensitive to interactions with "energy vampires," or people who feed off others' energy to compensate for a lack of their own.

It was key for Suzanne to learn to stand up for herself, set boundaries, and walk away from energy vampires and energy-draining environments whenever possible. She also learned how to create a protective energy shield around herself—by visualizing either an enveloping white light or an astronaut suit around her entire body—whenever she felt her energy starting to wane. You create this energy shield with your intention by saying to yourself: "I create an energy shield with the following properties: it will block out negativity, drain out any negativity I hold inside, and filter in all positivity." This simple energetic practice, adaptations of which are used by many healers, proved invaluable to

Suzanne; she started doing it several times per day and became better able to distinguish her own feelings and sensation from those of the people around her.

Over time Suzanne learned to acknowledge but separate herself from unwanted premonitions and intuitive "hunches." This protected Suzanne from feeling that her premonitions were controlling her rather than vice versa. She shared what she learned with her mother, who was grateful to finally have an explanation for what she had been experiencing her whole life. Then Suzanne learned to enhance her intuitive abilities and use her gift—once a source of great fear and anxiety—in the service of herself. She harnessed her natural-born intuitive capacity in her writing, really bringing her characters to life in a way few authors can. In her social life and personal life, she learned to check in with herself regularly and become more attuned to how she felt in her environment. Whenever she encountered an "energy vampire" or other energy-draining situation, she immediately put up her energetic protective shield and limited the amount of time spent there. She ended up feeling less exhausted, more productive, and overall happier and more balanced.

Exercise: Identifying Energy Vampires in Your Life

For this stream-of-consciousness writing exercise, set your stopwatch to five minutes and write without stopping on the topic Identifying Energy Vampires in Your Life. The Questions for Reflection are included as mere guideposts. As with life, let your writing take you where it may.

1. What kinds of qualities in other people do you find emotionally draining or exhausting? What kinds of people do you find it difficult to be around?

2. Are there currently any such people in your life with whom you don't feel you have set appropriate boundaries?

3. What would setting firmer boundaries with these people look like? What would be the benefit of setting such boundaries?

4. What keeps you from doing this?

As an action step to follow this journaling exercise, this week set firmer boundaries with one energy vampire in your life. This may mean saying no when you would ordinarily say yes. It may mean limiting the time you spend with them or the mental energy you give them in your mind when you are not with them. It may mean visualizing an energetic protective shield around you, as Suzanne did, when you are in the presence of this person.

Exercise: Restoring Your Energy by Connecting to Your Heart

As effective as it may be to set firmer boundaries with the people you find emotionally draining, an even more powerful way to restore yourself emotionally is to fill your heart with love.

This exercise is designed to help you connect with your heart and amplify your capacity to love yourself and others. From this space, you can send core heart feelings to people you love and, better yet, people you find difficult or draining in any way. When people send love and care to somebody with whom they are having problems, the relationship often improves. This may be due to an attitude shift in the sender, a heart opening in the receiver, a combination of both, or something else entirely. Whatever the mechanism, sending core heart feelings to others puts you more into alignment with the other person, yourself, and your capacity for love, compassion, and healing.

When you are ready, sit in a comfortable position and begin.

1. Find a quiet place, close your eyes, and begin to relax by slowly focusing on your breath. Take several slow deep breaths:
   - Inhale through your nose for the count of two.
   - Hold your breath for the count of four.
   - Exhale through your nose for the count of eight.
   - Repeat for five breath cycles.

2. Now pretend that you are breathing slowly through your heart. With each inhalation, imagine your heart expanding as it fills with love and white light. With each exhalation, imagine your heart contracting as it releases negative energy and darkness.

3. Now remember the feeling of love, care, or appreciation you have for someone whom it's easy for you to love. This can be a person dear to you, a pet, or even a spiritual source (e.g., God).

4. Place this person, pet, or entity in your heart center and feel what it is like to love, care for, and appreciate them. Send them love. Feel the love they have for you. Try to stay with these feelings for at least five minutes. If five minutes is easy for you, try to increase this to ten minutes, and eventually fifteen minutes. The longer you can sustain this state, the better you will feel.

5. As thoughts enter your mind, bring your focus gently back to the area around your heart.

6. If the energy feels too intense or even blocked, repeat breathing through your heart (Step 2) five more times.

7. From a state of heart-centered awareness, begin to send and receive love to and from people whom you love. On your inhalation, say or

think, "I receive love from people I love." On your exhalation, say or think, "I give love to people I love." Do this while you breathe for at least two minutes.

8. Next, begin to send love to the people in your life with whom you are having difficulties, including the energy vampire you identified in the above exercise. This could be a boss, friend, spouse, partner, or neighbor. Imagine the person on the other end receiving the love you send. On your inhalation, say or think as you breathe, "I receive love from everybody in my life." On your exhalation, say or think as you breathe, "I give love to everybody in my life." Do this for at least two minutes.

As you connect to your heart, you may also feel more connected to your intuition and a deep sense of inner knowing. If you receive any such messages or guidance during this exercise, write them down so you can review them later. After you complete this exercise, you may want to journal about what emerged for you.

EMPATHY, MIND-READING, AND PSYCHICS

Suzanne's heightened sensitivity and capacity for empathy were so powerful, sometimes even overwhelming, that she often felt like she had telepathy with the people close to her. She knew what others were thinking without knowing how or why she knew this. Suzanne was deeply intuitive. Some may even call her psychic. Although I certainly do not have many patients in my practice who present with psychic or telepathic capabilities like Suzanne, I have had multiple patients consult psychics before or during the course of our work together.

Whenever my patients consult psychics, I always greet their experiences with curiosity and an open mind—though I was a bit startled when one patient asked a psychic whether she should take the medication I prescribed to her! (To my relief, the psychic said she should.) A psychic once told another patient to reduce the dose of the Prozac I'd prescribed to her. She sensed that her current dose was too much for the patient. The patient and I discussed the psychic's recommendation and decided to try reducing the dosage. Over the next month, my patient's condition improved. I asked her to thank the psychic on my behalf for the medical consultation!

When psychiatrist Diane Hennacy Powell was working on the psychiatric consult service at Harvard Medical Center, a statuesque woman of African-American and Native American descent named Cheyenne came in with a suspected heart attack. After examining her, the medical staff thought she might be psychotic, so they called in Dr. Hennacy Powell for a psychiatric consultation.

"I see ghosts here," Cheyenne told Dr. Hennacy Powell. "It's really freaking me out and I want to leave."

Rather than concluding that she was mentally ill and signing her into the locked ward, Dr. Hennacy Powell sat down and talked to her. Cheyenne claimed to be psychic. "I'm getting a reading about you," she said. "Do you mind if I share the information?"

"No. Go ahead," Dr. Hennacy Powell replied.

"Your husband's a chemist." This was true. "And he's applying for a job right now in two cities." That very week he was interviewing for one position at Johns Hopkins in Baltimore and another one in San Diego.

Dr. Hennacy Powell was astounded by the accuracy of her remarks, and pressed her further by saying, "Which cities?" Cheyenne asked Dr. Hennacy Powell to name some cities. Dr. Hennacy Powell started listing cities, to which Cheyenne responded, "San Diego and Baltimore." Cheyenne told Dr. Hennacy Powell that, in his heart, her husband wanted to go to one, but they'd end up in the other one. That made sense to Dr. Hennacy Powell. Her husband had been born in Johns Hopkins and was the thirteenth generation in his family to live in Baltimore. That was where he belonged, in his heart of hearts. But when the better academic opportunity arose in San Diego, that's where they went.

During the time they talked, the woman made many predictions about Dr. Hennacy Powell's life that, years later, came true. She said she'd have only one child, a daughter, and she did. She said that, eventually, Dr. Hennacy Powell would give up psychiatry to write books, and she did.

Was this woman at the hospital indeed psychic? Or did her predictions perhaps subtly influence Dr. Hennacy Powell's later decisions to have one child and write books? Or was this just a function of Dr. Hennacy Powell selectively remembering the things this woman predicted correctly and forgetting her incorrect predictions?

The patient agreed to get her medical bloodwork done while she was there, but she said the results would come back normal, and they did.

The encounter left Dr. Hennacy Powell's sense of reality shaken. What could explain this woman's insight into a stranger's life that day? It was as if this woman had read Dr. Hennacy Powell's mind and forecasted her future! If this woman was truly psychic, how in the world did she know what she knew? Through this experience, Dr. Hennacy Powell realized that things are not always what we've come to believe.[6]

TELEPATHY AND THOUGHT TRANSFERENCE

The word "telepathy" derives from the Greek prefix *tele*, meaning "distant" and *patheia*, meaning "feeling or perception." It is defined by the *Collins English Dictionary* as "the communication between people of thoughts, feelings, desires…through mechanisms that cannot be understood in terms of known scientific laws."[7]

Many psychiatrists, psychologists, psychoanalysts, and therapists have written about these sorts of "telepathic" experiences. Even Sigmund Freud, who was skeptical of the supernatural, believed there to be a "kernel of truth" in the experience of telepathy, which he called "thought transference."[8] In his book *Dreams and Occultism,* he described it as an event where "mental processes in one person—ideas, emotional states, impulses—can be transferred to another person through empty space without employing the familiar methods of communication by means of words and signs."[9]

Even when we are not deliberately trying to cultivate telepathic capabilities, it's a familiar occurrence to be thinking about someone just before they call or e-mail. My father and I experience this on a regular basis. A song may enter your mind and, moments later, a loved one begins humming the same tune without any communication between you. My father and stepmother experience this occurrence with regularity. Or you may recall an old friend from high school you have not thought about in years and bump into them later on the street. Psychiatrist Berthold Schwarz kept a diary about coincidences like this in his family and later published them in a book entitled *Parent-Child Telepathy.*[10] Hans Berger, a German psychiatrist who invented the electroencephalogram (EEG), which measures brain waves to diagnose conditions like seizures, was inspired to create this machine after an extraordinary telepathic experience with his sister. She sent him a telegraph saying that she was very concerned that something bad had happened to him on the same day he had almost been killed while riding a horse![11] Coincidences like this may bewilder us and stand out in our mind as significant. Yet a skeptic would point out all the other times we have thought about somebody and they did not call or when we may have had a premonition and been wrong.

A number of psychoanalytic thinkers have developed methods for tuning in to the nonverbal unconscious material of another person. The psychoanalytic approach developed by Freud deliberately encourages access to this level of consciousness. By having the patient lie down without looking at the analyst and encouraging free-association (i.e., "tell me anything that comes into your mind when you think about that red elephant in your dream"), Freud believed the patient would be able to access the depth of their unconscious mind. Another method Freud frequently employed was dream analysis. He believed dreams to be the "royal road to the unconscious" by providing key insights into the inner conflicts a patient was working to resolve. Helping patients to become conscious of the content of their unconscious mind is one tool of traditional psychotherapy. As patients become more aware of their unconscious struggles, they gain the freedom to make different choices in resolving these conflicts. Freud was also one of the first to realize that a powerful force at work in the bond between a patient and therapist is emotional attachment, at the conscious and unconscious level. By developing and employing all these psychoanalytic methods, Freud was taking full advantage of our inherent interconnectedness. His friend and colleague Sándor Ferenczi called this the "dialogue of the unconsciouses."[12]

Neurobiologists continue to search for explanations for these fascinating, unusual experiences. Some say telepathy occurs because of a conversation between two people's limbic systems,[13] or two people's right amygdalas,[14] and/ or some activity in people's mirror neurons.[15] A mirror neuron is a neuron that fires both when we act and when we observe the same action performed by another. Thus, the neuron "mirrors" the behavior of the other, as though the observer were him or herself acting. In this way, mirror neurons are believed to be involved in our capacity for empathy or knowing the mind of another,[16] perhaps even telepathy. Despite existing hypotheses, the scientific mechanism for experiences like telepathy remains a mystery.

UNCONSCIOUS DIALOGUES

Since opening myself up to ideas of spirituality ten years ago, my awareness of telepathy and other expressions of our interconnectedness has increased exponentially in my life. On a regular basis, I have a fleeting thought about a patient I have not heard from in months and within twenty-four hours that patient contacts me. It has occurred with such regularity that when it happens now, I will sometimes even pull the patient's chart in preparation for their call.

Recently, I had an interesting experience with Carlie, a patient I'd been treating for five years. Prior to one of our appointments, I recall receiving a text from Carlie saying that her mother and sister would be joining her in the session that day. So I set up the room for three patients instead of one and went into my waiting room to invite them in.

I was quite surprised to see that Carlie was alone. "Where are your mother and sister?"

Carlie looked confused. "What do you mean?"

"I got your text. Weren't your mother and sister going to join you?"

"They were. But how did you know that? I never texted you." Carlie looked stunned. She told me that they had planned to come to the session but at the last minute had decided not to.

To my surprise, when I double-checked my cell phone, there were no texts from Carlie!

As a therapist, I become very close with my patients and embedded in the nuances of their inner worlds. It is therefore not surprising to me that my patients' inner worlds sometimes inadvertently bleed into mine, and vice versa. But the scientist in me wants to know exactly how and why this happens. How was I able to receive this seemingly telepathic communication from Carlie outside our usual channels of communication?

Psychiatrist Diane Hennacy Powell once unexpectedly said to her patient

Rolanda, "I think you may be stuck in this pattern because of what happened with your father when you were four years old." Rolanda was startled by Dr. Hennacy Powell's statement. "I've been working up the courage to tell you that," she said. Wondering if Rolanda had simply forgotten sharing this emotionally charged material at one of their previous sessions, Dr. Hennacy Powell checked her notes. She confirmed that Rolanda had never mentioned it. The expression of this unconscious bond deepened Rolanda's trust of Dr. Hennacy Powell and made their work progress.[17]

Telepathy manifested in a slightly different way—as a "slip of the tongue"—with an Eastern-Orthodox priest named Mark with whom I have been working for the last three years. About six months into treatment, Mark shared how difficult it was for him to come to therapy and explore parts of himself that he did not want to confront.

My response surprised me. I said something like, "Mark, you may want therapy to always feel like a massage, where you leave feeling relaxed and calm, but what is often most helpful is to discuss precisely those things that are most distressing and unsettling to you."

Relating therapy to a massage was a strange remark to make to a priest. As soon as the words escaped my mouth, I felt confused. Why had I said that? Not that there was anything wrong with the comment; it's just not a comment I would ordinarily make.

Mark looked at me in shock. In that session, he confessed to me that the real reason he had come to therapy was because he had been going to massage parlors for the last several years and felt extremely guilty about it.

My conscious mind was completely unaware of what Mark wasn't saying, but apparently, something had been communicated unconsciously that made me say what I said without even knowing why. Whatever the reason, the experience was quite powerful for both Mark and myself. This synchronicity was a turning point in our work together and enabled Mark to be honest with me about something he had never been honest about with anybody else.

Numerous psychiatrists have reported experiences of this nature in their work with patients. New York psychoanalyst Janine de Peyer published a paper in *Psychoanalytic Dialogues* entitled "Uncanny Communication and the Porous Mind." She describes a very similar "slip of the tongue" with one of her patients, Jordan.[18]

Jordan was anticipating having separation anxiety from her boyfriend, George, when she went on a retreat to New Mexico. Dr. de Peyer was asking Jordan about the possibility of Skyping with George while she was away. She meant to say "You could be in Timbuktu and still talk to him." Instead, she said "You could be in Tuckahoe and still talk to him." It seemed innocuous. Perhaps Dr. de Peyer had heard the name Tuckahoe on TV that morning and mixed it up with Timbuktu. But Jordan knew the difference. She had been talking to Dr. de Peyer about Tuckahoe, a place her family used to visit together when Jordan was a child, for the last thirty minutes in therapy without ever mentioning the name of the town! The emotional meaning of Dr. de Peyer's slip of the tongue was incredibly powerful for Jordan and, similar to my own experience, led to a significant breakthrough in their therapy. Dr. de Peyer's paper cites twenty-two similar cases published in the academic literature by psychiatrists, psychologists, and psychoanalysts since the days of Freud until the present.

Numerous doctors and therapists have also reported powerful, insight-generating dreams about patients,[19] yet sometimes the one with the insight is the patient! On two separate occasions, my patient Hans, the young violinist about whom I wrote in my introduction, had dreams about things in my personal life that he had no way of knowing about. In the first dream, which occurred about three years into our treatment, Hans saw the two of us together in my office during a session. Although I had short hair at the time, in Hans's dream I had flowing brown locks that went down to the floor. In his dream, I sat in an elevated chair while the tendrils flew all around the room, as if taking on a life of their own. Hans described the dream as having a grainy appearance, which he experienced when a dream was particularly meaningful to him. As we explored the dream, we realized that my long hair in the dream equated me in Hans's mind with a safe, kind yet complicated character in a novel he was writing who also had flowing brown locks. For me, however, the dream turned out to be unexpectedly literal.

I had long hair up until the age of twenty-five, when I cut it short while doing a research project in Thailand one summer during medical school. Long hair and the sweltering Thai heat did not mix. Curiously enough, I had started thinking about letting my hair grow out again about a week before Hans's dream. One of my friends suggested that I try some temporary hair extensions, and the day before I saw Hans, I had tried on flowing brown locks. I liked them and committed to growing out my own hair again. Then I took off the hair extensions, all in the comfort of my own home. The next day Hans told me his dream.

Had Hans unconsciously picked up my musings about my hair in our prior session? He could not have seen me with longer hair, since I had only tried the extensions on in my apartment. About a year after this occurrence, Hans dreamed that I had moved into a new apartment in Manhattan. His dream occurred the week I moved into a new apartment! These occurrences suggest that we are connected to each other on a deeper level than we realize. Our connections can run so deep that even mundane aspects of our daily experiences can overlap into each other's inner worlds. Predictive dreams, like those experienced by Hans, are not uncommon. Three days prior to his assassination, Abraham Lincoln had a dream about his own death.[20]

THE SCIENCE OF TELEPATHY

The Society for Psychical Research, founded in 1882, published findings from 149 cases of predictive dreams or "dream telepathy" in the historic work *Phantasms of the Living* by Edmund Gurney, Frederic Myers, and Frank Podmore. In most cases, the dreamer and the subject were either related or acquainted. Most of the dreams involved death or some sort of crisis. None of the dreamers had a history of psychic abilities or telepathy; nor were they prone to nightmares, which made these particular dreams stand out.[21] If such experiences are relatively common, could telepathic abilities be something we all possess? How can subjective and personal experiences of this nature be studied scientifically?

While the above stories offer ample anecdotal evidence of telepathy and other forms of mental interconnectedness, anecdotes alone do not constitute scientific proof. Perhaps the oldest well-known scientific experiment of telepathy is the Ganzfeld, which in German means "whole field." In the original Ganzfeld experiment, subjects are put into a state of relative sensory deprivation: they sit in a comfortable reclining chair in a soundproof room with halved Ping-Pong balls over their eyes. They wear headphones playing continuous quiet static and are told to speak for twenty minutes about any impressions that pop into their mind. This person is the "receiver."

At the same time, a "sender" observes a randomly chosen symbol (like a circle, square, or squiggly line) and tries to mentally transmit this symbol to the receiver. For thirty minutes, the receiver says out loud any image that comes into his or her mind. This is recorded by the experimenter (who does not know the symbol being transmitted). The receiver is then taken out of the Ganzfeld state and given a set of four possible symbols, from which they are asked to select the one which most resembles the images they witnessed. Most commonly there are three decoys along with the target, giving an expected "hit" rate of 25 percent.[22]

To overcome methodologic limitations in the study design, numerous refinements were made to the original Ganzfeld protocol. In its more recent incarnation, titled "digital autoganzfeld," an automated computer system is used to randomly select and display the symbols.[23] In 2010, researchers Lance Storm, Patrizio Tressoldi, and Lorenzo Di Risio analyzed twenty-nine Ganzfeld studies from 1997 to 2008, which contained a total of 1,498 analyzed trials. These trials produced 483 "hits," corresponding to a hit rate of 32.2 percent, which is significantly higher than the expect 25 percent hit rate.[24] These results were statistically significant, suggesting that there was indeed some telepathy at play among the study subjects.[25] As with any scientific discovery that challenges our existing paradigm, these results have been met with a healthy dose of skepticism and scrutiny.[26] The overall effect size is modest and difficult to replicate on demand, perhaps because "natural" telepathy occurs more frequently under circumstances when the "sender" is experiencing heightened physical, psychological, or emotional distress, which is hard to replicate in a laboratory setting.[27]

In a related experiment at University of California, Berkeley, psychologist Charles Tart gave himself electrical shocks while attempting to convey his pain telepathically to a person hooked up to machines in a nearby room (i.e., the receiver). The receiver was monitored for physiological changes, such as heart rate and blood volume. In contrast to the Ganzfeld experiment, which studied changes in the receiver's conscious mind, this experiment bypassed the conscious mind and focused only on changes at the autonomic (unconscious) level. The experiment was repeated with multiple receivers. While none of them reported any conscious awareness of Tart's pain, their bodies seemed to register some physiological changes quite clearly. While Tart was being shocked, the receivers' hearts beat faster. It was as if, unconsciously, they knew and empathized.[28]

The capacity to empathize unconsciously with another human being is something we all possess to different degrees, so the results of this experiment may not seem shocking. As a therapist, I will often pick up what my patient is feeling by being in the room with them. When a patient comes in sad or depressed, I can sometimes begin to feel depressed myself. When somebody comes in angry, I may start to feel angry. When appropriate, I will share what I am feeling in the moment with my patient. Psychiatrist Leston Havens writes, "How do we know what to tell the patient? We have to *experience* them, like water falling on Helen Keller's hand. Then we can begin to recognize them."[29] The way in which a therapist feels while in the room with a patient is an important tool for understanding what is going on with the patient and in the therapy.

BECOMING MORE TELEPATHIC

What is it that differentiates people who are a little more telepathic than others? This question has been asked by Ganzfeld researchers, therapists, and laymen alike. Parapsychologist Charles Honorton, together with social psychologist and Cornell professor Daryl Bem investigated personality traits that enhanced one's capacity for telepathy.[30] They found that these traits included a belief that telepathy was real (as opposed to a skeptical attitude toward it),[31] considering oneself to be an artistic or creative person,[32] having had a history of telepathic experiences,[33] practicing a mental discipline like meditation,[34] and emotional closeness to people with whom you are having the telepathic exchange.[35] In essence, more telepathic individuals are generally artistic, creative, likely to meditate, open to the unknown, and emotionally receptive. In summary, these are individuals who are more "right-brained." Some preliminary brain imaging studies have confirmed the association between telepathy and right-brain activation.[36,]

For the past fifty years, it was believed that the seat of intuition lay in the right hemisphere of our brain, whereas logic and language resided in the left hemisphere. In her book *Stroke of Insight*, Harvard-trained brain scientist Jill Bolte Taylor, PhD, describes what happened to her at the age of thirty-seven when she experienced a massive stroke that essentially inactivated the left hemisphere of her brain.[37] In the eight years of recovery following her stroke, Dr. Taylor oscillated between two psychological states: her present-focused, intuitive state (the one conducive to telepathy) and her logical, verbal state (the one that can, at times, block telepathy). Dr. Taylor describes her right mind as follows:

> *My right mind character is adventurous, celebrative of abundance, and socially adept. It is sensitive to nonverbal communication, empathic, and accurately decodes emotion. The right mind is open to the eternal flow whereby I exist as one with the Universe. It is the seat of my divine mind, the knower, the wise woman, and the observer. It is my intuition and higher consciousness. My right mind is ever present and gets lost in time.*

Being right-brained has been shown by researchers to also make one more telepathic.[38]

When we are born, we are predominantly right-brained or intuitive/instinctual. There is even data suggesting that babies are capable of reading minds.[39] Some say this state renders us connected to the universal consciousness, where we know everything but are not aware of it and do not know how to access or express it. As we get older and begin to learn, the right brain begins to take a backseat to the left brain, with intuitive/instinctual behavior replaced by learned behavior. As we continue to evolve, we become more left-brained, relying more on our technology and learned knowledge and less on right-brain instincts/intuition and collective consciousness. Science is very much a left-brained activity, whereas spirituality is largely a right-brained activity. Creating a healthy balance between the two enables us to have the cognitive flexibility to welcome change, access intuition, and be creative while remaining concrete and organized enough to meet our responsibilities and stay grounded in reality. For any well-balanced and functioning human being, both sides of the brain must be functioning in coordination with each other at all times.

The right brain is associated not just with telepathy, but also with creativity, intuition, altered states of consciousness, and universal consciousness. Activities like meditation, mindfulness, and certain forms of creativity can quiet the left brain and bring us into a more right-brained state of mind.[40] Another way of neutralizing the left brain and setting your right-brain potential free is through the use of sound, which is frequently used in healing. Certain sounds, including music and chanting, are important in religious and meditative traditions to help achieve deep, transcendental states of consciousness. After Harvard neurosurgeon Eben Alexander, MD, had a deeply spiritual near-death experience (NDE), he was able to use sound frequencies and harmonics found in the natural world to re-create the altered state of consciousness he experienced and revisit the extraordinary spiritual realms.[41] While the left brain is largely responsible for our feeling of individuality, the right brain helps us feel more interconnected with each other and the world.

This idea of our interconnectedness has profound implications for our lives and our relationship to others. When others suffer, we feel their pain. When we experience joy, it radiates out into the Universe. While the experience of oneness can never be fully and accurately put into words, it has been written about by poets, and frequently experienced by mystics and yogis, and to some degree by each of us in peak experiences.

For centuries, deep meditation has made practitioners aware of the oneness in all of life. Others have reported feeling a sense of interconnectedness while listening to great music, seeing an inspiring film, or experiencing creative breakthroughs. Parents feel these moments in their unconditional love for their child. Lovers may feel it during a sexual experience where the sense of separateness from their lover disappears. Learning to access this flow state within oneself and connect to this feeling of oneness is a powerful vehicle for growth, healing, transformation, and ultimately, fulfillment.[42]

In her pioneering book *Extraordinary Knowing*, psychoanalyst Elizabeth Lloyd Mayer writes about telepathy and other experiences of deep connectedness between human beings:

They reflect capacities to which we can't gain access in the customary ways. They're peculiar capacities in that they're least *likely to become available when we deliberately try to access them. We cannot reach these new sources of information simply by "tuning in" to something new; paradoxically, we must also "tune out" much of the ordinary information that continually bombards our senses. While some people appear born with an innate gift for doing that, it may be possible for the rest of us to learn to develop precisely the same quality of awareness, an awareness that might result in a subjectively felt state of profound connectedness to other human beings and to every aspect of the material world around us. If that state exists and we can achieve it, we may also develop distinct perceptual capacities, including an intuitive intelligence whose development and training our culture has largely overlooked. Refining and educating such intelligence has huge implications for how we see the world because it changes what we're able to see, changing what we're able to know as a result. It may render the intuitive knowing we call extraordinary and anomalous not only possible but downright ordinary.*[43]

12

Immortality

We are not human beings having a spiritual experience. We are spiritual beings having a human experience.

—Pierre Teilhard de Chardin

When patients ask me, "What's my prognosis?" I always tell them, "We all have the same prognosis: fatal." Despite our best efforts to avoid death, deny death, or defy death, one day our lives will inevitably come to an end, which begs the question: What's next?

Newton believed there was no afterlife. Socrates, in contrast, believed in the immortality of the soul and expected to befriend a community of like-minded truth seekers after his time on Earth had ended. According to Sigmund Freud, clinging to hope of an afterlife is a form of *infantile neurosis*: human beings need to create fantasies of an afterlife because we are too afraid to face the possibility that this life is all we've got. Most Americans do not agree with Sigmund Freud, however. According to the 2014 Religious Landscape Study conducted by the

Pew Research Center, 72 percent of Americans believe in Heaven, 21 percent do not, and another 7 percent don't know.[1]

By the law of conservation of energy, energy cannot be created or destroyed; it simply changes form. The amount of energy in the universe is constant—energy can be changed, moved, controlled, stored, or dissipated. However, it cannot be created from nothing or reduced to nothing. In essence, atoms are immortal. They never die. Although the forms and structures that atoms create eventually come apart and "die," the individual atoms themselves reconfigure, change form and live on. Thích Nhất Hạnh, a Vietnamese Buddhist monk and peace activist, discusses how modern-day concepts of death defy the law of conservation of energy:

The concept of death is that being turns into non-being. That is impossible. Can somebody become nobody? No. If we burn the piece of paper, we cannot reduce it to nothing. The paper will turn into heat, which will go into the cosmos, and turn into smoke, which will join the clouds in the sky. Tomorrow a drop of rain will fall on your forehead, and you will make contact with the piece of paper. The ashes produced by the burning will rejoin the earth, and one day they will manifest as daisies.[2]

Fritz-Albert Popp, a German biophysics researcher, suggests that death is a *decoupling* of our energy from matter (aka our cells and our bodies), so we can return to the field that connects us all.[3] Does this mean that people are still around *in some form* even after they die? Could that explain why people sometimes seem to receive communications from the dead?

VISITS FROM THE OTHER SIDE

On several occasions, my patients appear to have had visits from "the other side." Sharon's first love, Paul, committed suicide. She described him in the most romantic terms. He was a beautiful artist, singer, and songwriter who carried himself with style, confidence, and grace. While he was alive, he had struggled with severe bipolar disorder from an early age. Together he and Sharon withstood the trials and tribulations of his condition, but when he ultimately killed himself, Sharon felt a devastating sense of failure. She was so deeply upset that she began to feel suicidal herself.

In our second session, as Sharon was expressing her heartbreak over the loss of Paul, my door buzzer suddenly fell off my wall and onto my floor. This was the only time in all my years in private practice that this occurred. Sharon and I exchanged a look of surprise.

Sharon interpreted this synchronicity as a sign that Paul was there, consoling her in her grief. This thought provided Sharon with some relief from her pain and precipitated a positive turning point in our therapy.

A similar event occurred with Bob, whose beloved younger brother died in a car accident seven years before we began treatment. At one of our appointments, the lights in my office began flickering on and off every time Bob mentioned his brother. This time, I wondered aloud whether Bob's brother was with us that day. Bob looked at me quizzically at first, but ultimately welcomed my interpretation. It opened a powerful, cathartic discussion of Bob's beliefs about the afterlife and his continued connection to his brother even after his passing.

Curiously enough, the light flickering continued when Bob got home that day. As he was vacuuming his living room, one of the lamps in his apartment went out. Bob examined the lamp to make sure the bulb was screwed in tightly and the plug was stably in place. Seeing no problems, Bob went to get a new lightbulb. As he approached the lamp with a new bulb in hand, the light suddenly turned back on. It continued to burn brightly and only needed to be replaced a full year later. As it had for Sharon, the idea that his loved one was sending him signals from the other side was a source of great comfort for Bob.

Other patients have reported experiences where they felt loved ones had protected them from harm. My patient Meghan told me she was driving home late one evening and fell asleep at the wheel. The car veered off the road and hit the curb, jolting her awake just in time to slam on the brakes. When she got out of the car, she realized she was five feet away from the home where her grandmother grew up! Had she hit her brakes one second earlier or later, she would have run head-on into a light post or fire hydrant. Meghan felt that her grandmother had helped her avoid a potentially fatal catastrophe.

Experiences like Sharon's, Bob's, and Meghan's have led me to question the nature of life, death, and the soul. Could the buzzer falling off my wall and the flickering light in my office have been mere coincidences? Or do loved ones who have passed on have the potential to communicate with us, comfort us, and even protect us?

In an October 2014 article in *Scientific American*, Dr. Michael Shermer, editor-in-chief of *Skeptic* magazine, described an event that was so mysterious, it shook his own skepticism to the core. For a man who has essentially devoted his life to debunking the mystical and paranormal, this is a strong claim!

On his wedding day, his bride, Jennifer Graf, told him she was sad that her grandfather was not there to walk her down the aisle. Jennifer's grandfather died when she was sixteen, after having been the main father figure in her life.

Just as they were preparing for the ceremony, Michael and Jennifer heard music. They searched the house, only to discover that it was coming from a dresser drawer in the bedroom. In the drawer was her grandfather's 1978 Philips 010 transistor radio, which she had shipped to the United States from Germany a few months earlier.

Jennifer shares Michael's skepticism about the paranormal, but the music was hard to ignore. This synchronicity symbolized for Jennifer that her grandfather was there. The music was his gift of approval. It was a deeply meaningful experience to Jennifer and shook even a professional skeptic like Michael Shermer to the core.

Although this coincidence is certainly meaningful, Michael Shermer emphasizes that such inexplicable events as these "do not constitute scientific evidence that the dead survive or that they can communicate with us via electronic equipment. The emotional significance we attribute to such anomalous events grants them importance in our lives regardless of what caused them. If we live in accordance with the scientific credo to always remain open-minded in the face of inconclusive evidence and yet-unanswered questions, we should not discount all possible explanations for the mysterious." Could this uncanny experience have unexpectedly transformed a widely reputed atheist into an agnostic?

This story underscores one of the most important qualities in any search for truth and fulfillment: humility. Humility implies open-mindedness, wisdom, and maturity. While arrogance is far more popular, all it reflects is denial, close-mindedness, pride, and immaturity. As stated in a Hasidic proverb, "There is no room for God [or spirituality] in him that is full of himself." The wisdom of humility is what enabled a skeptic like Michael Shermer to be moved by the synchronicity he experienced on his wedding day, while tolerating the uncertainty it created.[4]

THE SMELL OF DEATH

Prior to his near-death experience (NDE), Harvard neurosurgeon Eben Alexander agreed with the many scientists and skeptics who argued that NDEs are simply delusions or fantasies produced by our brains while under duress. His own experience was so real and remarkable, however, that it opened him up to a whole new realm of being, suggesting that consciousness can continue even when the brain has been shut down.[5] Now a dedicated author and educator on the intersection of neuroscience, heaven, and the soul, Dr. Alexander believes, as I do, that true healing can be achieved when we realize that a Higher Power and the soul are real and that death is not the end of personal existence but only a transition.[6] But the idea of connecting with others outside of the usual channels of communication is not limited to telepathic experiences, dreams, and NDEs. Another realm where this idea has been explored and experienced by many is in what some call empathic or "shared death experiences."

At the exact time Betty began suffocating in her hospital bed in Oregon, her daughter Annie Cap began choking at work in England. Despite being thousands of miles apart, Annie believes she was having an empathic death experience—physically feeling her mother's fatal symptoms—because her mother, Betty, was reaching across the heavens to say "goodbye." Shortly after this experience, Annie's intuitive and psychic abilities dramatically increased, leading to a renewal of faith in this former nonbeliever. Through this experience, Annie was transformed and felt called to share her experience with others.[7]

Penny Sartori, PhD, who worked as an ICU nurse for seventeen years, began researching near-death experiences because of her proximity to death in her work. In her PhD dissertation, she documented cases where people who were present at the bedside of their dying loved one suddenly found themselves participating in a transcendent experience of a partial journey into death. She also documented cases where miles away from their dying loved one, people have suddenly and inexplicably been overwhelmed with intense emotion, only to realize that this coincided with the loved one's death.[8]

My friend Jonathan was playing cards with his friends one Saturday night when suddenly, without knowing why, he looked up from his cards. His acquaintance, who became a close friend after that fateful evening, looked over at Jonathan, noticeably concerned. "You just turned pale—are you okay?" Jonathan felt overwhelmed by emotions he could not comprehend. Out of his mouth came the words, "My father just died!"

There was no reason for him to anticipate his father's death. As far as anyone knew, he was perfectly healthy. Jonathan and his father had just spent the entire day on Friday talking and coming to a place of understanding and peace that they had never had before. Yet on Saturday night, Jonathan's father had a fatal heart attack, and all the way on the other side of town, Jonathan knew. Could the conversation Jonathan had with his father the night before have created the peace and closure his father needed to leave this world?

These kinds of experiences are relatively common, so it's quite possible that you or someone you know has had one, too. While our culture may view them as unusual, they are actually a natural part of the continual exchange of information we all receive through our connection with one another. Individuals who choose to cultivate their intuition are likely to become more aware of this ongoing source of knowledge—not only about death, but all kinds of things.

Whenever this normal connection to the world around us is perceived as strange or anomalous, it is deprived of its organic relationship to the ordinary flow of life. Under those conditions people who are aware of this knowledge can be marginalized, demonized, or even burned at the stake. When animals and other creatures seem to be aware of it, they are seen as uncanny, supernatural, or possessed. These strange superstitions get in the way of a scientific understanding of how the world works.

In 2007, the *New England Journal of Medicine* profiled Oscar, the resident cat at Steere House Nursing and Rehabilitation Center in Providence, Rhode Island. When a patient is about to die, Oscar shows up at their door to spend time with the resident and pay his respects. Apparently, Oscar has a reputation for predicting a patient's death better than any physician or medical test.

Nobody knows how Oscar does it, though Dr. David Dosa speculated in his article that Oscar may be attracted to an unknown pheromone or scent. While Oscar offers much-needed comfort to the terminally ill residents who would have otherwise died alone, his presence at a bedside is such a reliable sign of impending death that, when he appears, family members are always notified to come. In this way, Oscar is believed to have predicted more than one hundred deaths of nursing home patients.[9]

The world according to Newtonian physics sees human beings as essentially isolated from the world and our minds as isolated from one another. In contrast, quantum physics has shown that people are inherently interconnected to and indivisible from their environment and one another. Telepathy is one of the many ways in which this interconnectedness manifests. It may be that certain people, like psychics and mediums, have an exceptional capacity for interconnectedness with others, dead and alive, and therefore are able to obtain information about others that most people would have no way of accessing.

COMMUNICATION WITH DEPARTED SOULS

Henry, one of my patients who was quite skeptical of the paranormal, surprised me when he decided to go to a medium, somebody who can "channel" information from people who have died, after both his mother and father died unexpectedly in short succession. Fortunately, while with the medium during the reading, he recorded the session. When he shared it with me, it blew both of us away.

Knowing absolutely nothing about my patient and with no cues from Henry, the medium immediately started "communicating with departed souls." He said a man who had recently passed away was calling my patient "Fonzie," the nickname Henry's father always used for him. ("Fonzie" is short for Arthur Fonzarelli, the cool, super-masculine, lady-charmer lead character played by Henry Winkler in the 1974–1984 American sitcom *Happy Days*.)

This intense experience melted my patient's skepticism and enabled him to receive some powerful, healing messages from his father who had passed on. The most powerful of these messages for my patient was that the place where his father had gone was peaceful and beautiful. There was nothing to fear. Interestingly, at the end of his first medium session, Henry's father told him to drink a glass of water with lemon every morning. Henry had no idea why but decided to comply. For the next week, he drank a glass of water with lemon every morning. A few months later, Henry went to the doctor with complaints of low back pain radiating to his groin. The diagnosis was kidney stones, a natural treatment for which is drinking water with lemon!

A few years ago, a psychiatrist colleague of mine e-mailed me asking if I could recommend a medium for Altan, a Mongolian male patient with whom he had been working for the past year. Apparently, Altan had been told on two separate occasions that his late father, Gan, was trying to contact him. Since Altan and Gan had a very turbulent relationship, Altan was not particularly jumping for joy at this news. Besides, Altan was not convinced that it was possible to contact the other side.

The first time Altan had been told about Gan's attempts to contact him was five years before, when one of his friends consulted a medium. While his friend talked to her own father through the medium, Altan's father jumped in with a message—he really needed to speak with his son, Altan! When Altan heard this, he rolled his eyes, paid it no heed, and moved on with his life.

Imagine his surprise when it happened again five years later. Another one of Altan's friends had consulted a different medium and had the same experience. Gan was obviously quite persistent. Only then did Altan confide in my colleague and the two of them together decided that Altan would consult a medium to see if this experience could help heal the pain and anger Altan still held in his heart toward her. I provided Altan's psychiatrist with the name of the medium my patient Henry had used, which ultimately led to an unexpectedly warm reunion between Gan and Altan and the long-awaited apology that Gan had never been able to give Altan while he was alive.

In my life and work, I have struggled to make sense of stories like this along-side my patients. What do such experiences tell us about what happens after we die? Perhaps more importantly, what can we learn from them about how to consummate our life and fulfill our potential while we are alive? These pressing questions can lead to a common complaint I hear among my patients—death anxiety. While we began to explore this concept in chapter 7, Transforming Your Fear, my patient Gaston's case presents a slightly different perspective of how death anxiety may show up in one's life.

DEATH ANXIETY

Gaston, a sixty-eight-year-old retired oil tycoon, came to see me at the urging of his family because for the last three years, every time he had an appointment with his estate attorney to create his will, he would get sick, find a reason to cancel or, as had happened last week, have a panic attack and end up in the emergency room. Planning what will happen to your estate after you die necessitates accepting that one day you will die. Gaston did not like this idea and did everything he could, consciously and unconsciously, to avoid it. To appease his wife and children after his latest panic attack, Gaston found my information online and made an appointment to see me.

Gaston was quite a character. When I asked him what he did for a living, he answered, "As little as possible!" When I asked about his family, he shrugged it off. "I have a European system with my marriage. I am one hundred percent loyal, just not always faithful." For most of the year, he lived at his villa in the

Swiss Alps with his wife, Francesca, to whom he had been married for thirty-eight years. Until just the week before, he had also been dating a thirty-five-year-old nurse named Sabine, but he had just ended the relationship.

Sabine had been Gaston's nurse when he suffered a mild heart attack six months earlier. She enjoyed working with him and loved his quirky sense of humor. As soon as Gaston had been strong enough to leave the hospital, they'd started a romantic relationship. Then, as always happened to Gaston, his mistress wanted more than he was able to give her, so he broke it off. It was a familiar situation for Gaston. But this time was different. He could not stop thinking about Sabine. While he originally came to see me about his panic attack and death anxiety, a more pressing reason for his visit was to mend his broken heart.

"She wanted me to meet her child!" he said, shaking his head sadly. "I knew I could not give her what she really wants because I do not want to end my marriage. So I had to end things and I am heartbroken. We had a real connection. I've only had one other connection like this in my life. We had a real chemistry."

When Gaston described Sabine, he lit up. She was outgoing, fearless, and fun. He liked everything about her.

When I asked Gaston about his wife, he said he also loved her very much, but their chemistry had ended twenty-five years ago. In that time, it felt to him as if she had gotten older while he had gotten younger. Although they were actually both the same age, Gaston felt like she was eighty-five (always preoccupied with health issues and filling her days with nonstop doctors' appointments) and he was thirty-five (trying his best to live life to the fullest, as evidenced by his young mistresses).

Once I got to know Gaston a little better, I asked him why he'd chosen me as his therapist. The answer to this question is always very interesting, but in the case of Gaston, I had a hunch. I was close to Sabine's age and wondered if perhaps Gaston had, consciously or unconsciously, chosen somebody like Sabine (close in age, at least) to temporarily replace her as his therapist as he healed his heart and worked through his emotions. In essence, I would be his transitional relationship. He was amused by my interpretation and, with a flirtatious smile, answered, "Perhaps…"

As Gaston and I began our work, he slowly transferred his former dependence on Sabine to a dependence on his therapy and me. He came twice per week and told me all about his family, children, life, travels, and everything in between. Whenever the topic of dating younger women came up, Gaston gave me his signature response: "Why not? They make me feel young again."

I explored with Gaston some of his feelings about getting older and his efforts to ward off death anxiety by dating younger women, starting triathlon training, and other such activities. Six months into our treatment, Gaston announced that he was feeling better and was ready to leave therapy. He felt his broken heart had healed and he had met another woman he really liked: Fabiola, a twenty-five-year-old waitress.

Gaston is not alone in his use of therapy as a transitional space between relationships, though he had no intention of using his therapy to face his fear of death. As long as he could interest younger women, he was perfectly happy with the illusion that their proximity made him young, too.

The most powerful way to deal with death anxiety is to engage in the old adage of living each day as if it were your last, without fear or regret. Although death itself will lead to the end of our physical life as we know it, the recognition that life is finite may be the very thing that opens us up to our aliveness. Ways of dealing with death anxiety include embracing our authenticity, living with purpose, fostering meaningful connections, and embracing our freedom by taking full responsibility for our life. None of these things will make you immortal, but they will enable you to live the life you have on earth most fully. As Irvin Yalom writes, "Though the physicality of death destroys us; the idea of death saves us."[10]

Exercise: What Are You Waiting For?

As in the prior chapter, set your stopwatch for five minutes and write in stream-of-consciousness fashion on the topic What Are You Waiting For? The Questions for Reflection are included as mere guideposts. As with life, let your writing take you where it may.

Questions for Reflection

1. If you found out you were going to die tomorrow, how would you live your last day of life?

2. If you found out you were going to die in a week, how would you live your last week of life?

3. If you found out you would die in a year, how would you live your last year of life?

4. Of all the things you would do in your last day, week, or year of life, which ones have you not yet done? What has held you back? What are you waiting for?

In the coming month, choose one of the things on your list above and do it.

THE LIMITS OF MEDICAL SCIENCE

Curiously enough, the field of medicine, which has been so devoted to the exploration of the deepest layers of the psyche, has recoiled from taking a closer look at our universal fear of death. Among therapists and thinkers in the field, death anxiety is rarely a part of the conversation. Either they deny that it exists or they deny its relevance. They sometimes claim that fear of death is actually the fear of something else, which we explored in chapter 7. Although this may indeed be true in some cases, in other cases it may be a suspicious attempt at deflection. Perhaps these medical professionals are themselves afraid of unearthing their own fears of death, facing their own perplexity and despair, or admitting their own reliance on ideology—religious or otherwise—for explanations, comfort, meaning, and a sense of peace.

Atul Gawande, MD, author of *Being Mortal: Medicine and What Matters in the End,* said that he learned a lot of things in medical school but mortality wasn't one of them. He was surprised to find that medical textbooks said almost nothing about the process of dying or aging. As a physician, he was curious about how people experienced the end of their lives and how it might affect their loved ones and others around them. Yet the medical school curriculum seemed to consider these matters to be beside the point. Clearly medical school was meant to teach aspiring doctors how to save lives—not how to tend to the dying. "People live longer and better than at any other time in history," Dr. Gawande said. "But scientific advances have turned the processes of aging and dying into medical experiences… and we in the medical world have proved alarmingly unprepared for it."[11]

My friend, colleague, and classmate at Stanford University and Yale Medical School Dr. Paul Kalanithi was diagnosed with terminal lung cancer while completing his neurosurgery residency in 2013. In March 2015, he passed away at the age of thirty-seven, leaving behind an artfully introspective legacy titled *When Breath Becomes Air.* In this rich masterpiece, Dr. Kalanithi echoes Dr. Gawande's earlier sentiments on the limitations of science in reconciling death, dying, and the soul:

> *Although I had been raised in a devout Christian family, where prayer and Scripture readings were a nightly ritual, I, like most scientific types, came to believe in the possibility of a material conception of reality, an ultimately scientific worldview that would grant a complete*

metaphysics, minus outmoded concepts like souls, God, and bearded white men in robes. I spent a good chunk of my twenties trying to build a frame for such an endeavor. The problem, however, eventually became evident: to make science the arbiter of metaphysics is to banish not only God from the world but also love, hate, meaning—to consider a world that is self-evidently not the world we live in... Science may provide the most useful way to organize empirical, reproducible data, but its power to do so is predicated on its inability to grasp the most central aspects of human life: hope, fear, love, hate, beauty, envy, honor, weakness, striving, suffering, virtue.

As a result, many doctors have looked elsewhere for answers, turning to the religion of their childhood or adopting new ones—anything that might promise certainty in the face of a fatal prognosis. Others have come across surprising alternatives without looking for them at all.

Dr. Brian Weiss, who graduated from Yale Medical School, started his career as a conventional psychiatrist but over the course of his work had a series of inexplicable experiences that shocked him and seemed to provide evidence of the transcendence of the soul and proof of immortality. Before medical school, Dr. Weiss graduated Phi Beta Kappa, magna cum laude, from Columbia University in New York City. By the time he completed his psychiatry residency at Yale, his mind was disciplined to think like a physician and scientist. He was suspicious of anything that could not be proven using scientific methods. While he was aware of studies in parapsychology, they didn't hold his attention. They seemed "too far-fetched."

Then he met a patient named Catherine who would radically alter his way of thinking. After working with Catherine for eighteen months in an effort to allay her numerous unremitting, paralyzing fears (of water, choking, dying, heights, the dark, you name it) to no avail, he turned to hypnosis. To his surprise, Catherine remembered her "past lives" while in a hypnotic trance. Following the process, Dr. Weiss went with the "memories" and found that working through them effectively eliminated her symptoms, something no conventional methods had been able to accomplish. For the first time in her life, Catherine was happy and at peace.[12]

Dr. Weiss's work with Catherine provided him with an unexpected glimpse into the spiritual side of our existence using past-life regression under hypnosis, giving some credence to the idea of past lives. While our physical bodies have a finite life span, our souls are eternal and keep returning to earth to undertake new journeys, learn new lessons, experience new things, play different roles, and accumulate new memories. Each journey is an "incarnation," and the cycle of returning and embodying again is a "reincarnation." Through his best-selling books, Dr. Weiss brought ideas of reincarnation into mainstream consciousness.

No science that Dr. Weiss knew of could explain the radical transformation he observed in his patient. There were no plausible scientific explanations for the power of these past-life memories and their apparent impact on Catherine. Dr. Weiss speculated that under hypnosis her mind may have been able to access actual past-life memories. Perhaps she tapped into the collective unconscious referred to by Carl Jung?

Jung's concept of the collective unconscious came from his recognition that our unconscious mind contains more than just our personal unconscious. Jung saw that even without direct cultural transmission, there are archetypes or themes that are expressed universally in dreams, the arts, and daily life. He believed that these archetypes were a part our greater human heritage that we inherit not via DNA transmission but by tapping into the collective unconscious, which contains knowledge, wisdom, information, and memories of the entire human race. While the collective unconscious influences all aspects of our lives, we cannot be fully conscious of it and so only know it indirectly, by looking at its influences.[13]

Science is meant to investigate things that can be measured. According to the Dalai Lama, the trouble is that the mind and the self cannot be measured. From a Buddhist point of view, the mind and consciousness are currently outside the realm of science. Since there have been so many sophisticated scientific experiments about the experiences of dying people, the Dalai Lama is hopeful that the study will expand and one day lead to new discoveries. For now, the only way for science to explain the yet inexplicable—in this case, past lives—is to say that it does not exist. In doing so, however, the following problem emerges:

> [I]f it is scientifically proved that certain things do not exist, then theoretically speaking, it has to be accepted. For example, if reincarnation is thoroughly investigated in a scientific way and it is proved 100 percent that it doesn't exist, theoretically speaking, Buddhists would have to accept that. But you must see the difference between merely not finding proof and having tangible proof that something doesn't exist.[14]

The Dalai Lama is highlighting the important scientific principle that absence of evidence does not constitute evidence of absence.

THE PRESENCE OF SPIRIT GUIDES

In addition to the idea of past lives, another notable exception to the belief system of Western medicine is the presence of spirit guides. The reality of guiding spirits has not yet been validated by Western medicine, but it is a noteworthy subject, since it would provide evidence that we are indeed "guided" by something greater than ourselves.

Psychologist Michael Newton, PhD, author of *Journey of Souls*, has used past-life regression extensively and believes in spirit guides. Human beings, he says, have always created anthropomorphic figures to portray the spiritual forces they sense all around them. In this way, the act of praying is an attempt to reach out to a caring, familiar entity for love and inspiration. Newton finds the idea of one supreme God to be too distant and impersonal, so spirit guides fill the gap, serving as intermediaries.[15] In some religious traditions, angels serve the role of spirit guides.

Elisabeth Kübler-Ross, whose landmark 1969 book, *On Death and Dying*, changed the way a generation of physicians and caregivers worked with the terminally ill, would agree. She devoted her working life to the end-of-life counseling that others before her had been reluctant, perhaps afraid, to take up. In the final years of her own life, she turned to a channeler of the spirit world, who led her into meetings with her spirit guides. As she describes in her 1997 book, *The Wheel of Life*, her first experience with a spirit guide was dramatic:

> *One day a woman in Virginia asked me into her house and wanted to know if I believed in fairies. I told her that I wasn't turned on to fairies but would like to know about my guides. I believed that there were such things as guides, but up to that time I had never seen any.*
>
> *She handed me a Polaroid camera and asked me to take a picture of any part of her garden. I thought this was a strange request, but I took the shot nevertheless. As the picture developed, imagine my surprise when I saw a fairy right in the middle of it!*
>
> *There it was, pretty as ever, looking at me. So that afternoon I thought to myself, if a camera can take pictures of fairies, then it certainly could take pictures of guides! So I took my husband's expensive camera, went up a small hill, looked into the woods, and said aloud, "If I have a guide, I'd like to see him or her materialize in a photograph."*
>
> *I pointed the camera at the trees, took two pictures, went home and forgot about the whole thing. Weeks later when the pictures were*

developed, there, on one of them, was the figure of a tall American Indian with a hand stretched out toward me. Needless to say I was thrilled! That was my first encounter with one of my guides.[16]

Exercise: Connecting to Your Spirit Guides via Automatic Writing

Many believe we all have spirit guides to help us complete our soul corrections and actualize our soul contribution potentials. These are entities that exist at a much higher spiritual level than us, who guide us and communicate with us in various ways, such as through synchronicities, gut feelings, intuitive insight, inspired thoughts, dreams, even sending certain people into our lives and arranging chance meetings when we most need them.

Since spirit guides work through various means—such as creating "signs" or synchronicities and facilitating intuitive inner knowing—there are many ways in which we can connect to our guides. Whether you are a skeptic doubtful of this process, an agnostic willing to be assured, or a believer refining your skills of connection, this exercise is designed to help connect you with your spirit guides.

One way in which you can connect to your spirit guides is through the process of automatic writing—asking your spirit guides a question in written form and being open to whatever they respond back to you in written form. This is the means through which best-selling author Neale Donald Walsch wrote his best-selling series Conversations with God. We will explore this exercise together here.

1. Open your journal to a new page.

2. Write down some questions you would like to ask your guides. These could be questions about any part of your life in which you would like

some guidance. Your spirit guides are loving and compassionate. They do not judge, so feel free to ask anything, no matter how troubling. Some sample questions include:

- What do I need to release?
- What is the source of this struggle?
- How can I achieve my dreams?
- What is the purpose of my life?
- Is this a healthy relationship for me?
- What positive changes can I make right now?
- Do you have any advice for me right now?

3. Now take several slow deep breaths as follows:
   - Inhale through your nose for the count of two.
   - Hold your breath for the count of four.
   - Exhale through your nose for the count of eight.
   - Repeat for five breaths.

4. Now go back to the questions you just wrote. Reach into the inner depths of your being and begin to write down your answers to these questions, as if the answers were coming from your spirit guides. Keep going as if you're having a conversation with them. In your writing, you may greet your guides and ask them their names. Although it may seem as if you're just writing answers from your imagination, your spirit guides can communicate with you through your imagination and your thoughts. At first it will feel weird, as if you're communicating with yourself or with an imaginary friend. But if you can suspend your judgment and freely allow yourself to converse with your guides, you may be startled by the information you receive. Be sure to be open to whatever answers come. You may or may not anticipate the answers, and you may or may not like and/

or agree with them. If in doubt, just keep going. When you feel like you have your answers, thank your guides for their support.

5. Take a look at your answers and then put your journal away for safe-keeping so that you can review what you wrote at a later time.

Connecting to your spirit guides is like tapping into the depth of your unconscious mind. Your guides are there to help you in any way they can and, more importantly, in any way you allow. The more open and allowing you can be, the more help you will receive. Over time you'll see that you are being guided in the right direction and you'll trust your guides—who communicate with you through your inner wisdom—even more.

LIFE AFTER DEATH

For Dr. Kübler-Ross, there was no question of life after death and no need to fear death whatsoever. She likened death to the shedding of our bodies like a butterfly sheds its cocoon. The profound difference is that death is, according to her book *Life Lessons*, "a transition to a higher state of consciousness where you continue to perceive, to understand, to laugh, and to be able to grow." If we were able to put aside our fears, we might be surprised to discover that death is very possibly one of the most wonderful experiences of our lives.[17] This involves making the perceptual shift similar to what was suggested by Pierre Teilhard de Chardin in the opening quote of this chapter. We need to go from seeing ourselves as human beings having an occasional spiritual experience to inherently spiritual beings having a temporary physical experience.

So many people wonder about such questions that Raymond Moody's book *Life After Life: The Investigation of a Phenomenon—Survival of Bodily Death* was a smash bestseller that has now sold more than thirteen million copies around the world. Moody published it after conducting a small study of one hundred people who had been medically revived after being clinically dead.

What he found was that, in general, when someone is dying, he hears a loud ringing or buzzing, then feels as if he is moving through a long, dark tunnel. Suddenly, he finds himself in the same room, but outside his own body. He sees himself from a distance. Maybe people are trying to resuscitate him or crying. He watches the scene as if he's a spectator.

Soon the spirits of dead relatives and friends appear. A warm being of light asks him, nonverbally, to evaluate his experience. He is shown an instant replay of his life. He is drawn to a mysterious border between this life and the next but finds that he cannot cross it. Sometimes it is not yet his time. Sometimes he has to go back to Earth. Usually he doesn't want to return, but if he does, he is "overwhelmed by intense feelings of joy, love, and peace."[18]

Beliefs about what happens after death appear in virtually every civilization throughout recorded history. There is some evidence that even in prehistoric times people may have been buried with a sense of the afterlife to come. Dr. Peter Fenwick, an internationally renowned neuropsychiatrist, developed a profound interest in end-of-life experiences when he received a letter from Pauline Drew describing the day before her mother died. Pauline's mother suddenly stared intently out the window and told her daughter, "Please don't ever be afraid of dying." She said she had seen a beautiful light and felt herself irresistibly drawn toward it. The appeal was so great and the effect so peaceful that she had to fight the urge to sink into it and never come back. The next morning, Pauline's mother died, but Pauline was forever changed by her words.[19]

Whether we can face death with equanimity and joy depends a great deal on how authentically we have lived. All throughout our lives, we get nudges and reminders about the direction that best suits our soul, the ways we can contribute to the world, the better course of action. A life well lived is one in which we have worked to complete our soul correction and actualize our soul contribution. If we fail to pay attention or ignore the guidance life gives us, we can easily end up in the wrong place, living according to someone else's values and feeling alienated from ourselves. Staying focused and living authentically will allow us to not only live a more fulfilled life, but also guarantee a good death.

As Kübler-Ross wrote, "It is not the end of the physical body that should worry us. Rather, our concern must be to live while we're alive—to release our inner selves from the spiritual death that comes with living behind a facade designed to conform to external definitions of who and what we are."[20]

DEATH AND TIME

Death is predicated on the concept of linear time. We are alive as physical, living and breathing bodies for a certain number of years, after which our bodies cease to function and we, as we know ourselves, cease to be. Everything in our life is measured in designated intervals of linear time, beginning with the nine months we are in utero from conception to birth. We scrupulously keep track of time, bemoan its passing, measure our accomplishments against it, and await the next milestone. We may ask ourselves, particularly in our waning years, if time is infinite, why do we have so little of it?

But what if time is not truly linear? What if it is actually possible to go forward or back in time? What then do we make of the concept of death?

Science writer and MIT professor Alan Lightman explores this question in his 1993 bestseller, *Einstein's Dreams*. In a series of vignettes assembled into a novel, Lightman illustrates thirty conceptions of nonlinear time, such as the following:

> *Suppose time is a circle, bending back on itself. The world repeats itself, precisely, endlessly. For the most part, people do not know that they will live their lives over. Traders do not know that they will*

make the same bargain again and again.... In the world in which time is a circle, every handshake, every kiss, every birth, every word, will be repeated precisely.[21]

Lending some credence to the idea that time does not function as we might think it does, Cornell social psychologist Dr. Daryl Bem conducted many experiments on this subject. When he gave two randomly selected groups of students a simple test, he asked one group not to study for the test at all and the other group to study only *after* taking the test. Surprisingly enough, the students who studied afterward did better than the group that had not studied at all! Studying for a test will surely increase your test score, but how can this be possible if you study *after* the test?

Scientists all over the world were encouraged to replicate his seemingly anomalous results. Bem's experiment has been carried out ninety times in thirty-three different laboratories in fourteen different countries. A meta-analysis of the data suggests that, indeed, his findings are for real.[22] Studying after a test improves your test score. Had I known this trick, I could have saved myself a lot of time in college and medical school!

So what is going on here?

Bem hypothesizes that these results represent the effects of *time slippage*, the ability to tap into your so-called future self to make use of what that future self might know.[23] This is a general form of *precognition*, when we know something before it actually happens. Bem's results turn the modern-day concept of cause and effect on its head and provide support for the phenomenon of *retrocausation*, where the effect (doing well on a test) occurs *before* the cause (studying for the test). Maybe time can move backward after all?

Appalled and fascinated by these results, the American Association for the Advancement of Science (AAAS) sponsored several conferences for physicists and researchers to figure out what is really going on here.[24] In the conference proceedings, published by the American Institute of Physics, it was written: "It seems untenable to assert that time-reverse causation (retrocausation) cannot occur, even though it temporarily runs counter to the macroscopic arrow of time."[25] Has the AAAS officially suggested that time can move backward? Why didn't anybody tell me earlier? There are a few things in my past I was hoping to alter just a bit...

Time slippage, retrocausation, precognition, and time moving backward are inherently incompatible with our everyday Newtonian conception of physical reality. Numerous researchers have suggested compelling metaphors with quantum theory to explain what is going on[26] as well as other theories that are more testable than simple metaphor.[27]

If nonlinear conceptions of time exist, what does this say about our ideas of death? Whatever the answer, death of the body is our destiny. We all want to survive, so we instinctively resist death. The most powerful way to overcome death anxiety is to live a life of fulfillment: living authentically, living with purpose, and perhaps most importantly, living in the present. After all, the past is gone and the future is not yet here. The present moment is all we have. It is all we have ever had. Yet often our minds get in the way of our embracing the present. We relive the past and plan for the future. These behaviors are healthy and normal. They are essential to living a fulfilled life. Yet the capacity to quiet the mind, embrace the silence and be present with our experience is one of the most important tenets of cultivating true fulfillment.

Journalist Lynne McTaggart, who was skeptical of all things quantum before she researched and wrote her award-winning book *The Field*, points out that there is no such thing as time in the quantum world of the infinite field of consciousness of which we are all a part. It is a realm of pure potential, existing in "one enormous present." Time and space are tools used by our consciousness and filtered through our brains to enable us—inherently infinite beings—to exist in the finite here and now. According to McTaggart's extensive research, both time and space are imaginary! This implies that every place and event exists in a vast "here and now."[28]

The very act of being present and embracing the here and now can be our reservoir of calm in any flurry of chaos and commotion. If you are completely present, your worries recede and you are able to honestly and spontaneously experience "what is" in its totality. Jewish theologian Martin Buber makes this point in saying, "In spite of all similarities, every living situation has, like a newborn child, a new face, that has never been before and will never come again. It demands of you a reaction that cannot be prepared beforehand. It demands nothing of what is past. It demands presence, responsibility; it demands you."

Exercise: The Point of Power Is in the Present Moment

While the method for being present is fairly simple, it's the practice that matters most. Most people don't learn to be present because they don't practice, not because it's too hard to do. The way to be present with whatever you're doing is to learn to focus completely on doing that one thing. Choose one thing today with which you would like to be wholly and completely present—it could be absolutely anything in your day. Now begin the following steps:

1. As you begin to do this activity, pay attention to every aspect of it.

2. Take a moment to consciously collect all the information about your experience through your five senses: touch, sight, hearing, smell, even taste.
   - How does this experience feel?
   - What does it look like?
   - How does it smell? Sound? Taste?

- What emotions come up as you do it?
- What is going on in your body as you undertake this experience?

3. Now become aware of what thoughts enter your mind. As you become aware of your thoughts, you'll notice them jump to other things.

4. Use your awareness to gently bring yourself back to your present task. Keep gently returning your awareness back to the present moment, time and again. It can become tiring at first if you're not used to it, in which case certainly take as many breaks as you need and return once you feel ready.

I invite you to practice this exercise at least three times per day in the coming week. Over time you'll notice the worries and distractions in your life melt away as you begin to enjoy the present moment much more. Be joyful in whatever you're doing, grateful that you're able to do that specific task, and fully appreciative of every little movement and tactile sensation of the task. In this way, you become much more mindful in your daily life.

For this exercise, little presence reminders are useful to help you come back to the present. You can find presence reminders everywhere: your child's voice, your colleague appearing before you, a regular event on your computer, the noise of traffic. Practice, repeatedly, in small, easy, beautiful steps. Each step is a wonder in itself, and each practice helps you to find that calm in the middle of the traffic of your life.

By living in a constant state of presence, we begin to appreciate the miraculous in the mundane. As Albert Einstein once said, "There are only two ways to live your life. One is as though nothing is a miracle. The other is as though everything is a miracle."

Conclusion

WHERE TO FROM HERE?

And the end of all our exploring
Will be to arrive where we started
And know the place for the first time.

—T. S. ELIOT

On a global scale, fulfillment begins when we realize our collective unity. Since quantum physics has shown that we are all interconnected as matter and energy, there is no arbitrary distinction from an energetic standpoint between you and me. There is only the delusion of separateness that Albert Einstein referred to as the "optical delusion of consciousness." This delusion alone is powerful enough to eradicate civilization as we know it because when we harm others, we do not realize that we are actually harming ourselves.

For this reason, the fate of our species depends on shifting our consciousness, individually and collectively. This shift entails taking responsibility not just for ourselves and our own actions, but for others and for the world. Spiritual teacher Jiddu Krishnamurti made this point in saying, "The heart of man is in his own keeping. To end violence, we must relentlessly keep freeing ourselves of the violence within. Inner strife projected externally becomes world chaos." Jewish theologian Martin Buber elaborated on this idea in saying, "Everything depends on inner change; when this has taken place, then, and only then does the world change." To end the world's darkness, we must consistently unearth and transform the darkness within, which is at the heart of every soul correction.

As discussed in this book, three implicit core beliefs may give rise to darkness within:

I am unaware of my soul.

I give away my power.

I am disconnected and alone.

At the root of these three implicit core beliefs are lack of authenticity, addictions, incapacitating fears, toxic relationships, lack of meaning and purpose, and the many negative extensions of the ego: hatred, jealousy, anger, pride, control, et cetera. Recognizing that the path to fulfillment is not outside of us, we must do the inner work of connecting to our soul, cultivating authenticity, completing our soul corrections, and fulfilling our soul contribution potential. As Mahatma Gandhi pointed out, "You must become the change you wish to see in the world."

By elevating our own consciousness, we elevate the global collective consciousness of humankind and shift our implicit core beliefs to:

I am deeply connected to my soul.

I take my power back and create the life I want to live.

I am interconnected with everybody and everything.

Making this shift involves transforming fear to love and living in alignment with love—the divine essence of our soul—every day of our lives. Love is the most potent form of light in this world. Turning on the light is the only way to remove darkness from ourselves and from the world. In this way, a life lived in alignment with love, caring, and compassion for the self and others is a necessary prerequisite for fulfillment.

The quest to become whole is as old as humankind. My hope is that this book has helped you to move at least one step closer to wholeness and fulfill-ment in your own journey. Before a caterpillar becomes a butterfly, it must undergo the daunting transformation of allowing its earthbound form to trans-form. If it resists the process, it simply dies.

Most people's transformation experience of releasing their limited earth-bound forms begins with a dark night of the soul. In the depths of despair, we begin searching for ways to see the world anew and pull ourselves out from our darkness. At first we seek solace in the things we know: theories, people, and experiences. If these are ineffective, we eventually find our way inside ourselves. We begin to connect to our soul and listen for what we really need. In an act of creativity and healing, our darkness becomes the very impetus through which our pains of loneliness and longing are eased. When our exile from ourselves is over, we've come home at last.

Along this path, there is guidance every step of the way if we are open to it. It speaks to us in myriad ways, from synchronicity and intuition to telepathy, dreams, and premonitions. The barrier between the conscious and the uncon-scious, the sacred and the mundane, is more permeable than we think. There is an incredible power that comes with penetrating the layers of reality that reveal the interconnectedness of all things.

We do not need to be religious or even spiritual to receive spiritual guidance, only open-minded and humble. The Bible says, "Open for Me an opening the size of the eye of a needle and I will open for you the Eternal Gates."[1] In other words, if you are open, even a tiny bit, to being guided and shown miracles in your life, they will be shown to you. You must only request this with a pure heart, an open mind, and a deliberate intent of the outcome being "for the greatest good of all involved."

Kabbalah describes the journey of wholeness and fulfillment as the elevation and redemption of lost sparks of your soul.[2] Sparks of your soul are scattered all over the world for you to reclaim by connecting with certain people, having certain experiences, and gleaning the wisdom your soul needs to learn along the way. With each experience, you chisel away at your own sacred block of precious marble, slowly revealing the angles, curves, and crevices of the magnificent being deep within. The radiance of the rock is enhanced day after day by your persistence, courage, devotion, and willingness to take risks and work through whatever challenges cross your path.

If you are committed to this journey, it is by nature asymptotic—you can get closer and closer but never truly arrive. Arriving is not the goal here. It never has been. Because if you arrived, there would be no more to discover. And you would have revealed to yourself and the world all that remains when the music is gone, when the ticking clock of daily life pauses once again for breath between seconds. And now, as the present becomes the past and these ideas gain immortality, I type these last words, step outside, and begin to walk toward the rising sun.

Acknowledgments

If I have seen further, it is by standing on the shoulders of giants.

—Isaac Newton

Writing a book is like giving birth to a child. I am infinitely grateful to the many beautiful souls who have helped me to usher my baby into the world.

I am most indebted to the patients who have kindly agreed to have an adaptation of their stories used in this book in the service of helping others going through similar struggles. Thank you for sharing your hearts and souls with me and allowing me to help you. It is an honor for which I am grateful every day of my life.

To my dad and Raya, my first readers of each chapter hot off the press. Thank you for your consistent enthusiasm, thoughtful and honest criticism, and unconditional love. You guys were my initial barometers of how the outside world would react to these ideas. To my mom and Charles for believing in me and for your consistent encouragement, love, and support.

To Cassie Hanjian, my wonderful literary agent, and her associates at Waxman Leavell Literary Agency. Thank you for believing in this book, always being so wonderfully on top of everything, being patient with me through the challenges, and ultimately helping this book see the light of day. To Sarah Pelz, my treasured editor, and her associates at Hachette Book Group's Grand Central Life & Style imprint. I am most grateful for your generosity of spirit, brilliant vision, and refined skill in masterfully shepherding this book from its genesis. A special thanks to Sheila Curry Oakes for supporting this project after Sarah's perfectly timed baby made her beautiful way into the world. Thank you also to Katherine Stopa, Karen Murgolo, Elisa Rivlin, Jeff Holt, Nick Small, and Amanda Pritzker for your guidance and expertise. And to Eric Rayman for your brilliant legal advice.

To my dear friend and writing partner, Masum Momaya, PhD, whose rich insight, huge heart, and brilliant mind helped shape many of the pages in this book. To my invincible assistant, Anuta Rathe, truly a Godsend without whom life as I know it would be virtually impossible. Thank you for rereading many versions of this book and masterfully serving as the "general manager" of my life for the past ten years. I don't know what I would do without you! Many thanks to Donna Beech for her invaluable assistance in preparing the manuscript and assisting with research for this book. Your time, guidance, and wisdom were greatly appreciated, and I couldn't have accomplished getting this into print without your generous support. To Pedro Ruiz, MD, and Thomas Stewart, MD, for being wonderful mentors and role models to me in the field of psychiatry. Thank you for believing in me and supporting this unconventional project. To Eben Alexander, MD, for supporting this book since its inception and, through your vital work, making this world a better place.

My deep gratitude to Ragy Girgis, MD, for miraculously showing up in my life at just the right moment and helping to strengthen the science in this book. To Rabbi Jonathan Feldman, PhD, for his consistent support and friendship and for helping me with this book's Torah references. To Gibbs Williams, PhD, for his encyclopedic knowledge of Freud and Jung, and his kindness in sharing this wisdom with me. To Marva Allen, in whose writing workshop at the Academi of Life the seed of this book was planted. Your support was invaluable to this work's inception, and I am

Acknowledgments

most grateful for your continued kindness and encouragement. To Eric Maisel, in whose writing workshop at Kripalu the seed of this book flourished into a proposal. Thank you for showing me "how"! To my dear friends Jacqueline Cohen and Josh Pickard for allowing me to use The Shack as my writing haven. To Malcolm Thomson and David Kekst, who were invaluable in helping my book find a home.

To numerous friends and family members who have read, reread, and thoughtfully edited many parts of this book as it was being born: Larell Atkins, Karen Bishko, Daniel Bober, MD, Sharon Bridbord, Carrie Capstick, PhD, Jacqueline Cohen, Kathy Falk, MD, Rabbi Jonathan Feldman, PhD, Judy Fletcher, Howie Friedman, PhD, Jessica Kattan, MD, Sheryl Kurland, Anatoly Libgober, PhD, Jonathan Libgober, PhD, Ayonija Maheshwari, MD, David Moyer, Dave O'Keefe, John Allen Paulos, PhD, Roger Price, Diane Redleaf, Carlos Saavedra, MD, Sheila Salama, MD, Gino Scapillati, Sasha Siem, Jocelyn Soffer, MD, Renee Tordjeman, and Jackie Vayntrub, PhD. To my dear friend Ron Shefi, a gifted and intuitive healer, for his unique perspective, wisdom, and support. He sadly passed away while this book was being written. To other friends who provided invaluable support in ways I could not even have imagined: Dr. Bacer Baker, Yana Golbin, Ondine Harris, Maxim Jago, Aiyah Maraka, John Napolitano, Peggy Rometo, Tara Sheehan, and Linda Swain.

I also wish to thank certain people for helping me not only to write this book, but also to become the person who is capable of writing this book. A sincere thanks to the mentors and guides, some of whom shall remain unnamed, who have helped me to ascend the spiritual ladder to a point where I can finally spread my wings and fly: Rav and Karen Berg, Patty Casby, Sara Choi, Alice Colonna, David Ghiyam, Henry Grayson, Robert Salvit, Maureen St. Germain, and Sarah Yardeni.

And, finally, I offer my heart's gratitude to my husband, Jesse, for being my rock and inspiration, believing in me, and helping me to find fulfillment.

Notes

Introduction

1. Eric R. Maisel, PhD, "Rethinking Mental Health," *Psychology Today*, February 15, 2016, https://www.psychologytoday.com/blog/rethinking-mental-health/201602/anna-yusim-humanistic-psychiatry.

2. Luke 4:23, New Testament, New International Version Bible.

3. In *Obsessive Actions and Religious Practices* (1907), his earliest writing about religion, Freud suggests that religion and neurosis are similar products of the human mind: neurosis, with its compulsive behavior, is "an individual religiosity," and religion, with its repetitive rituals, is a "universal obsessional neurosis, from: Peter Gay, ed., *The Freud Reader* (New York: W. W. Norton & Co. 1995), 435.

4. Sigmund Freud, *Civilization and Its Discontents* (London: Hogarth Press, 1946), 7–22.

5. Clare Dunne, *Carl Jung: Wounded Healer of the Soul: An Illustrated Biography* (New York: Continuum International Publishing Group, 2002), Prelude.

6. This quote was written in the paper "Science, Philosophy and Religion" that Einstein prepared for initial meeting of the Conference on Science, Philosophy and Religion in Their Relation to the Democratic Way of Life, at the Jewish Theological Seminary of America, New York City (Sept. 9–11, 1940).

7. Christopher Cook, "Addiction and Spirituality," *Addiction* 99, no. 5 (May 2004): 539–51.

8. Interview with Dr. Gibbs Williams for film *An Open Mind* on May 6, 2016, in New York City.

9. Gallup, *2014 Gallup Poll on Religion*, accessed on February 2, 2017, http://www.gallup.com/poll/1690/religion.aspx.

10. Human Friedrich Unterrainer, A. J. Lewis, and A. Fink, "Religious/Spiritual Well-Being, Personality and Mental Health: A Review of Results and Conceptual Issues," *Journal of Religion and Health* 53, no. 2 (April 2014): 382–92, doi: 10.1007/s10943-012-9642-5.

11. Kimberly K. Laubmeier, S. G. Zakowski, and J. P. Bair, "The Role of Spirituality in the Psychological Adjustment to Cancer: A Test of the Transactional Model of Stress and Coping," *International Journal of Behavioral Medicine* 11, no. 1 (2004): 48–55.

12. Craig S. Hassed, "Depression: Dispirited or Spiritually Deprived?" *Medical Journal of Australia* 173, no. 10 (December 2000): 545–47. PMID: 11194740.

13. Tim Read, Nicki Crowley, and Christopher Cook, "The Transpersonal Perspective," in *Spirituality and Psychiatry*, eds. A. Sims, C. Cook, A. Powell (Glasgow: Bell & Bain Limited, 2010), 212–232.

14. Esme Fuller-Thomson, S. Agbeyaka, D. M. LaFond, and M. Bern-Klug, "Flourishing After Depression: Factors Associated with Achieving Complete Mental Health among Those with a History of Depression," *Psychiatry Research* 242, no. 11 (April 2016): 111–120, doi: 10.1016/j.psychres.2016.04.041.

15. Katie Witkiewitz, E. McCallion, and M. Kirouac, "Religious Affiliation and Spiritual Practices: An Examination of the Role of Spirituality in Alcohol Use and Alcohol Use Disorder," *Alcohol Research* 38, no. 1 (2016): 55–8.

16. Helen Matzger, L. A. Kaskutas, and C. Weisner, "Reasons for Drinking Less and Their Relationship to Sustained Remission from Problem Drinking, *Addiction* 100, no. 11 (November 2005): 1637–46.

17. Murali S. Rao, "Spirituality in Psychiatry?" *Psychiatry* (Edgmont) 2, no. 9 (2005): 20–22, PMID: 21120102.

18. D. E. King and B. Bushwick, "Beliefs and Attitudes of Hospital Inpatients about Faith Healing and Prayer," *Journal of Family Practice* 39, no. 4 (1994): 349–52.

19. Alan B. Astrow, A. Wexler, K. Texeira, et al.: "Is Failure to Meet Spiritual Needs Associated with Cancer Patients' Perceptions of Quality of Care and their Satisfaction with Care?" *Journal of Clinical Oncology* 25, no. 36 (2007): 5753–7.

20. Harold G. Koenig, Michael E. McCullough, David B. Larson, *Handbook of Religion and Health* (Oxford: Oxford University Press, 2001), 97–117.

21. Kenneth S. Kendler, X. Q. Liu, C. O. Gardner, et al., "Dimensions of Religiosity and Their Relationship to Lifetime Psychiatric and Substance Use Disorders," *American Journal of Psychiatry* 160, no. 3 (2003): 496–503.

22. Pehr Granqvist et al., "Attachment and Religious Representations and Behavior" in *Handbook of Attachment: Theory, Research, and Clinical Applications: 2nd Edition* (New York: Guilford Press, 2008), 906–33.

23. Mary D. Ainsworth, "Attachments across the Life Span," *Bulletin of the New York Academy of Medicine* 61, no. 9 (November 1985): 792–812.

24. Harold G. Koenig, "Research on Religion, Spirituality, and Mental Health: A Review. *Canadian Journal of Psychiatry* 54, no. 5 (2009): 283.

25. Albert Einstein, "Letter from Albert Einstein to Distraught Father Who Lost His Young Son and Had Asked Einstein for Some Comforting Words" in *The New Quotable Einstein,* ed. Alice Calaprice (Princeton: Princeton University Press, 2005), 206.

26. Eric R. Maisel, PhD, "Rethinking Mental Health," *Psychology Today,* February 15, 2016, https://www.psychologytoday.com/blog/rethinking-mental-health/201602/anna-yusim-humanistic-psychiatry.

Chapter 1

1. Donald W. Winnicott, "Ego Distortion in Terms of True and False Self," in *The Maturational Process and the Facilitating Environment: Studies in the Theory of Emotional Development* (New York: International UP Inc., 1965), 140–152.

2. Søren Kierkegaard, *The Sickness Unto Death* (Princeton, NJ: Princeton University Press, 1941), 18.

3. Tian Dayton, "Creating a False Self: Learning to Live a Lie," *HuffPost Healthy Living* (November 17, 2011), http://www.huffingtonpost.com/dr-tian-dayton/creating-a-false -self-lea_b_269096.html.

4. Rainer Maria Rilke, *Rilke's Book of Hours: Love Poems to God*, 8th ed., trans. Anita Barrows, Joanna Macy (New York: Riverhead Books, 1997), 11.

5. Martin Heidegger, *Being and Time*, trans. J. Macquarrie, E. Robinson (New York: Harper & Row, 1962), 41–49, 244–252, 293–311.

6. Alice Miller, *The Drama of the Gifted Child* (New York: Basic Books, 2008), 21, 45.

7. Irvin Yalom, *Love's Executioner* (New York: HarperCollins, 1989), 17.

8. Lucy L. Brown, B. Acevedo, and H. E. Fisher, "Neural Correlates of Four Broad Temperament Dimensions: Testing Predictions for a Novel Construct of Personality," *PLoS One* 11, no. 8 (November 13, 2013): e78734, doi: 10.1371/journal.pone.0078734. eCollection 2013.

9. Thomas R. Insel, "The Challenge of Translation in Social Neuroscience: A Review of Oxytocin, Vasopressin, and Affiliative Behavior," *Neuron* 6, no. 65 (March 25, 2010): 768–79, doi: 10.1016/j.neuron.2010.03.005.

10. Helen Fisher, Arthur Aron, and Lucy L. Brown. "Romantic Love: A Mammalian Brain System for Mate Choice," *Philosophical Transactions of the Royal Society B: Biological Sciences* 1476, no. 361(2006): 2173–186, doi:10.1098/rstb.2006.1938.

11. Anderson, W. T. (ed.) (1996). *The Fontana Postmodernism Reader* (London: Fontana), 132–40.

12. Hazel Markus and P. Nurius, "Possible Selves," *American Psychologist* 41, no. 9 (Sept. 1986): 954–96.

13. Sy Atezaz Saeed, D. J. Antonacci, and R. M. Bloch, "Exercise, Yoga, and Meditation for Depressive and Anxiety Disorders," *American Family Physician* 81, no. 8 (April 15, 2010): 981–6.

14. Alexandra Zgierska, D. Rabago, N. Chawla, K. Kushner, R. Koehler, and A. Marlatt, "Mindfulness Meditation for Substance Use Disorders: A Systematic Review," *Substance Abuse* 30, no. 4 (Oct.–Dec. 2009): 266–94, doi: 10.1080/08897070903250019.

15. Fadel Zeidan, J. A. Grant, C. A. Brown, J. G. McHaffie, and R. C. Coghill, "Mindfulness Meditation-Related Pain Relief: Evidence for Unique Brain Mechanisms in the Regulation of Pain," *Neuroscience Letters* 520, no. 2 (June 29, 2012):165–73, doi: 10.1016/j.neulet.2012.03.082. Epub 2012 Apr 6.

16. Indranill Basu Ray, A. R. Menezes, P. Malur, A. E. Hiltbold, J. P. Reilly, and C. J. Lavie, "Meditation and Coronary Heart Disease: A Review of the Current Clinical Evidence," *Ochsner* 14, no. 4 (winter 2014): 696–703.

17. Adam B. Levin, E. J. Hadgkiss, T. J. Weiland, G. A. Jelinek, "Meditation As an Adjunct to the Management of Multiple Sclerosis," *Neurology Research International* 2014, 704691 (July 1, 2014), doi: 10.1155/2014/704691.

18. Dharma S. Khalsa, "Stress, Meditation, and Alzheimer's Disease Prevention: Where the Evidence Stands," *Journal of Alzheimer's Disease* 48, no. 1 (2015):1–12, doi: 10.3233/JAD-142766.

19. Mircea Eliade, *Shamanism, Archaic Techniques of Ecstasy*, Bollingen Series LXXVI (Princeton, NJ: Princeton University Press, 1972), 3–7.

20. Interview with Shaman Fernando Broca in New York City for film *An Open Mind*, October 6, 2016, New York City.

Chapter 2

1. A History of the Brain. Stanford Early Science Lab. History of the Body. https://web.stanford.edu/class/history13/earlysciencelab/body/brainpages/brain.html.

2. G. J. C. Lokhorst and Timo T. Kaitaro, "The Originality of Descartes's Theory about the Pineal Gland," *Journal of the History of the Neurosciences* 10, no. 1, (2001): 6–18. ISSN 0964-704X.

3. Lennart Heimer, Gary Van Hoesen, Michael Trimble, Daniel Zahm, "The Triune Brain Concept and the Controversy Surrounding It," in *Anatomy of Neuropsychology: The New Anatomy of the Basal Forebrain and its Implications for Neuropsychiatric Illness* (Amsterdam; Boston: Academic Press-Elsevier, 2008), 15–16, 19.

4. Daniel Kahneman, *Thinking, Fast and Slow* (New York: Farrar, Straus and Giroux, 2011), 19–31.

5. Lissa Rankin, MD, *The Fear Cure* (Carlsbad, CA: Hay House, 2015), Kindle Location 371.

6. Donna Jackson Nakazawa, "15 Ways to Get Someone Out of Your Head," *Psychology Today*, May 26, 2014. https://www.psychologytoday.com/blog/the-last-best -cure/201405/15-ways-get-someone-out-your-head.

7. Larry R. Squire, F. E. Bloom, S. K. McConnell, J. L. Roberts, N. C. Spitzer, and M. J. Zigmond, eds., "Long-Term Potentiation," *Fundamental Neuroscience*, Second Edition (New York: Academic Press, 2003), 1277–91.

8. Erica R. Glasper, T. J. Schoenfeld, and E. Gould, "Adult Neurogenesis: Optimizing Hippocampal Function to Suit the Environment," *Behavioural Brain Research* 227, no. 3 (February 14, 2012): 380–3, doi: 10.1016/j.bbr.2011.05.013. Epub 2011 May 23. http://www.ncbi.nlm.nih.gov/pubmed/21624398.

9. Allan A. Abbass, S. J. Nowoweiski, D. Bernier, R. Tarzwell, and M. E. Beutel, "Review of Psychodynamic Psychotherapy Neuroimaging Studies," *Psychotherapy and Psychosomatics* 83, no. 3 (April 12, 2014): 142–7, doi: 10.1159/000358841. Epub 2014 Apr 12.

10. Benedetta Leuner, J. M. Caponiti, and E. Gould, "Oxytocin Stimulates Adult Neurogenesis Even Under Conditions of Stress and Elevated Glucocorticoids," *Hippocampus* 22, no. 4 (April 2012): 861–8, doi: 10.1002/hipo.20947. Epub 2011 Jun 20. http://www .ncbi.nlm.nih.gov/pubmed/21692136.

11. Pasquale G. Frisina. J. C. Borod, S. J. Lepore, "A Meta-Analysis of the Effects of Written Emotional Disclosure on the Health Outcomes of Clinical Populations," *Journal of Nervous and Mental Disease* 192, no. 9 (September 2004): 629–34.

12. Jon Kabat-Zinn, PhD, "An Outpatient Program in Behavioral Medicine for Chronic Pain Patients Based on the Practice of Mindfulness Meditation: Theoretical Considerations and Preliminary Results," *General Hospital Psychiatry* 4, no. 1 (April 1982): 33–47, http://www.sciencedirect.com/science/article/pii/0163834382900263?np=y.

13. Bruno Bettelheim, *Freud and Man's Soul: An Important Re-Interpretation of Freudian Theory* (New York: Vintage, 1983), 70.

14. Maria Popova, "How Our Minds Mislead Us: The Marvels and Flaws of Our Intuition," *Brain Pickings*, accessed December 1, 2016, https://www.brainpickings.org/2013/10/30/daniel-kahneman-intuition/.

15. Anne Lamott, "Anne Lamott Shares All that She Knows: 'Everyone Is Screwed Up, Broken, Clingy, and Scared,'" *Salon* (Apr 10, 2015), http://www.salon.com/2015/04/10/anne_lamott_shares_all_that_she_knows_everyone_is_screwed_up_broken_clingy_and_scared/.

16. Baháʼuʼlláh, *Gleanings from the Writings of Baháʼuʼlláh*, (Wilmette, Illinois: Baháʼí Publishing Trust), 158–63.

17. Paramahansa Yogananda, *God Talks with Arjuna: The Bhagavad Gita* (Los Angeles: Self-Realization Fellowship, 2001), 225–227.

Chapter 3

1. Anna Freud, *The Ego and the Mechanisms of Defense* (London: Hogarth Press and Institute of Psycho-Analysis, 1937), 54.

2. Carl Jung, "Psychology and Religion," in *CW 11: Psychology and Religion: West and East* (Princeton, NJ: Princeton University Press, 1938), 140.

3. Carl Jung, "The Philosophical Tree," in *CW 13: Alchemical Studies* (Princeton, NJ: Princeton University Press, 938), 335.

4. Carl Jung, "Good and Evil in Analytical Psychology," in *CW 10. Civilization in Transition.* (Princeton, NJ: Princeton University Press, 1959), 872.

Chapter 4

1. Living Wisdom from the Kabbalah Centre: "Kabbalistic Concepts: Making the Correction" (December 9, 2013), https://livingwisdom.kabbalah.com/making-correction.

2. Michael Toms, *An Open Life: Joseph Campbell* (Harper Collins, 1990), 26.

3. Karen Berg, *Finding the Light Through the Darkness* (New York: Kabbalah Centre Publishing, 2016), 3.

4. Kabbalah University, "Living Kabbalah System Level 1, Lesson 12," accessed April 13, 2017, https://university.kabbalah.com/living-kabbalah-system-level-1/112-tools-proactivity.

5. William Shakespeare, *Hamlet* (England: Cambridge University Press, 2003), 1.3,78.

6. Katherine Woodward Thomas, *Calling in "the One": 7 Weeks to Attract the Love of Your Life* (New York: Harmony Books, 2004), 163–64.

7. Henry David Thoreau, *Walden, or, Life in the Woods* (Philadelphia: Henry Altemus Company, 1899), 10.

8. Herman Hesse, *Demian*, trans. Stanley Appelbaum (New York: Dover Publications, 2000), 83.

9. Robert Jaworski, *Synchronicity: The Inner Path of Leadership* (San Francisco: Berrett-Koehler Publishers, 2011), 119.

10. Thomas Moore, *Soul Mates: Honoring the Mysteries of Love and Relationship* (New York: HarperCollins, 1994), xvii.

11. Joan Z. Borysenko, PhD, *Inner Peace for Busy People* (Sydney: ReadHowYouWant, 2009), 346.

Chapter 5

1. Maxwell Maltz, *Psycho-Cybernetics* (New York: Tarcher-Perigee, 2015), 3.

2. Harville Hendrix, PhD, *Getting the Love You Want, 20th Anniversary Edition: A Guide for Couples.* (New York: Macmillan, 2007), 38.

3. Louise Hay, *Mirror Work: 21 Days to Heal Your Life* (Carlsbad, CA: Hay House, 2016), 48–49.

4. Sharon Salzberg, Jon Kabat-Zinn, *Lovingkindness: The Revolutionary Art of Happiness*, (Boulder: Shambhala, 2002), 25.

5. Jack Kornfield, *The Wise Heart: A Guide to the Universe Teachings of Buddhist Psychology*, (New York: Bantam Books, 2008), 350.

Chapter 6

1. Poem: "There Is a Candle in Your Heart," from *Hush Don't Say Anything to God: Passionate Poems of Rumi*, translated by Sharam Shiva (Jain Pub Co., October 1, 1999).

2. Letter from Dr. Carl Jung to Bill Wilson: Kusnacht-Zurich, Seestrasse 228, January 30, 1961, accessed August 9, 2016, http://www.soberrecovery.com/recovery/the-famous-letter-from-carl-jung-to-bill-wilson-founder-of-alcoholics-anonymous/.

3. N. M. Avena, P. Rada, and B. G. Hoebel, "Evidence for Sugar Addiction: Behavioral and Neurochemical Effects of Intermittent, Excessive Sugar Intake," *Neuroscience & Biobehavioral Reviews* 32, no. 1 (2008): 20–39, e-pub 2007 May 18.

4. N. M. Hetherington and J. I. MacDiarmid, "'Chocolate addiction': A Preliminary Study of its Description and its Relationship to Problem Eating," *Appetite* 21, no. 3 (December1993): 233–46.

5. Nora D. Volkow, G. G. Koob, and A. T. McLellan, "Neurobiologic Advances from the Brain Disease Model of Addiction," *New England Journal of Medicine* 374, no. 4 (January 28, 2016): 363–71, doi: 10.1056/NEJMra1511480.

6. Rose A. Rudd, et. al., "Increases in Drug and Opioid-Involved Overdose Deaths—United States, 2010–2015," *Morbidity and Mortality Weekly Report* 65, no. 50–51 (December 30, 2016): 1445–1452.

7. Rosemary Brown with Laura MacKay, "Addiction Is the Symptom, Not the Problem," *The Fix*, Mar 20, 2016, https://www.thefix.com/addiction-symptom-not-problem.

8. This exercise is adapted from the Heart Lock-In technique of HeartMath. See Doc Childre, Howard Martin, and Donna Beech, *The HeartMath Solution: The Institute of HeartMath's Revolutionary Program for Engaging the Power of the Heart's Intelligence* (New York: HarperCollins, 2011), 213–14.

9. J. F. Kelly and M. C. Greene, "The Twelve Promises of Alcoholics Anonymous: Psychometric Measure Validation and Mediational Testing as a 12-Step Specific Mechanism of Behavior Change," *Drug and Alcohol Dependence* 133, no. 2 (December 1, 2013): 633–40, doi: 10.1016/j.drugalcdep.2013.08.006.

Chapter 7

1. Sigmund Freud, "Thoughts for the Times on War and Death," in *The Standard Edition of the Complete Psychological Works of Sigmund Freud, Vol. 4* (London: Hogarth Press, 1953), 304–305.

2. Marianne Williamson, *A Return to Love: Reflections on the Principles of a Course in Miracles* (New York: HarperCollins, 1992), 190.

3. Marianne Williamson, *Tears to Triumph: The Spiritual Journey from Suffering to Enlightenment* (New York: Harper Collins, 2016), 1–19.

4. Robert M. Sapolsky, *Why Zebras Don't Get Ulcers*, Third Edition (New York: Holt, 2004), 21.

5. Ibid., 4–18.

6. Ibid., 215–25.

7. Karl Albrecht, PhD, "The (Only) 5 Fears We All Share," (March 22, 2012), Brainsnacks blog, https://www.psychologytoday.com/blog/brainsnacks/201203/the-only-5-fears-we-all-share.

8. X Zeng, C. P. Chiu, R. Wang, T. P. Oei, and F. Y. Leung, "The Effect of Loving-Kindness Meditation on Positive Emotions: A Meta-Analytic Review," *Frontiers in Psychology*, 6, (November 2015): 1693, doi: 10.3389/fpsyg.2015.01693. eCollection 2015.

Notes

Chapter 8

1. Karen Berg, *The Kabbalah Center Daily Consciousness E-Newsletter*, July 4, 2015.

2. Rabbi Philip S. Berg, *Kabbalah for the Layman* (New York: The Kabbalah Learning Centre, December 1991), 14–17.

3. Lewis B. Smedes, *Shame and Grace: Healing the Shame We Don't Deserve* (New York: HarperCollins, 1993), 141.

4. John Gardner, *Grendel* (Knopf Doubleday Publishing Group, 2010), 133, 159.

5. Viktor E. Frankl, *Man's Search for Meaning* (Boston: Beacon Press, 1992), 75–76.

6. David R. Hawkins, MD, PhD, *Letting Go: The Pathway of Surrender* (Carlsbad, CA: Hay House, 2014), Kindle Location 714.

7. Aaron Beck, "The Past and the Future of Cognitive Therapy," *Journal of Psychotherapy Practice and Research* 6, no. 4 (fall 1997): 276–84.

8. Doc Childre, Howard Martin, and Donna Beech, *The HeartMath Solution: The Institute of HeartMath's Revolutionary Program for Engaging the Power of the Heart's Intelligence* (New York: HarperCollins, 2011), Kindle Locations 2826–2833, 2869–2871.

9. Joseph Le Doux, *The Emotional Brain*, (New York: Simon & Schuster, 1998), 178.

10. T. Gard et al., "Greater Widespread Functional Connectivity of the Caudate in Older Adults Who Practice Kripalu Yoga and Vipassana Meditation than in Controls," *Frontiers in Human Neuroscience* 9 (March 16, 2015): 137, doi: 10.3389/fnhum .2015.00137, eCollection 2015.

11. Barry Boyce, "The Healing Power of Mindfulness," *Mindful*, Feb 28, 2011, http:// www.mindful.org/the-healing-power-of-mindfulness/#.

12. Daniel J. Siegel, *Mindsight* (New York: Bantam, 2010), 86.

13. Natasha Odou and Jay Brinker, "Self-Compassion, A Better Alternative to Rumination than Distraction as a Response to Negative Mood," *Journal of Positive Psychology* 10, no. 5 (Sept 2015): 447–57.

14. J. R. Wolkin, "Cultivating Multiple Aspects of Attention through Mindfulness Meditation Accounts for Psychological Well-Being through Decreased Rumination," *Psychology Research and Behavior Management* 8 (June 29, 2015):171–80, doi: 10.2147/ PRBM.S31458, eCollection 2015.

15. A. Chiesa, A. Serretti, and J. C. Jakobsen, "Mindfulness: Top-Down or Bottom-Up Emotion Regulation Strategy?" *Clinical Psychology Review* 1, no. 33 (February 2013): 82–96, doi: 10.1016/j.cpr.2012.10.006, Epub 2012 Oct 23.

16. Jordi Quoidbach, June Gruber, Moira Mikolajczak, et al., "Emodiversity and the Emotional Ecosystem," *Journal of Experimental Psychology* 143, no. 6 (December 2014): 2057–66.

Chapter 9

1. Paul Levy, Catching the Bug of Synchronicity, Website and blog of Paul Levy. http://www.awakeninthedream.com/catching-the-bug-of-synchronicity/ Accessed on 12/11/16.

2. Interview with Dr. Gibbs Williams for film *An Open Mind* on May 6, 2016, in New York City.

3. Letter from Sigmund Freud to Carl Jung: Vienna IX, Berggasse 19, April 16, 1909 (reproduced with permission of Ernst Freud, London), appearing in: C. G. Jung (author), Aniela Jaffe (author, editor), Clara Winston (translator), Richard Winston (translator) Kindle Edition, *Memories, Dreams, Reflections* (Vintage Reissue edition; sold by Random House, January 6, 2011), 361.

4. Williams Gibbs, A Theory and Use of Meaningful Coincidences (Synchronicities): http://www.gibbsonline.com/synchronicity.html (accessed 10/1/16).

5. Milton Rokeach, *Three Christs of Ypsilanti: A Narrative Study of Three Lost Men*, (New York: Random House, 2011), xiii.

6. Bertrand Russell, *Power: A New Social Analysis*, second edition (London: Routledge Classics, 2004), 3.

7. Michael Shermer, *The Believing Brain: From Ghosts and Gods to Politics and Conspiracies—How We Construct Beliefs and Reinforce Them as Truths* (New York: Times Books, 2011), 263–66.

8. E. Cardena, S. J. Lynn, and S. Krippner, eds., *Varieties of Anomalous Experience: Examining the Scientific Evidence*, second edition, (Washington, DC: American Psychological Association, 2014), http://dx.doi.org/10.1037/10371-000.

9. Newseum Institute, Newseum Exhibits Online, "Yes, Virginia, There Is a Santa Claus," http://www.newseum.org/exhibits/online/yes-virginia/.

10. Lisa Belkin, "The Odds of That," *New York Times*, Aug 11, 2002, accessed September 6, 2016, http://www.nytimes.com/2002/08/11/magazine/the-odds-of-that.html.

11. Ibid.

12. John Allen Paulos, *Irreligion: A Mathematician Explains Why the Arguments for God Just Don't Add Up* (New York: Macmillan, 2007), ix.

13. Carl Jung, from "The Conjunction," *Mysterium Coniunctionis, Collected Works*, XIV, (New Jersey: Princeton University Press, 1955–56), 384–85.

Chapter 10

1. Max Born and Emil Wolf, *Principles of Optics 7th Edition* (New York: Cambridge University Press, 1999), xxv–xxxiii.

2. David Harrison, "Complementarity and the Copenhagen Interpretation of Quantum Mechanics," *UPSCALE*, Department of Physics, University of Toronto, 2002, retrieved June 2008.

3. University of Winnipeg, *de Broglie's Waves*, accessed January 9, 2016, http://theory.uwinnipeg.ca/physics/quant/node6.html.

4. Maximilian Schlosshauer, Johannes Kofler, and Anton Zeilinger, "A Snapshot of Foundational Attitudes toward Quantum Mechanics," *Studies in History and Philosophy of Modern Physics* 44, no. 3 (January 6, 2013): 222–30. arXiv:1301.1069, doi:10.1016/j.shpsb.2013.04.004.

5. Werner Heisenberg: "The Copenhagen Interpretation of Quantum Theory," in *Physics and Philosophy* (George Allen and Unwin, 1959), chapter 3.

6. Lynne McTaggart, *The Field, Updated Edition: The Quest for the Secret Force of the Universe* (New York: HarperCollins, 2012), 85.

7. Eugene Weigner, Jagdish Mehra, and Arthur S. Wightman, eds., *Philosophical Reflections and Syntheses* (Berlin: Springer, 1995), 14.

8. John Marburger, *On the Copenhagen Interpretation of Quantum Mechanics*, accessed September 6, 2016, http://henry.pha.jhu.edu/Marburger.pdf.

9. Albert Einstein as cited by Bruce Rosenblum and Fred Kuttner in *Quantum Enigma: Physics Encounter Consciousness* (Oxford: University Press, 2006), 125.

10. Rajiv Mehrotra, *All You Ever Wanted to Know About His Holiness the Dalai Lama on Happiness, Life, Living and Much More* (Carlsbad, CA: Hay House, 2009), 96.

11. Rhonda Byrne, *The Secret* (New York: Atria, 2006), 24.

12. Wayne W. Dyer, *Inspiration: Your Ultimate Calling* (Carlsbad, CA: Hay House, 2006), 55.

13. Marianne Williamson, *The Law of Divine Compensation: On Work, Money and Miracles* (New York: Harper Collins, 2012), Kindle Location 52.

14. Rhonda Byrne, *The Secret* (New York: Atria, 2006), 51.

15. Fritjof Capra, interviewed by Renee Weber in *The Holographic Paradigm* (Shambhala/Random House, 1982), 217–18.

16. Walter Heitler, "Erwin Schrödinger, 1887–1961," *Biographical Memoirs of Fellows of the Royal Society* 7 (1961): 221–226.

17. Erwin Schrödinger, *My View of the World* (Woodbridge, CT: Ox Bow Press, 1983), 18–22, 37.

18. Douglas De Long, "The Brain and the Mind," *The Llewellyn Journal*, accessed September 6, 2016, https://www.llewellyn.com/journal/article/628.

19. Ervin Laszlo, *The Interconnected Universe: Conceptual Foundations of Transdisciplinary Unified Theory* (Singapore: World Scientific, 1995), 97–102.

20. Charles D. Laughlin, "Archetypes, Neurognosis and the Quantum Sea," *Journal of Scientific Exploration*, 10 (1996): 375–400.

21. Robert Kanigel, *The Man Who Knew Infinity: A Life of the Genius Ramanujan* (New York: Charles Scribner's Sons, 1991), 280–88.

22. Robert K. Merton, "Singletons and Multiples in Scientific Discovery: A Chapter in the Sociology of Science," *Proceedings of the American Philosophical Society*, 105: 470–86, 1961. Reprinted in Robert K. Merton, *The Sociology of Science*, op. cit., 343–70.

23. Julia Cameron. *An Artist's Way: A Spiritual Path to Higher Creativity* (New York: Penguin Putnam, 2001), Kindle Loc. 2345–2388.

24. "Languages of Dreaming: Anthropological Approaches to the Study of Dreaming in other Cultures," in J. Gackenbach and A. Sheikh, eds., *Dream Images: A Call to Mental Arms* (Amityville, NY: Baywood, 1991), 203–20.

25. E. J. Edelstein and L. Edelstein, *Asclepius: A Collection and Interpretation of the Testimonies* (Baltimore: Johns Hopkins Press, 1945), 209–11.

26. B. Steiger, *Medicine Power: The American Indian's Revival of His Spiritual Heritage and its Relevance for Modern Man* (Garden City: Doubleday, 1974), 72.

27. Deirdre Barrett, "The 'Committee of Sleep': A Study of Dream Incubation for Problem Solving," *Dreaming* 3, no. 2 (1993): 115–122, accessed April 9, 2008, http://www.asdreams.org/journal/articles/barrett3-2.htm.

28. Henry Reed, "Dream Incubation," *Journal of Humanistic Psychology* 16, no. 4 (fall 1976): 53–70.

29. Deirdre Barrett, *The Committee of Sleep: How Artists, Scientists, and Athletes Use Dreams for Creative Problem-Solving—And How You Can Too* (Oneiroi Press, 2010).

30. Shaul Bar, *A Letter That Has Not Been Read: Dreams in the Hebrew Bible* (New York: Hebrew Union College Press, 2001), 78–107; A. L. Oppenheim, "Mantic Dreams in the Ancient Near East," in *The Dream and Human Societies*, edited by G. E. von Grunebaum and R. Caillois (London: Cambridge University Press, 1966), 341–350.

31. Billy Phillips, *Kabbalah Student.com* (blog), Secrets, "Frightening and Liberating," Jan. 5, 2015, accessed September 5, 2016, http://kabbalahstudent.com/frightening-and-liberating/.

32. Lynne McTaggart, *The Field, Updated Edition: The Quest for the Secret Force of the Universe* (New York: HarperCollins, 2012), Kindle Location 1690–1693.

33. David R. Hawkins. *Power Vs. Force: The Hidden Determinants of Human Behavior* (Carlsbad, CA: Hay House, 2012), Kindle Location 913–1217.

34. Doc Childre, Howard Martin, and Donna Beech. *The HeartMath Solution: The Institute of HeartMath's Revolutionary Program for Engaging the Power of the Heart's Intelligence* (New York: HarperCollins, 2011), Kindle Locations 3301–3303.

35. Ibid.

Chapter 11

1. Lenore Terr, *Too Scared to Cry: Psychic Trauma in Childhood* (New York: Hachette Book Group, 2008), 125–67.

2. Judith Orloff, *Dr. Judith Orloff's Guide to Intuitive Healing: 5 Steps to Physical, Emotional, and Sexual Wellness* (New York: Three Rivers Press, 2000), 163–64.

3. T. Singer and O. M. Klimecki, "Empathy and Compassion," *Current Biology* 24, no. 8 (September 22, 2014): R875–8, doi: 10.1016/j.cub.2014.06.054.

4. W. T. Boyce and B. J. Ellis, "Biological Sensitivity to Context: I. An Evolutionary-Developmental Theory of the Origins and Functions of Stress Reactivity," *Development Psychopathology* 17, no. 2 (2005): 271–301. PMID: 16761546.

5. B. P. Acevedo, E. N. Aron, A. Aron, M. D. Sangster, N. Collins N, and L. L. Brown, "The Highly Sensitive Brain: An FMRI Study of Sensory Processing Sensitivity and Response to Others' Emotions," *Brain and Behavior* 4, no. 4 (July 2014): 580–94, doi: 10.1002/brb3.242, e-pub 2014 Jun 23.

6. Diane Hennacy Powell, *The ESP Enigma: The Scientific Case for Psychic Phenomenon* (New York: Walker & Company, 2009), 8 (and personal conversation with Dr. Powell on April 23, 2015).

Notes

7. Janine de Peyer, "Uncanny Communication and the Porous Mind," *Psychoanalytic Dialogues* 26, no. 2 (2016):156–74.

8. Claudie Massicotte, "Psychical Transmissions: Freud, Spiritualism, and the Occult," *Psychoanalytic Dialogues: The International Journal of Relational Perspectives* 24, no. 1 (2014): 88–102.

9. Sigmund Freud, *The Standard Edition of the Complete Psychological Works of Sigmund Freud*, vol. XXII, lecture XXX, "Dreams and Occultism," James Strachey trans. (London: Hogarth Press, 1936), 38. http://users.clas.ufl.edu/burt/deconstructionandnew mediatheory/Freuddreamsoccultism.pdf.

10. Berthold Schwarz, *Parent-Child Telepathy* (New York: Garrett Publications, 1971).

11. Diane Hennacy Powell, *The ESP Enigma: The Scientific Case for Psychic Phenomenon* (New York: Walker & Company, 2009), 7 (and personal conversation with Dr. Powell on April 23, 2015).

12. S. Ferenczi, *The Clinical Diary of Sándor Ferenczi*, J. Dupont, ed. (Cambridge, MA: Harvard University Press, 1995), 84.

13. R. Buck, "The Neuropsychology of Communication: Spontaneous and Symbolic Aspects," *Journal of Pragmatics* 22 (1994): 265–78, doi:10.1016/0378-2166(94)90112-0.

14. A. N. Schore, *Affect Regulation and the Repair of the Self* (New York: Norton, 2003), 81–83.

15. V. Gallese, "Mirror Neurons, Embodied Simulation, and the Neural Basis of Social Identification," *Psychoanalytic Dialogues* 19 (2009): 519–36, doi:10.1080/1048188090 3231910.

16. Sandra Blakeslee, "Cells That Read Minds," *New York Times* (January 10, 2006), accessed August 9, 2016, http://www.nytimes.com/2006/01/10/science/cells-that-read -minds.html.

17. Personal Interview with Dr. Diane Hennacy Powell for documentary film *An Open Mind*, New York, April 23, 2015.

18. Janine de Peyer, "Uncanny Communication and the Porous Mind," *Psychoanalytic Dialogues* 26 (2016): 156–174.

19. Ofra Eshel, "Where Are You, My Beloved?: On Absence, Loss, and the Enigma of Telepathic Dreams," *International Journal of Psychoanalysis* 87 (2006): 1603–1627; Michael Ullman, "Dream Telepathy: Experimental and Clinical Findings," in *Psychoanalysis and the Paranormal: Lands of Darkness* (London: Karnac Books, 2003), 15–46; Sigmund Freud, "Dreams and Telepathy," in *The Standard Edition of the Complete Psychological Works of Sigmund Freud, Volume 18*, ed. and trans. J. Strachey (London: Hogarth Press, 1922), 195–220.

20. Ward Hill Lamon, *Recollections of Abraham Lincoln 1847–1865* (Lincoln: University of Nebraska Press, 1994): 116–117. http://rogerjnorton.com/Lincoln46.html.

21. E. Gurney, F. Myers, and F. Podmore, *Phantasms of the Living* (London: Trubner Co. 1986), 1: 202.

22. John Palmer, "ESP in the Ganzfeld," *Journal of Consciousness Studies* 10 (2003): 6–7.

23. A. Goulding, J. Westerlund, A. Parker, and J. Wackermann, "The First Digital Autoganzfeld Study Using a Real-Time Judging Procedure," *European Journal of Parapsychology* 19 (2004): 66–97.

24. L. Storm, P. E. Tressoldi, and L. Di Risio, "Meta-Analysis of Free-Response Studies, 1992–2008: Assessing the Noise Reduction Model in Parapsychology" (PDF), *Psychological Bulletin* 138, no. 4 (July 2010): 471–85.

25. D. I. Radin, "Thinking about Telepathy," *Think*, 1 (2003): 23–32, doi:10.1017/S1477175600000415.

26. R. Hyman, "Meta-Analysis That Conceals More Than It Reveals: Comment on Storm, et al.," *Psychological Bulletin* 136 (2010): 486–90.

27. Janine de Peyer, "Uncanny Communication and the Porous Mind," *Psychoanalytic Dialogues* 26 (2016): 156–74.

28. Lynne McTaggart, *The Field, Updated Edition: The Quest for the Secret Force of the Universe* (New York: HarperCollins, 2012), 127–28.

29. Website of Psychiatrist Leston Havens, MD: https://www.lestonhavensmd.com/pdf/notes-on-existential/.

30. Daryl J. Bem and Charles Honorton, "Does Psi Exist? Replicable Evidence for an Anomalous Process of Information Transfer" (PDF), *Psychological Bulletin* 115, no.1 (1994): 4–18, doi:10.1037/0033-2909.115.1.4, retrieved 2007-07-31.

31. T. R. Lawrence, "Gathering in the Sheep and Goats: A Meta-Analysis of Forced-Choice Sheep-Goat ESP Studies, 1947–1993," in *Proceedings of the 36th Annual Convention of the Parapsychological Association* (Durham: Parapsychological Association, 1993): 75–86.

32. M. J., & H Schlitz, and C. Honorton. "Ganzfeld psi performance within an artistically gifted population." *Journal of the American Society for Psychical Research*, 86 (1992): 83–98.

33. Daryl J. Bem and Charles Honorton, "Does Psi Exist? Replicable Evidence for an Anomalous Process of Information Transfer" (PDF), *Psychological Bulletin* 115, no.1 (1994): 4–18, doi:10.1037/0033-2909.115.1.4, retrieved 2007-07-31.

34. Daryl J. Bem, J. Palmer, and R. S. Broughton, "Updating the Ganzfeld Database: A Victim of its Own Success?" (PDF) *Journal of Parapsychology* 65, no. 3 (September 2001): 207–18.

35. R. S. Broughton and C. H. Alexander, "Autoganzfeld II: An Attempted Replication of the PRL Ganzfeld Research," *Journal of Parapsychology* 61 (1997): 209–226.

36. William G. Roll et. al., "Neurobehavioral and Neurometabolic (SPECT) Correlates of Paranormal Information: Involvement of the Right Hemisphere and its Sensitivity to Weak Complex Magnetic Fields," *International Journal of Neuroscience* 112 (2002):197–224; Michael A. Persinger et al., "Remote Viewing with the Artist Ingo Swann: Neuropsychological Profile, Electroencephalographic Correlates, Magnetic Resonance Imaging (MRI), and Possible Mechanisms" *Perceptual and Motor Skills* 94 (2002): 927–949.

37. Jill Bolte Taylor, *My Stroke of Insight* (New York, Viking, 2008), 37–46, 137–45.

38. Daryl J. Bem and Charles Honorton, "Does Psi Exist? Replicable Evidence for an Anomalous Process of Information Transfer" (PDF), *Psychological Bulletin* 115, no. 1: (1994): 4–18, doi:10.1037/0033-2909.115.1.4, retrieved 2007-07-31.

39. C. M. Heyes and C. D. Frith, "The Cultural Evolution of Mind Reading," *Science* 344, no. 6190 (June, 20, 2014):1243091, doi: 10.1126/science.1243091.

40. Ron Shefi, *Spiritual Psychology* (Paradise Books, 2013), 16–19.

41. Eben Alexander and Ptolemy Tompkins, *The Map of Heaven: How Science, Religion and Ordinary People Are Proving the Afterlife* (New York: Simon & Schuster, 2014), Kindle Loc 1937–2784.

42. Henry Grayson, *Mindful Loving* (New York: Gotham Books, 2003), 199–218.

43. Elizabeth Lloyd Mayer, *Extraordinary Knowing: Science, Skepticism, and the Inexplicable Powers of the Human Mind* (New York: Bantam Books, 2007), Kindle Location 247–256.

Chapter 12

1. 2014 Religious Landscape Study, Belief in Heaven, conducted by Pew Research Center, http://www.pewforum.org/religious-landscape-study/belief-in-heaven/.

2. Thích Nhất Hạnh, "You Are Here," September 6, 2011, https://leptospira.word press.com/.

3. Fritz-Albert Popp, "Biophotonics: A Powerful Tool for Investigating and Understanding Life," in *What Is Life?* ed. H. F Durr, F. A. Popp, and W. Schommers (Singapore: World Scientific, 2016), 279–306.

4. Michael Shermer, "Anomalous Events That Can Shake One's Skepticism to the Core," in *Scientific American* (October 1, 2014), accessed September 6, 2016, https://www.scientific american.com/article/anomalous-events-that-can-shake-one-s-skepticism-to-the-core/.

5. Eben Alexander and Ptolemy Tompkins, *The Map of Heaven: How Science, Religion and Ordinary People Are Proving the Afterlife* (New York: Simon & Schuster, 2014), Kindle Location 1970–2012.

6. Eben Alexander, *Proof of Heaven: A Neurosurgeon's Journey into the Afterlife* (New York: Simon & Schuster, 2012), 200–202.

7. Annie Cap, *Beyond Goodbye: An Extraordinary True Story of a Shared Death Experience* (New York: Paragon Publishing, 2011), 26–51.

Notes

8. Penny Sartori, *Wisdom of Near-Death Experiences: How Understanding NDEs Can Help Us Live More Fully* (London: Watkins Publishing, 2014), 85–110.

9. D. M. Dosa, "A Day in the Life of Oscar the Cat," *New England Journal of Medicine* 357, no. 4 (July 26, 2007): 328–9.

10. Irvin D. Yalom, *Staring at the Sun: Overcoming the Terror of Death* (London: Piatkus, 2008), 7.

11. Atul Gawande, MD, *Being Mortal: Medicine and What Matters in the End* (New York: Metropolitan Books, 2014), 6.

12. Brian L. Weiss, *Many Lives, Many Masters: The True Story of a Prominent Psychiatrist, His Young Patient, and the Past-Life Therapy That Changed Both Their Lives* (New York: Grand Central, 1996), 9–10.

13. Carl Jung, "Conscious, Unconscious, and Individuation (1939)," in *Collected Works Volume 9, Part 1: Archetypes and the Collective Unconscious, trans. R.F.C Hull* (Princeton: Princeton University Press, 1969), 286–287.

14. Rajiv Mehrotra, *All You Ever Wanted to Know about His Holiness the Dalai Lama on Happiness, Life, Living, and Much More* (Carlsbad, CA: Hay House, 2009), 80–83.

15. Michael Newton, *Journey of Souls: Case Studies of Life Between Lives* (Woodbury, MN: Llewellyn Publications, 1994), Kindle Locations 1317–21.

16. John Harricharan, *A Conversation with Dr. Elisabeth Kübler-Ross*. Insight 2000. http://www.insight2000.com/kubler-ross.html.

17. Elisabeth Kubler-Ross, *On Life After Death* (New York: Random House, 2008), 26.

18. Raymond Moody, *Life After Life: The Bestselling Original Investigation That Revealed "Near-Death Experiences"* reprint ed. (New York: HarperOne, 2001), 13.

19. Peter Fenwick and Elizabeth Fenwick, *The Art of Dying* (London: Bloomsbury Academic, 2008), 6.

20. Elisabeth Kübler-Ross, *Death: The Final Stage of Growth* (New York, Scribner, 1975), 164.

21. Alan Lightman, "14 April 1905" in *Einstein's Dreams* (New York: Vintage Books, 1993), 6–7.

22. D. Bem, P. Tressoldi, T. Rabeyron, and M. Duggan, "Feeling the Future: A Meta-Analysis of 90 Experiments on the Anomalous Anticipation of Random Future Events, Version 2." F1000Res. 2015 Oct 30 [revised 2016 Jan 29] 4:1188, doi: 10.12688/f1000research.7177.2, eCollection 2015.

23. Daryl J. Bem, "Feeling the Future: Experimental Evidence for Anomalous Retroactive Influences on Cognition and Affect," *Journal of Personality and Social Psychology* 100 (2011): 407–425.

24. D. P. Sheehan, ed., "Quantum Retrocausation—Theory and Experiment," *AIP Conference Proceedings* (San Diego, California; Melville, New York: American Institute of Physics, 2011), 863.

25. D. P. Sheehan, ed., "Frontiers of Time: Retrocausation—Experiment and Theory," *AIP Conference Proceedings* (San Diego, California; Melville, New York: American Institute of Physics, 2006), 1408, p. vii.

26. Dean Radin, *Entangled Minds: Extrasensory Experiences in a Quantum Reality* (New York: Paraview Pocket Books, 2006), 240–74.

27. Edwin C. May and Sonali B. Marwaha, "Part I: Theories of Psi" in *Extrasensory Perception: Support, Skepticism, and Science Vol. 2: Theories of Psi* (Santa Barbara: Praeger, 2015), 1136–80.

28. Lynne McTaggart, *The Field, Updated Edition: The Quest for the Secret Force of the Universe* (New York: HarperCollins, 2012), 164.

Conclusion

1. The Distress of Separation, Song of Solomon 5:2, New International Version Bible.

2. Kabbalah Series on the Paradise Principle by Kabbalist Rabbi Yitzchak Schwartz, accessed October 1, 2016, http://www.paradiseprinciple.com/papers/kabbalah_series.html.

About the Author

Anna Yusim, MD, a graduate of Stanford University and the Yale University School of Medicine, is a psychiatrist in private practice in New York City. She has helped more than one thousand patients lead happier, more meaningful lives. She lives with her husband in Manhattan. For more information, visit www.AnnaYusim.com.